EXCERPTS FROM SOME OF THE STORIES

We had a skinny dip in Lake Erie Climbed down a cliff, discarded o sufficiently isolated spot submitted ___ies to the tossing and tumbling waves of this ___eat Lake." We let the waves roll over us and wash us roughly over stones to shore. What glorious freedom! Climbed the cliff again and discovered some delicious wild strawberries.

—*Annette Scherer Robbins* (The Fortunate Four—
In the Summer of 1935)

Ken and I sat down together one day and read through all of our love letters and then destroyed them. They were too mushy for our kids to read!

—*Ruth Swanson* (Destiny Through Time)

In reliving my life, I realize it has really been pretty much the way I had wished it to be. First, I wanted to fall in love with a nice Jewish fellow. You see, I always had quite a clear idea of the way I would like to live my life. I can honestly say my dreams have pretty much come true.

—*Jeanette Scherling* (Let's Have a Picnic)

It turned out that I did meet someone special—through a strange twist of fate and, I believe . . . a little help from our guardian angels. The year was 1925, and I was beginning my freshman year of college. . . . Since there was no money to purchase flowers for my wedding, we went out in the fields and picked daisies and wild asparagus ferns to decorate the church. We created beauty with what we could borrow from nature.

—*Dorathy Lysne* (Bouquets of Daisies and Wild Asparagus)

As children we spent a lot of time in the woods and pasture, where there was always something interesting to do. We would climb young trees and as they would bend, we would just hang on with our hands and drop down until we almost touched the ground. Then we would let go and the trees would spring back up again. What a feeling of freedom! Then we would lie on the cool grass, gaze at the blue sky, and watch the fluffy clouds float by . . . just dreaming.

—*Eva Olson* (The Little Girls)

After the wedding, we stopped at a little restaurant and had sardines and crackers. This was on Tuesday, November 23, 1926, and then I wasn't able to see my husband again until Thanksgiving. You see, our marriage had to be kept a secret!

—*Winifred Miller* (Caught Between Two Worlds)

I remember your wearing green gabardine pants and white shoes and how you sat on the chair backwards holding your pipe in your hand. I still remember how wonderful you looked the first time I saw you without a shirt with your suspenders over your naked skin. You were wonderful and sweet, and I loved you very much. (Portion of a letter to her husband.)

—*Cloe Hulbert* (My Bud, You Would Have Just Loved Him)

My mother wanted more than anything to become a dancer. However, this was around 1918, and the profession was frowned upon. "Nice girls" didn't do that. So she chose another love—music—and enrolled in what is now the Julliard School of Music.

—*Lucile Johnson* (Pearls, Lace, and the Gift of Music)

The future seems so uncertain for me. Oh, for a real wonderful future! There is the popular slang phrase, "Not much of a future but oh . . . what a past." I would like to be able to say, "Not much of a past, but oh, what a future!" Who knows, perhaps five years from now I'll be able to say, "I told you so. Your future was rosy, but time could only reveal each rose bud as it opened." My greatest ambition is something unattainable—if I were to become a concert artist—a soloist who would hold hundreds spellbound!

—*Violet Anne Rehnberg* (Dreams in a Bottle)

The fortune-teller told me that I would be married within two years. I wonder what will really happen. She also said that I would make a big success of music, traveling a lot after I was married.

—*Marcella Flory* (Dreams in a Bottle)

There is a place where late summer breezes whisper in the old maples and the setting sun casts a magical golden light. This place is Xanadu Island. It holds the secret of the mystery woman and the lost diamond.

—*Alice Vollmar* (The Legends of Xanadu)

THE
FORTUNATE FOUR
& OTHER JOURNEYS OF THE HEART

JOY KUBY

Beaver's Pond Press, Inc.
Edina   Minnesota

ISBN 1-59298-007-4

Library of Congress Catalog Number: 2003105084

Book design and typesetting by Mori Studio

Printed in the United States of America

First Printing: 2003

Second Printing: 2004

07 06 05 04   6 5 4 3 2

Beaver's Pond Press, Inc.

7104 Ohms Lane, Suite 216
Edina, MN 55439
(952) 829-8818
www.beaverspondpress.com

to order, visit www.BookHouseFulfillment.com
or call 1-800-901-3480. Reseller discounts available.

⚜

I dedicate this book to my grandmother, Eva Olson,
whose life spanned over three centuries.
She worked hard, yet she took the time to appreciate the beauty of nature.
She had a gentle spirit with a quick tear for the misfortune of others,
and she showed us how to age gracefully.
She never lost her wit, her great sense of humor, or her desire to learn.
I was blessed to be a part of her journey.

⚜

Contents

Acknowledgments   ix

Preface   xi

Introduction   xiii

THE JOURNEY OF A LIFETIME

The Fortunate Four—In the Summer of 1935
*Annette Scherer Robbins, Irene Hoebel, Elizabeth Bridgman,
and Garneth Buchanan*   3

A BRUSH WITH DESTINY

Let's Have a Picnic   *Jeanette Scherling*   69

Bouquets of Daisies and Wild Asparagus Fern
Dorathy Lysne   79

Destiny Through Time   *Ruth Swanson*   85

Lost Love   *Eva Olson*   93

The "Bride and Groom" Show   *Donna Grinvalds*   98

A CELEBRATION OF THE JOURNEY

Hilda and Eva—The Little Girls   *Eva Olson*   135

Caught Between Two Worlds   *Winifred Miller*   146

The Journey from Hollywood   *Dr. Chris Matteson*   153

Viola Gets a School   *Viola Daetz*   180

Sing from Your Heart   *Charlotte Sonnichsen*   187

The Journey on the Train   *Lee Anderson*   193

Clear Blue Skies and Cool Deep Waters
Arlene Graham   205

The Winding Road to Monterey Bay   *June Usher*   217

The Master Storyteller   *Verdi Nelson*   223

THE MYSTERY OF A PHOTOGRAPH

Mother and Child   261

That Special Day   262

No Regrets   *Phyllis Ranallo*   263

The Wedding Album   266

Pearls, Lace, and the Gift of Music   *Lucile Johnson*   272

LOVE LETTERS—SWEETER THAN CHOCOLATE

Hello, Sweetheart!   *Anonymous*   279

My Bud, You Would Have Just Loved Him
Chloe Hulbert   280

The Little Red Rambler *Eva Olson* 294

Loving You, Emil *Donna Grinvalds* 297

6

LOVE AND LAUGHTER

The Iceman *Inez Kullberg* 327

Where's the Beef? *Hilda Swanson* 330

Strolling with a Stranger *Ruth Swanson* 333

A Change of Plans *Irene Christiansen* 334

Riding the Streetcar *Ginny Elmer* 342

7

DREAMS IN A BOTTLE
AND OTHER BURIED TREASURES

The Legends of Xanadu 345

Dreams in a Bottle 351
Violet Rehnberg, Verona Bangs, Helen McKinzie, and Marcella Flory

On a Final Note 365

About the Author 373

Acknowledgments

Special thanks to my personal coach, Melanie Keveles. Without her encouragement and skill at keeping away the gremlins of doubt, this book would still be only a dream.

My heartfelt appreciation goes to all my wonderful friends for their support throughout this project, particularly Darlinda Alexander and Linda Christian for proofreading and critiquing my stories. It was a pleasure to work with my editor, Hope Levine, whose suggestions were most valuable.

Thanks to my supportive husband for putting up with my many late nights on the computer as I worked on the stories for the book.

Most of all, my deepest gratitude goes to all of the spirited women I interviewed for this book. I sincerely thank each of you for speaking from the heart and for sharing your personal journey. You have made my life much richer by knowing you, and I have gained many new friends.

I also thank you, my readers, for honoring these women by reading their stories.

PREFACE

This book is the culmination of a dream that began over ten years ago. It began as a soft whisper from my guardian angel to "write a tribute to women." The desire grew over time, and I began interviewing women and simply listening to the stories that they had to tell of their personal journeys. There were heart-tugging love stories, stories where destiny played a part in their lives, stories of lifelong friendships, and stories that show we all make a difference.

As a baby boomer, life before the 1950s was often a mystery to me. I knew there were many incredible stories from my mother's and grandmother's generations that were soon to be lost forever. They were like precious gifts that had been wrapped up with a bow and were not being shared. I had a strong desire to write about their journeys through life—to show their passions, hopes, dreams, and fears—for in learning about their journeys we can better understand ourselves.

I began seeking out women from previous generations that I might listen to their stories. Many of the women were still living active lives, but several were widows living in small apartments in retirement communities. The apartments were condensed versions of their lives, with only room for their most cherished possessions. Their bodies may have become wrinkled and worn out, but these women had spirited stories about their journeys through life.

Even though we were years apart in age, a most special bond was created. We laughed and cried as they opened up their hearts to me and shared their intimate stories. They gave me goodbye hugs; we often had follow-up conversations by phone; they sent notes in the mail; and we had stimulating conversations over lunch. I treasure all of these women. I fell in love with each woman's story, and their stories became like my little children—something to cherish and protect. *The Fortunate Four & Other Journeys of the Heart* is a compilation of these stories. A note of reflection is also often included at the beginning or end of the story. I now pass along these stories for you to enjoy.

INTRODUCTION

Many books have been written about the lives of famous women; this is not one of them. This book is a tribute to women from ordinary walks of life who experienced much of the twentieth century, and it provides an opportunity for us to connect with the stories they have to tell. These women had adventurous spirits, were looking for love, and shared many of the same emotions that women of today experience.

We are each shaped by the era in which we live. The lives of the women in this book were greatly shaped by war, the Great Depression, their immigrant parents, and the changes taking place in the world around them. These stories tell of a calmer, simpler time in the past—a time when, out of respect, adults were referred to as "Mr." Bridgman, "Aunt" Etta, and "Mrs." Matuska. A time when close-knit communities had a central place to gather, talk, and play. A time when lifelong friendships were treasured. A time when, despite one's lot in life, there was hope that tomorrow would be better. A time when love and happiness flourished, even with few material possessions.

The time is right for these stories to be told, for it will soon be too late— these remarkable women will have passed on. Their journeys will end in silence if their precious stories are not shared.

These are stories of our mothers and our grandmothers—women who were once young and in love and filled with hopes and dreams for the future. Women who showed incredible spirit, courage, and passion for life. Women who opened their hearts and let us catch a glimpse into their souls. These are their stories.

I

THE JOURNEY
OF A LIFETIME

*Friends are quiet angels
who lift us to our feet
when our wings have trouble
remembering how to fly.*

AUTHOR UNKNOWN

THE FORTUNATE FOUR—
IN THE SUMMER OF 1935

Annette Scherer Robbins, Irene Hoebel,
Elizabeth Bridgman, and Garneth Buchanan

W hat young lady has not entertained dreams in her heart of romance, adventure, and travel to places unknown?

These dreams came true in the summer of 1935 for four young women—Annette Strand, Betty Klein, Irene Holth, and Irene's younger sister Garneth—students at Hamline University in Minnesota. They were thankful for the generosity of a wealthy benefactor who had made a most unusual offer—to sponsor a summer-long trip for them to see much of the eastern United States. Their journey created a bond that would last a lifetime and helped mold the women they were to become. Sixty-one years later, in the spring of 1996, they were reunited in Irene's apartment in the Kenwood Retirement Community to reflect on the memories of this trip traveled so many years ago. This is the story of their extraordinary journey. It is told by Irene, with excerpts from Annette's journal.

It was a feeling of joy and excitement to share the afternoon on that spring day in 1996 with my friends and traveling companions of so long ago. Betty, Annette, Garneth, and I had looked forward to this afternoon to reminisce together about our lives and to savor the warmth of our friendship. We had been apart much too long.

We had stayed in touch over the years, and several of us had been together at various times. Yet this was the first time all four of us had been together with the opportunity to truly reflect on our journey of 1935. We were now between the ages of 79 and 82, and we giggled and howled with laughter as if we were once again young college students.

Caterers delivered chicken-salad sandwiches, chips, fruit, and coffee. Over our delicious lunch, we talked about our grandchildren, books we had read, and seminars we had attended, but we mostly talked about our 1935 journey. We had called ourselves "The Fortunate Four"—or in moments of refinement, "The Four Young Ladies." Our trip had been mixed with adventure—climbing Mt. Washington by moonlight and skinny-dipping in Lake Erie; romance—being serenaded before bedtime by nice young fellows we met at a dance; experiencing new foods—Betty never got over her passion for English muffins; meeting wonderful people; and gaining a real appreciation for the beauty of our country.

This is Our Story

In the summer of 1935, Annette, Betty, and I were college juniors and my sister Garneth was a freshman. The country was deep in the heart of the Depression. Although we were from families of modest means, we were fortunate to have scholarships to attend Hamline University in St. Paul,

Minnesota. We had never traveled far from home, so we were both thrilled and surprised when the opportunity to travel across the country together was suddenly presented to us. But maybe I'd better start back at the very beginning.

Mr. Donald Bridgman, who was to become our benefactor, had invited us four young ladies for dinner at Mrs. Jones' Tea Room that spring on April 22. There he offered us the trip of a lifetime—we would tour the eastern United States and Canada by car. What excitement!—being offered an all-expense-paid nine-week trip with no strings attached except to have fun, keep within our budget, and keep a journal of all our experiences.

So who was this mysterious man, and why was he making such a generous offer? Mr. Bridgman was a bachelor, a successful lawyer, and a Hamline trustee. (His father, George Henry Bridgman, was a Methodist minister and Hamline's first president from 1883 to 1912.) Donald Bridgman was grateful for the part Hamline had played in his life. He had already made substantial donations and set up several scholarships. Since we were all "smart girls," we got in on the scholarships as freshmen. A few years earlier Annette, Betty, and I had also been part of a group of ten freshmen whom Mr. Bridgman and his lawyer friend, Mr. Drew, had sent to the World's Fair in Chicago. Perhaps Mr. Bridgman was impressed by the nice thank-you notes we had written upon our return; or perhaps he thought that we needed a little culture; or he simply thought us worthy of such a trip. At any rate—we were thrilled at this opportunity, and we began making our plans.

The Itinerary

Mr. Bridgman carefully supervised the itinerary and had his secretary type the agenda of where we would be going. We were each given $2.50 a day for expenses, and an additional $2.50 per day was allocated for the car. Mr. Bridgman even took us to the bank to apply for our first American Express traveler's checks. We were also given letters of introduction to friends of Mr. Bridgman's and to friends of various members of the Hamline faculty. Mr. Drew, a bachelor friend of Mr. Bridgman's, had graduated from Wesleyan in Connecticut, and he sent along letters of introduction to his wealthy friends in the Adirondacks, the Catskills, Martha's Vineyard, and New York.

Betty and Garneth would begin the journey on June 29, 1935, by picking up Annette and me at Lake Geneva, where we would be attending lectures at a YWCA college camp. From there we would skirt around Chicago, heading for Greenfield Village. We would continue on to Detroit, Michigan, and then into Canada to see Niagara Falls. Our route would follow the St. Lawrence River to Montreal and Quebec. We would then drive south along the Atlantic from Bar Harbor, Maine, down to Williamsburg, Virginia. Our plan was to return to Minnesota by Labor Day.

Of course, none of us owned a car. Fortunately, my mother offered her car for the summer. My mother, Mrs. Hazel Holth, was a widow and owner of a corner grocery store. My sisters and I lived with my mother above the store. I realize now that my mother made a generous offer. She gave up her car for the summer even though it was also her delivery wagon. I don't know if I ever really thanked her.

Betty worked for Mr. Bridgman for three weeks prior to the trip while his secretary was on vacation. She used the $50 that she earned during this time to get the 1930 Studebaker in shape for the long journey. Mr. Bridgman gave us goals and asked each of us to keep track of our thoughts and experiences in a journal, which we did. One of Betty's goals, for example, was to study architecture and geology.

Our Journey

At our luncheon in 1996, we laughed over Betty's recollections of the first day of the journey as she and Garneth left to meet up with Annette and me in Lake Geneva where we had been attending a camp. Betty said,

> The car was packed and Garneth and I took to the road on June 29, 1935. It was only 4:30 a.m. and the sun had not yet risen, but we were eager to connect with Irene and Annette at Lake Geneva where we would begin our journey together. Our first stop was to say goodbye to Mr. Bridgman at the Lemington Hotel in Minneapolis where he lived with his widowed mother. Of course, there were no freeways at that time. There were just two-way roads, hardly wider than the two cars. I had been noticing, with Garneth at the wheel, that we kept edging to the left of the center-line. I didn't quite know what to say. Finally I said, "Garnie, I notice the cars coming toward us are moving off onto the shoulder." She immediately moved to the right of the lane, and that's all that was said. Surely, we owed our safe passage to Lake Geneva to the charity of the others on the road.

Annette was the only one of us who could really drive, so we jokingly said that we "practically killed a lot of people." Annette became the principal driver, and the rest of us learned as we went.

At our luncheon, we were all thrilled that Annette had brought her journal and photo album of the journey. For the rest of us, our journals may have been misplaced during one of the many moves throughout a lifetime or were perhaps stored in a box of possessions . . . but where? We looked at the younger images of ourselves in the photo album. I said, "You know, we were pretty cute." As Annette read aloud from her journal and turned the yellowed, worn pages, our minds and hearts were transferred back to that simpler time of youth.

Annette began by reading from her daily log of June 29, 1935:

We saw everyone off at the YWCA camp, bid them goodbye, and then had the rest of the day to shift for ourselves. We waited longingly for Garneth and Betty to join us. They arrived at 6:30 p.m. Were we glad to see them! It was a happy reunion for the Four Young Ladies.

The following morning, we were up by 5 a.m. after a rather restless night. With one suitcase per person, hiking boots, picnic supplies, and a spare tire tied to the front bumper, we were ready for the journey to begin. Annette drove through Chicago, since she was the most experienced driver. We drove 350 miles and stayed that night at a tourist home in Michigan. (During most of our trip, we stayed at tourist homes, which were private homes or cabins. They could be rented from fifty cents to a dollar and fit into our budget.)

In the next two days, as we traveled through Michigan, we toured the University of Michigan, Greenfield Village, and the Edison Institute Museum; saw the chair in which Lincoln was assassinated; and saw the courthouse where he practiced law. We also toured the Ford plant in Detroit and drove up to Ontario, our first time in Canada.

Skinny-dipping in Lake Erie

We were enthralled by the magnificence of the Great Lakes. I don't know whose idea it was, but we decided to go skinny-dipping in Lake Erie. It was a beautiful morning and nobody was around for miles—there were only trees and beaches. We stripped off our clothes, swam, and splashed. What a feeling of freedom! We were all modest girls, so it surprised us (and does, to this day) that we actually did this.

Annette had a descriptive entry in her journal about this experience—

July 2.

> *A skinny-dip in Lake Erie this morning about 9 a.m. Climbed down a cliff, discarded our clothes, and being in a sufficiently isolated spot submitted our unclad bodies to the tossing and tumbling waves of this "Great Lake." We let the waves roll over us and wash us roughly over stones to shore. Irene looked pink enough (from the cold water) to have been severely spanked. I guess the rest of us did, too. What glorious freedom. Climbed the cliff again and discovered some delicious wild strawberries.*

Niagara Falls

We saw such beauty across the country. Niagara Falls was one unforgettable scene for the four of us who had grown up amidst the 10,000 lakes of Minnesota but had never experienced such magnitude.

Again, Annette's journal described it so well.

(July 2 continued)

We drove along the Niagara River at Sunset—to, oh, the most spectacular Niagara Falls. Saw the roaring, dashing upper rapids first—clear green color. Then to behold the falls proper from various angles—what a privilege to look at this gorgeous natural phenomena—this God-given wonder of beauty and power! Saw both the Canadian and American falls as daylight faded. Then the huge, powerful floodlights were focused on the hurling, rushing waters. Colored lights flooded the falls, and what an array of reflected grandeur shown all about. The mist and spray (heavy as rain as it beat against our faces and bodies) made beautifully colored rainbows. We viewed the falls in our raincoats. Dripping wet as we were, it was hard to drag ourselves away. We left this enchanted mass of falling beauty at 10:30 p.m. and found a comfortable, well-furnished tourist home nearby. As I sit here now, writing an inadequate account of an all too glorious day, I can still hear the thundering roar of Niagara Falls.

The Canadian Tour Continues

To stay within our budget of $2.50 per day, most breakfasts required us to be very frugal. Breakfasts were usually comprised of an orange or banana and doughnuts. (We could purchase seven bananas for five cents.) I can't believe we can actually look at another orange or banana to this day. A trip through the Canadian Shredded Wheat factory was very good timing.

Annette wrote:

July 3.

Went through the Canadian Shredded Wheat factory and saw the processes that this healthful wheat-and-water cereal goes through in the making. We chanced to visit the place at a most con-venient time and, having only had an orange for breakfast, were treated to a dish of shredded wheat and bananas.

After dinner we walked about a mile and a half down to Lake Ontario—a calm, blue, serene expanse of water. Irene and Betty took a swim; Garneth and I had sponge baths and sat on the beach. We met a couple of young fellas who walked back with us, and one came to call on us at 9:30—all dressed up. He said he was lonely. Walked down to the pond with him.

We had a few challenges driving through Canada and read-ing the French road signs. I was astonishingly dumb. We kept coming upon a road sign that read, Vitesse 25. I thought it was saying the town of Vitesse was 25 miles away. It actually meant that the speed was 25 miles per hour.

Let's Dance

Being four college students, of course we loved to dance. We couldn't pass up the opportunity to attend a few dances along our journey.

July 7.

Rising later than ever—not up until 10 a.m. All four of us went to a dance last night at the lodge near our cabin. Not much of a dance but had a ride into Three Rivers and met some fellas—the one whom I was with was Ernie Frost. They all serenaded us before we went to bed. They were also out to bid us "bon voyage" when we left this morning on our way to Quebec.

July 9.

Last night we presented our first letter of introduction that was given to us by Mr. Drew. It was presented to Mr. and Mrs.

Annette, Irene, Garneth, and Betty in the Guibords' garden.

Guibord. They have a lovely large home—a white colonial, three stories with a beautiful lawn and garden.

The garden includes a rock garden, goldfish pool, little brook, and numerous trees and flowers. We found them to be the most charming people. Mrs. Guibord insisted that we have coffee with them. We had a delightful breakfast, especially the fresh hot bread. They gave us a very well-conducted tour of the city of Quebec. We accepted an invitation to lunch with these friendly people, helped wash the dishes, and then said goodbye at 2:30 p.m.

Along the way to Wilmington, we had a glorious view of the approaching mountains—the Adirondacks.

Climb Every Mountain

We certainly did a great deal of mountain climbing. I remember all of the hosts at the tourist homes were very nice to us. When I didn't have appropriate hiking shoes, a woman loaned me hers. I hiked up the mountain in her worn-out shoes, feeling every grain of sand; but that's how nice people were to us—they were willing to offer us what they had. Our first experience at mountain climbing—up White Face Mountain—was unforgettable.

July 10.

It took me awhile to arrange my bed so as to miss the leaks in the roof last night, but I was finally successful. Awoke at 6 a.m. Dismal and rainy outlook, but I was determined to climb White Face Mountain anyway. I got the others talked into it, too, although at first they were a bit hesitant in tumbling out of comfortable beds just to go off and climb a mountain in the rain.

Dressed in boots and breeches, took a canteen, compass, 2 slickers, and a bag lunch and left Pilgrim Cottage (the first place we've spent two successive nights) at 7 a.m. to begin our "first mountain climb" up White Face. (It's the second highest peak in the Adirondacks—4,800 ft.) A most thrilling experience following the trail up the mountain—rocky, winding, narrow, deep in pine and birch forests at times, and very shady, or out on a rocky summit in the warm sunshine. We climbed up the streambed in places where it was rushing madly down the mountainside; wet boots and feet couldn't be avoided.

We stopped several times along the way up to fill the canteen with ice-cold delicious spring water. Left our slickers on a tree after 3 miles of climbing and Irene discarded her sweatshirt a little further on. Got so hot about half way, so we shed our shirts—walked along in

**Garneth, Irene, & Annette
Resting after the first 3 miles—
only 7 more miles to go.**

brassieres and pants and boots. (Betty wasn't wearing a brassiere, but we excused her.) Sunned ourselves on a flat rock after the first four miles. What a beautiful view of the surrounding mountains as we neared the summit of White Face.

Reached the TOP—after 7 miles of ascent—at 1 p.m., proud of our achievement. Had a vigorous lunch of crackers, cheese spread, cookies, and oranges. Started down at 2 p.m. We were enveloped in the clouds—felt the soft mist of rain on our hair and faces—strange and cool. Near the end of the trail, Garneth and I got lost; found Irene and Betty were lost, too—but what a good laugh we had when we discovered we weren't. Stuffed ourselves with $1.00 dinner at the hotel and then drove to Lake Placid to see the movie "Oil for the Lamps of China."

The resort owner had put us up in one of his cabins. We thought, "That's so nice—let's have dinner in his restaurant." The evening after our big climb, we went into quite a fancy dining room and found out after we ordered that the dinner cost us each a dollar! We just about died! We had never paid a dollar for dinner in our lives. We ate all that was set before us. (Was it worth a dollar? I imagine it was good—not that we knew the difference between good and bad food at that age.)

The Home of Emily Dickinson

Many historic homes were open to the public as museums. We got used to thinking that any time there was a sign on the house we could go in and check it out. We were at breakfast, and I asked the waitress, "Can you tell me where we would find the home of Emily Dickinson?" (She was the most famous person of whom I had ever heard.) The waitress said, "Is she new in town?"

Anyway, we managed to find her house on our own and rang the doorbell. A tall, statuesque woman with a hat appeared. (I had never heard of anybody wearing a hat in the house.) We explained who we were and that we hoped to see Emily's room. The woman called to somebody. It turned out to be a young man who was her secretary. She said, "These girls want to see Emily's room." They were mystified, but they allowed it. It was actually a wonderful tour.

They told us a great deal about the family. Emily's father was artistic. He bought a lot of art, of which his wife didn't approve. So when he got a new piece, he would take it to the attic and leave it there. Later, at an opportune time, he would take it down from the attic and hang it. His wife would say, "Did you just get that?" "Oh no," he would reply, "I've had that for a long time."

There was a little path from the house to the garden. Emily called it "A path just wide enough for two who love." I have remembered it all these 70 years since.

Annette had written the following about this interesting day spent in the home of Emily Dickinson.

July 13.

> *It's just 9:30 p.m. Finished a hot bath, and from where I lie in a bed on a large sleeping porch, I can see the dark outlines of a distant mountain and the shadowy figures of nearby trees; the slowly fading twilight is still visible. We're in a lovely home in the country in New Hampshire, not far from Claremont, with Vermont just across the other side of the Connecticut River. For the night, we have at our disposal a large, well-furnished bedroom with two huge four-posted beds (with innerspring mattresses), lounge chair, and this large comfortable sleeping porch. Oranges and bananas for breakfast. I like the radio music playing downstairs, too.*

But on with the details of today—a most fascinating hour spent at the home of Emily Dickinson. We were welcomed by her niece (a 70-year-old lady), Mrs. Martha Dickinson Bianchi. She recently published "Emily Dickinson Face to Face." The home smelled very old, dark, and musty. Everything had been kept in place for years, just as it used to be in Emily's time. We saw some of Emily's original poems, her choice of books, chinaware, her beautiful garden, and the narrow path only wide enough for "two who love."

Emily and her sister Lavinia were dearest and closest of friends all through life. Though they lived in different homes after Lavinia's marriage, they used to put out candles in their bedroom windows when they said "goodnight." The estate has beautiful lawns, gardens, trees, and shady wooded paths. Something very old, quiet, and intellectually creative about these rooms where Emily used to write her poetry.

One remarkable thing is that the Dickinson home is not open to the public ordinarily and is not at all commercialized. What a delight it is, too, not to find it that way. Mrs. Bianchi has devoted herself entirely now for a number of years to making Emily Dickinson "immortal," seeing that she gets the recognition that she deserves as "the greatest woman poet of the English language."

The home is rather difficult to find. It has a high gray picket fence and is well screened off by large trees and hedges from the road. (An elderly man down the road told us, "Mrs. Bianchi is quite eccentric.") Whatever others think, she suits her role perfectly—tall, thin, gray-haired, wrinkled, heavily circled eyes. Talks in a rather high voice, makes one feel her authority and breeding; she travels in Europe every winter and returns to the Dickinson home each April.

On Emily's tombstone:

EMILY DICKINSON
(1830 – 1886)
Born 1830
Called back 1886

Automobile Episodes

We were so fortunate to never have any major car problems as we traveled more than 8,000 miles in nine weeks, not even a flat tire. There were, however, a few minor incidents. Annette's journal reminded us of these.

Our trustworthy car

July 14.

It's extremely beautiful out tonight—full moon in the White Mountains. Saw the moon come over the mountains as we were driving along this evening. In attempting to park the car off the highway, we slipped into an unseen rut and put the car at a tippy angle, but some people from Oklahoma stopped and helped us out of the ditch.

Irene had a minor accident with the car this morning, also. In trying to start it, a spark from a backfire made a flame under the hood and nearly frightened her to death. She screamed, "The car is on fire!" Betty ran toward the car and told her to turn off the ignition and release the brake. (The latter was the most insensible command I ever heard of, for the car was on a wooded hill.) It rolled back several yards, shaving off part of an apple tree. Threw sand on the flame and with the others pushing from behind, I drove it up on the driveway again.

Climbing Mount Washington by Moonlight

Again, I don't remember whose crazy idea this was, but we decided to heighten our sense of adventure and climb Mount Washington by moonlight. It was rather spooky because there wasn't anyone around. We made sure we all stayed together.

A short pause up the Carriage Road. Not far to Summit House, but sleepy and exhausted. Annette, Garneth (reclining), & Irene

July 17.

Went to see a movie at Berlin (five miles away)— "Hooray for Love." A most perfect setting for romance driving back along the river in the mountains by the light of a full moon. Craved romance, but no means of satisfying it, so sought adventure instead. We decided to climb Mt. Washington, 6293 ft. up the Carriage Road (8 miles) by moonlight!

This day had a queer beginning, starting with our crazy idea to climb Mt. Washington (the highest peak east of the Rockies and north of North Carolina) by moonlight. Dressed in boots and breeches by 11 p.m. and drove out to the Glen House where we left our car. Started up the Carriage Road (built in 1861) at 11:30 p.m. We had a full moon all the way up—except where the road was too deep in the pines.

What adventure—climbing by moonlight; just we four girls alone on the narrow, winding mountain road. Rather uncanny and scary at first; the whole atmosphere reminded me of the "Werewolf." Stayed close together and tried to think little of strange mountain sounds at midnight. Stopped frequently for rest and refreshments (prunes and milk chocolate). Found ourselves in the clouds more than once.

Reached the Summit House at 5:45 a.m. after a six-hour climb. Had breakfast there and talked to some of the people. Temperature 43 degrees and very windy. Very sleepy while indoors. Started back by way of a trail at 7:20 a.m. Took the Tuckerman Ravine Trail to Hermit Lake down a very dangerous and steep head-wall on to the Rayond Trail. Still snow in the ravine. A hard descent all the way—down cliffs, over cascades, roots of trees, streams. Hardest physical exercise I've ever had. Reached Glen House at 1:30 p.m. much exhausted.

Maine

July 18.

Left our mountain town for Maine and the rocky Atlantic coast. Came on through Bangor; still surrounded by some mountains and lots of woods. At last—more pines and the sea. Saw our first glimpse of the sea from Bar Harbor on Mount Desert Island—much of a summer resort town and somewhat expensive. Got a comfortable cottage for the night. Ate supper at a place that specialized in seafood. I had a huge shrimp salad, Betty had "Lobster ala Newburg," and Garneth had clam chowder. We walked down to the ocean this evening, along the walk in the bay. Both cool and warm air currents struck us. Many couples out for a stroll. Spent the night in Bar Harbor.

In shorts - Betty, Annette, Garneth, and Irene

July 20.

Cold shower to wake me up for the day—invigorating! Spent most of the morning in Portland, Maine.

Spent an hour and a half in the charming old home of Henry Wadsworth Longfellow [1807 – 1882] in the very heart of the city (admission 25 cents). Saw the room and desk where Longfellow wrote "The Rainy Day." (I like it.) We saw much interesting furniture, many pictures, and homey relics and belongings of the Longfellow and Wadsworth families.

We came to Orchard Beach mid-afternoon. Thrilled over our first swim in the Atlantic; high tide, very salty waves breaking over us.

July 21.

Walked about the wharves at Rockport—sailing boats, sloops, gulls, old fishing shacks, and men and boys busy about the wharves. Just outside of Rockport was an exhibition of marine pictures. Lovely pictures of the sea. We met the young, good-looking artist himself— William Presnal. A huge rustic barn is his studio—a fireplace, a ship *model, a few trinkets, and his paintings on the wall. Talked to him for an hour and a half. He showed us a nude sketch he had made. Critiqued it. Irene posed for him. They seemed to get along well together. Learned that a "reasonable sum" for a small painting is $15 to $20. We all had lunch at the Mayflower Cafeteria in Gloucester. "All good things must come to an end; and good things are always short and sweet!" said artist Presnal.*

We watched men clean and barrel fish on the wharves. Got used to the smell. We went on a real "fishing schooner." The captain, a friendly, large, and weather-beaten man, let us roam all over his boat. Talked to the cook. There were 12 men on the crew. Had an actual ride on the schooner over to another wharf.

Boston

We spent about five days in Boston. Along the journey, we connected with numerous Hamline friends. Besides seeing the sights, there was always a chance for a summer romance. Annette was a bit "struck" by a guy from Hamline. His name was Homer Elford. He was a Hamline graduate and living out East training to go into the ministry. They spent time together at a few of our stops—Boston was one of them. Garneth also had a romance along the way. Bob was a scientist at a marine research center on the East Coast. They went together quite awhile after the trip.

July 22.

Had fun waking up in a canopy bed this morning. (The first one I'd slept in.)—I owe it all to dear old Salem. We had English muffins for the first time last night and ordered them again for breakfast. They're tasty!

Went through the Peabody and Essex museums; two such places with vast amounts of interesting material in each is a big job for one morning. Saw Nathaniel Hawthorne's birthplace—old—1655. Came on to Lynn, Massachusetts, by late afternoon. Swam at a fine beach. There was more salt water and roaring waves and sun on the sand. We arrived in Boston by 7 p.m. and hunted awhile for rooms. Betty and I went to a movie, "It Happened One Night," with Gable and Colbert. It was excellent!

July 23.

Our first full day in Boston. We walked downtown (about a mile) to the Sattler Hotel where our sightseeing tour began. Saw most of the historical sites of Boston proper. Drove out to Cambridge, saw Harvard, Radcliffe, University of Boston, and Boston School of Technology.

We met Homer Elford at 4 p.m. Spent the rest of the day with him—all four of us. Tromped around town—down to the market, into the railroad station, and out to the harbor and dock.

July 24.

We drove out to Stoneham (a suburb of Boston) to spend the day with Homer. He showed us around the First Congregational Church, where he is one of the three ministers. Saw his friend Nick again—a talkative chap.

We visited Louisa May Alcott's home (Orchard House at Concord, Mass.). Everything in the house seemed to be just as one would imagine it from her book "Little Women"—Jo's room, Beth's piano, Amy's art room, etc. The Alcott home is surrounded by trees and hills in back—very lovely. Part of the large tree (around which Meg danced on her wedding day) still stands on the front lawn. Homer and I came out of the house sooner than the others. We sat on the front lawn of the Alcott home and talked.

We all drove back to Stoneham and had dinner with Homer and Nick. I spent the evening with Homer. He and I drove out to Lynn Beach and walked along the beach and sat on the sand by the ocean. We watched and listened to the waves roll in and romanced. Both of us were in a very receptive mood. "A picture, a memory, a hope."

Student Ministers - Homer (on left) and a friend, Roland

July 25.

We drove down to the post office through the busiest part of Boston. Got caught in a "one-way" street and was sufficiently embarrassed by the scolding of other motorists and pedestrians. They yelled and swore at me—my! my! Such rudeness to an out-of-town guest! There are too many one-way streets without sufficient forehand notice of them.

8 p.m. I met Homer at the School of Theology. Had accordion and violin music on the boat—fun and a pretty sunset. Drove and walked along the Clark's River with Homer.

July 26.

This is our last full day in Boston. This day "the four young ladies" separated for the first time—each going her own way. I walked downtown at 11:30 a.m. and went through the lovely gardens in Boston Commons—lakes, trees, fountains, flowers, bridges, and statues. There was an orchestra for people to enjoy out of doors. It's nearly 50 acres, with not a building on it.

Homer came at 3 p.m. My, he looked handsome! (White checked flannels, dark coat, and white tie) I wore my 2-piece pale-green sport dress and white shoes. We were off together for the rest of the day. We drove to North Hampton, New Hampshire (50 miles), and met his dear chum and roommate, Jerry. He's also a student minister. (Jolly, energetic, and likeable—can sing beautifully.)

Homer and I took a swim in a rather chilled ocean at Hampton Beach. Went to the Christian Endeavor Banquet at 9:00 p.m. Nice. Homer gave a talk on "Life Plus" (a thrill for me). Had the urge to "fall in love" with him right there. We drove down to the ocean. Saw part of the rehearsal for the "Hermit's House" and then drove back to Boston. Homer gave me an "Evening in Paris" atomizer set. Sweet of him!

July 27.

We left Boston this morning. Enjoyed it. It was especially nice to have begun a friendship with Homer, too—besides seeing a lot of Boston.

Cape Cod and Martha's Vineyard

We felt fortunate to have contacts along the way given to us by Mr. Bridgman, Mr. Drew, and various Hamline faculty. Professor Brightman was one of our contacts. He was waiting for us when we arrived on the shores of Martha's Vineyard.

July 28.

We drove out to the tip end of Cape Cod at Race Point. Ocean on three sides—white, coarse sand to play in and an ice dip in the blue Atlantic. The coldest water I've been in so far. We looked at and climbed about on an old shipwrecked boat on the beach (quite a large old sailing vessel).

Ate our Sunday dinner at Provincetown on the Cape. Ordered fried scallops that didn't quite meet with my delight. Ate some of Betty's mackerel. Provincetown has very narrow streets and typical shingled fishing cottages, many shops, and piers.

July 29.

Woke up spasmodically this morning from 5 a.m. on. Got up at 6:45 while the other three were sleeping. I slipped out quietly and went down to the dock to meet Homer and Jerry before they left on the 8:20 a.m. boat for Martha's Vineyard. Nice to see Homer again after two days. Homer gave me a letter from him—my first one!

We girls had a motorboat ride into the bay—made merry with song and laughter and were soaked by the ocean spray.

Bath and dressed up at 4 p.m. to meet Homer at the dock at 5:20—back from the Island. A real reunion after only a day! Homer and the four of us had dinner at the Ideal Restaurant— swordfish this time. Good. Our last evening together, Homer and I. Drove over to Falmouth. Stopped near a little bay and talked frankly about ourselves and the future. I think we understand each other. Drove back to Woods Hole. (It's our last night here.) It's hard to say goodbye to my new friend. I like him very much. We said goodnight instead.

July 30.

Our last day at Woods Hole and enjoyable Cape Cod. Packed and down to the boat pier by 8:20 a.m. We left on a white, comfortable steamer for Oak Bluffs on Martha's Vineyard. A beautiful day—sunshine going over and back, blue sky and ocean, sea gulls playing around the boat. An interesting arrival at Oak Bluffs in trying to identify Professor Brightman upon our coming off the boat. We made two mistakes and then a tall, slender, gray-haired, and nice-looking middle-aged man shouted across the gate to us, "Say, there, are you the Hamline girls?" This was followed by a hearty handshake all around and introductions. Professor Brightman showed us around the town and harbor, bought us some saltwater taffy, and then took us to his summer cottage. We met Mrs. Brightman and two of their children, Mariam and Bob. Chatted on their veranda.

Two delightful hours of real ocean swimming at the Beach Club. Lots of sunshine. Nice ride back to Woods Hole. We drove to New Bedford to spend the night.

New Bedford

The crashing waves of the sea held such a fascination for us. We couldn't get enough of their hypnotic beauty.

One of our tourist homes

July 31.

Awoke in our tourist home in New Bedford about 8 a.m. Drove out to Colonel Green's Mansion to see the fully restored whaling vessel, built in 1840. Walked through it—a fine ship. The captain took his wife and children along on the voyages. The voyages lasted five to seven years, with a stop at some foreign port to get supplies every five months.

Near Whitehall, we saw Purgatory (deep crevices in the cliff rocks with ocean waters washing into them) and Paradise (two projecting layers of rock with shelf between.)

We took a beautiful walk along the cliff by the ocean—angry waves breaking against the rocks (swells, waves, and breakers, says Betty). I like to sit on the cliff and watch the sea—so restless and impetuous. Hope I'll come back to it again some day.

Rhode Island

It was not very common for young ladies to wear shorts in 1935. When we did, it was usually noted in the journal. Most of the people in the tourist homes were just wonderful. The woman that Annette wrote about here was an exception.

August 1.

Awoke at 8 a.m. from a fine night's sleep in our lovely country home in Rhode Island. Stopped along the highway to get a dozen peaches and a dozen doughnuts for breakfast. Drove around the campus of Yale University at New Haven, Connecticut. At Middletown, we saw Wesleyan University where Mr. Drew and Mr. Guibord attended college. Ivy-covered red brick buildings.

We all wore shorts today. We came into Southport where we are to call on Miss Perry—not home until 6 p.m. We found a tourist home out a ways and took it in order to get out of the rain. No bath or pressing facilities—disliked the landlady's attitude very much.

After dinner, we called on Miss Virginia Perry at Southport. She lives in a beautiful brick and gray-shingled mansion. The maid

*answered the door. Had ginger ale and cookies. We were told more
about what a well-planned trip we had than about old Southport.
Miss Perry, a society woman, had a rather "indifferent" Eastern
tone of voice, but was nice and hospitable. She had a dog, Taffy.*

New York City—Here We Come!

Can you imagine four naïve young ladies from Minnesota
arriving in the big city of New York? As we walked down Fifth
Avenue, we were thrilled to be a part of the noise, speed, and
activity all around us in this large city. We toured several
museums, and we rode the trolley and the subway. We also
paid about $2 apiece to sit in the cheap seats for four plays
on Broadway—*Tobacco Road, The Children's Hour, Personal
Appearance,* and *The Old Maid.*

One of our contact families, Mr. and Mrs. Nelson and
their three children, lived in Mt. Vernon, New York, which
was an hour-and-a-half ride by subway to downtown New
York. How fortunate we were to live with these friendly people during our eight-day stay in New York City. Annette's
journal reflected the varied experiences of our memorable
time there and the wonderful breakfasts that were prepared
for us. It was a welcome change from our usual oranges or
bananas and doughnuts.

August 2

*Left Fairfield, Connecticut, about 9 a.m. on our way to New
York City. Arrived at Mount Vernon, N.Y., about 11 a.m. and
stopped at the Nelson home (Fred Nelson's parents) where we're to
have our headquarters while visiting the "big city." The Nelsons are
friendly and hospitable. Mr. Nelson drove us down to the subway
station where we left for downtown New York. The subway was
abominably noisy—a deafening roar at a rapid speed!*

We walked down Fifth Avenue. Thrilled with the immensity, noise, speed, and modernity of New York. It's the largest city of the world—over 7 million people living and working here. Actually thrilled after riding in the dark (to daylight) subway and then emerging to find myself in the heart of New York City. Felt excitement!

Took a double-decker bus ride to upper New York (10 cents). We rode on top in the open air—bumpy and jerky, but fun. Saw the Empire State Building—105 floors, slender, firm, and handsome like a well-formed youth. Saw Grant's tomb and the new Washington Bridge. We took another bus back through the Harlem district and got off at 42nd Street.

We purchased tickets for "Tobacco Road" (for tomorrow night) at Gray's Drugstore (corner of 42nd and Broadway). Took a ferry across to Staten Island and saw the Statue of Liberty. What a beautiful view of the New York skyline on the return trip—gray outline in the evening mist. Took a tour of Chinatown and Greenwich Village in a taxi. Subway ride back to Mt. Vernon by 11:30 p.m.

August 3.

Awake at 8 a.m. after our first night in the Nelson home at Mount Vernon. Breakfast here at 8:45. Delicious! Honeydew melon, breakfast food, coffee and rolls. Took subway downtown and transferred three times to get off at 50th and Broadway. We had lunch at Woolworth's; then spent two hours or more in Radio City (Rockefeller Center). Took the NBC Studio tour through the RCA building—an intensely interesting and well-trained guide. We visited several studios; saw a rehearsal in one. (Heard a crooner sing "OK—Toots—What Would You Suggest?")

We saw Grand Central Station, the Chrysler Building, and the Library. We were lured into an auction shop—some system of attracting and keeping an audience. Bid on something and got it.

We ate supper at a cafeteria on 49th and Broadway. Then we went to our first play in New York City—"Tobacco Road." It was excellent for the type of life it portrayed. It was set on Lester farm in Georgia along an old tobacco road about backcountry people—poor, uncouth, crude, dirty-cussing, plain-speaking men and women; rank with frankness about sexual promiscuity, very suggestive. Might shock some people. Cussin', spitting men. Rode back on the subway and to bed by 2 a.m.

August 4.

A hot bath felt good this morning and then another good breakfast. Drove to visit Grant's Tomb. (Mrs. Grant is buried there, too.) We saw a small part of Columbia University. (That's where Betty would like to do graduate work.)

We took a new type of streetcar to 50th and Broadway. Went to Music Hall in Radio City to see Shirley Temple in "Curly Top." Good picture and excellent stage show. The theatre is a beautiful, spacious example of modern architecture. Sat in the show from 3:30 until 8 p.m.—worth the time.

August 5.

Another one of Mrs. Nelson's delicious big breakfasts. Took the subway down to Bowling Green. We went through the aquarium— interesting fish but not an attractive building. Walked through the Bowery, Ghetto, and Italian section. Real slumming. Streets all cluttered up with peddlers' stands and outdoor selling shops of every sort of merchandise and food. Not much room for people to pass by. Things were being sold very cheaply. Bought a slice of water-melon for 2 cents and a piece of fresh coconut for 1 cent.

We took a trolley up to Macy's (the largest department store in the world.) Had a personally conducted tour through the back-stage part of it. Very interesting—hospital, bureau of standards room, stock room, and employees' floor. All of us had tired feet today—ached. We bought our tickets for "The Great Waltz." Stretched our meals today in 11 places! We saw "Personal Appearance" with Gladys George and Merna Pace. Highly amusing, surprising beginning and ending. Went backstage and saw Merna Pace afterwards—pretty and charming.

August 6.

Woke up at 8:30 a.m. and had a big breakfast again. We had a leisurely

Watermelon in Ghetto, lower New York

morning, writing in diary, ironing, etc. We left for downtown at 11:30 a.m. Spent all afternoon at the Metropolitan Art Museum. It is the third best art museum in the world—surpassed only by the Paris and London ones. It takes a long while to walk through it—a good hike. I liked the Italian paintings particularly—Leonardo de Vinci, Titian, and Michelangelo.

We drove out to Playland (Rye Beach Amusement Park) after dinner. An evening of thrills and fun. Went on two roller coasters. One of them was terrific—90 miles an hour—jerky as the dickens and many sinking drops. I held on for dear life; glad when it was over.

August 7.

    We took the subway about 10 a.m. for the Bronx Park to see the zoo. It's one of the largest and best of its kind in the U.S. It provides, as far as possible, the natural setting for the animals instead of having them all cooped up in cages. Took the subway to 42nd and ate lunch at the large Woolworth store across from the library.

    We called on Mr. Fowler at his office, using our fourth and last letter of introduction from Mr. Drew. Cordial and friendly—he invited us to spend the weekend at his cottage in the Catskills (called Twilight Park). Went with Mr. Fowler to see the new Christ Church. (It's the finest Methodist church in New York.) He gave us a personally conducted tour through all six floors of it.

    Went to "The Great Waltz"—a perfectly splendid production. It's the story and music of Strauss (Jr. and Senior)—divine waltzes. Grand finale with "The Blue Danube" on a revolving stage. Home at 1 a.m.

August 8.

    Out of bed at 10 a.m. and had our sixth mammoth, delicious breakfast at the Nelsons'. We didn't get to sleep until nearly 2 a.m. this morning—late in getting back from "The Great Waltz." (After the production, Bob Nelson and his father were at the subway station in two cars to meet us.)

    We left for the subway this afternoon at 12:45 p.m. Stopped off at Wall Street and went to the Irving Trust Co. to wire for more money from the Minneapolis Bank. We took the subway again and traveled across Brooklyn to Coney Island. Arrived at the famous amusement park and beach about 3 p.m. We ate our lunch and supper at well-distributed places and intervals. Bought tickets for the Steeplechase (50 cents) for 31 different events (rides, sideshows,

Relaxing
in the
Nelsons'
Garden

*and circus.) Lots of fun. We had some "four for a nickel" pictures
taken, which turned out fairly well. A ride on a roller coaster called
the "Tornado"—dark tunnels and bad curves—but not terrifically
thrilling. Must be getting immune from riding on so many.*

August 9.

*Breakfast at the Nelsons' again. Another letter from Homer. I
took Anna (Mr. and Mrs. Nelson's daughter) with me on the subway for downtown. Did a hurried bit of shopping at Macy's. Took
me 20 minutes to buy a dress—first black one I've ever had.*

*Anna and I walked through Central Park—a very large city
park with lakes, bridges, rocks, zoo, and carousel.*

The Catskills

We had such a great time in New York City! It was difficult to
say farewell to the "big city" and our wonderful new friends,
the Nelsons, (plus all the delicious breakfasts) after our week's
stay. However, we were also eager to experience the Catskill
Mountains and continue on with the rest of our journey.

August 10.

Enjoyed our last big delicious breakfast at the Nelsons'. They sat down at the table with us. There are seven children in the family. We said goodbye and left Mt. Vernon about 11 a.m. for our weekend trip in the Catskills. These mountains are famous for their "Rip Van Winkle" legends. They have a characteristic blue haze about them. We ate our lunch at Poughkeepsie and also visited the Vassar College there.

A snapshot with the Nelson Family

We had real mountain grades for our car to climb. Reached Twilight Park and the home of the Fowlers (Mr. Drew's friends) at 5 p.m. It's a charming, comfortable, well-furnished cottage halfway up the mountain with two precipices below. Mrs. Fowler is very charming and cordial. (Had already met Mr. Fowler in New York last Thursday.) They have a self-conscious, mechanically-bent son, Carl. Mr. Fowler showed us his terraces and gardens. The maid served a chicken dinner.

August 11.

I awoke after a wonderful night's sleep in the Catskill Mountains in the Fowlers' cottage in Twilight Park. All of us went to the Union Church—a beautiful, rustic church in the heart of

Twilight Park. The minister preached a sermon on "Gratitude." It made me think of how grateful I should be for life and friends and the blessed opportunities that come my way—as the trip, for example. My prayer each night, brief and simple as it is: "Oh, dear God, make me truly appreciative of all I have to enjoy and help me to understand the rest."

It's lovely to find oneself here in the peaceful, serene, and beautiful quiet of the Catskills—to drink in the kindness and hospitality of the Fowlers. (Our thanks to dear Mr. Drew and the four letters of introduction he gave us, which helped to enrich our trip with new friends.) We were begged to stay to dinner, but left right after church— back to New York. Took rooms in the YWCA in Mt. Vernon.

August 12.

We left the YWCA shortly after 8 a.m., stopped in the Bronx for Betty's sister, Amy Klein, and said goodbye to New York. We followed Route 1 to the George Washington Memorial Bridge (a beautiful new suspension bridge over the Hudson—50 cents toll) and then crossed the river into New Jersey.

New Jersey

It was nice to have Betty's sister Amy join us for a few days along our journey. This is also where we felt the first waves of sweltering heat. As Annette recorded in her journal, "It's hotter than Hades!"

We drove through Asbury Park—an exclusive, expensive summer resort on the beach of New Jersey. At 3 p.m., we reached glamorous, fascinating Atlantic City (population 60,000, but millions go there annually). It has a boardwalk nine miles long, shops, cafes, stands, huge piers, and surf bathing.

We had a thrilling bit of ocean bathing. Played and plunged against and with roaring, twisting, and tumbling breakers. A strong undertow and waves nine feet high.

Smiling bathers on the beach below the famous boardwalk at Atlantic City. Betty, Irene, Annette, and Garneth

August 13.

We slept in a large dormitory in the YWCA in Atlantic City. There were about 80 compartments, each screened off with white curtains on four sides; included a single bed, chair, and locker with a mirror on it. We left Atlantic City at 9 a.m.

Drove through Trenton, New Jersey. Found our first real heat wave today—hotter than Hades! We went to Princeton and tromped around the campus of Princeton University. The Princeton campus is large with fine buildings—a quadrangle of lovely styled architecture.

Pennsylvania—The Heat Goes On

We had seen so much natural beauty along our travels—from the majestic mountains to the breaking ocean waves. We all disliked the dirty, dusty city of Philadelphia. Of course, it didn't help that we were visiting for the first time in the middle of a heat wave.

Annette wrote:

> It was on to Philadelphia of 2 million and our famed historic city (very hot, dirty, and old-appearing). We went through Independence Hall where the Declaration of Independence was signed and where the Liberty Bell (found here) proclaimed its adoption on July 4, 1776. (The bell cracked in 1843.)

> August 14.

> My little dingy room in the YWCA in Philadelphia looked out—with its one window—on a sunless court; consequently, when I woke up this morning amid Betty's raps on my door, it was still dark even at 8 a.m.

> We got peaches for breakfast from an impatient fruit man. "You'll have to hurry and make up your minds, girls. Can't you see I have work to do?" We drove through the slummy district of Philadelphia, much like the ghetto of New York—only much dirtier, more garbage and refuse on the streets. We all heartily disliked this third largest city in the U.S. We found it much too dirty, old, dead, and HOT.

> We took Betty's sister Amy to the Pennsylvania Station where she took a train for New York. Saw a smattering of Fairmont Park and then experienced our first car trouble after traveling 5,200 miles without a bit of it, not even a flat. A stranger stopped and fixed it first. The carburetor was not feeding enough gas. It stalled again on the way out of the city. Had it towed to a garage, had the fuel pump adjusted, and new points put in. Wasted at least three hours. Saw Bryn Mahr College and then spent half of the afternoon at Valley Forge.

August 15.

I was awakened by all three of my co-travelers this morning at 8 a.m. in our tourist home in York, Pennsylvania. For our break-fast, we stopped a man driving a fruit truck—peaches and bananas. Spent most of the morning in Gettysburg seeing the famous battle-field of the civil war. Had a very competent guide accompany us in our car and explain points of interest on this extensive battlefield. A pleasant dose of history—really educational.

August 16.

Awakened last night at 3 a.m. by the two women next door in the YWCA at Baltimore. The hottest night I have ever spent. Rolled my pajama legs up and turned the top down—terrific heat! Bananas for breakfast—seven for a nickel!

Washington, D.C.—Our Nation's Capital!

There was so much to see in this historic city! During our visit to Washington, D.C., Garneth and I stayed with our uncle and aunt. After much searching, Annette and Betty found a room on Massachusetts Street. Then we would meet up each day and the Four Young Ladies would spend long sightseeing days together. The heat continued, but that didn't slow us down.

We drove on to Washington, D.C., in the afternoon—lots of mail waiting for us at the Holths' uncle's home. Dinner at the Holths'. It's very hot here in the nation's capital. We drove down by the Capitol and government buildings to see them lit at night. A beautiful sight!

August 17.

Began our longest sightseeing day—from 9:20 a.m. to 6 p.m. We browsed around the Library of Congress first and saw the original copy of the Declaration of Independence and the Constitution. Lunch in a drugstore. We went through the unfinished Supreme Court Building. Greek pillars—marble—glorious. Toured the Capitol. Proud of the nation's capital—more trees than any other city in the country—broad avenues—white beautiful buildings. We took an elevator up to the Washington Monument—fine view. We visited the Lincoln Memorial and reflecting pool.

A view of the Capitol

August 18.

Betty drove while I conducted the tour through the northeast and northwest part of the city. We visited the Smithsonian Institute. Saw the "Spirit of St. Louis." We had dinner at the Holths' at 5:30—very good. All of us went to a "Sunset Symphony Concert" in the evening beside the Potomac. Three conductors, a three-quarter moon out. It was a very lovely concert in the out-of-doors. Had ice cream refreshments at the drugstore.

August 19.

Visited the White House—basement, corridor, and East Room. We looked at the chinaware used by different administrations. Hurried up to the Capitol to listen in on the U.S. Senate for a while. Only a small group of senators answered roll call—not a very important day, I guess.

The Four Young Ladies in Washington, D.C.

We left the Capitol to go through the Bureau of Printing and Engraving where all paper money (from $1.00 to $10,000) and stamps (from 1 cent to $5.00) are made. It takes 30 days to complete one bill and 3 days to make a stamp. Saw a great deal of money in a 20-minute tour.

We drove by the Ford Theatre where Lincoln was shot and also saw the house across the street in which he died.

Shopped and ate dinner. Betty and I enjoyed the last of an outdoor band concert on the Capitol steps.

August 20.

Again, peaches and doughnuts made up our breakfast. We drove down to Mt. Vernon to visit George Washington's estate. A beautiful estate on the wooded green banks of the Potomac.

We had a "fish ball" dinner at the Holths'. Not particularly keen about this Norwegian dish. We left Washington at 6:30 p.m. to board a steamer for Norfolk, Virginia. (Will arrive tomorrow at 8 a.m.) Betty and I have a tiny stateroom together—snug and comfortable.

We sat out on deck, ate our supper—which Mrs. Holth had put up for all of us—talked, and watched the lights of the city fade in the distance. A dark night—lots of breeze—cool—perfect for a bit of romancing if there were only someone to share it. Ordered watermelon in the dining room. It was huge.

August 21.

The slight tossing of the boat awakened me at 6 a.m. Betty awoke, too, so we slipped on our coats and went out on deck to watch the waves and see the morning sun in its full glory. It was rather warm in our small cabin—but fun to have been on a steamer all night. Back into my upper bunk and slept again until 7:20. Our boat docked at Norfolk, Virginia, at 8:15—a 13 1/2 hour trip in all down the Potomac and into the Chesapeake Bay.

We drove out to Virginia Beach (called the summer playland of the South) for a swim. A rough sea—huge waves and powerful breakers. A strong undertow, too. It takes one off guard—hard to keep one's footing when the sand begins to shift underfoot and the swift current forces one to be carried along in its direction. Curiosity and desire for something new and exciting in sport got me introduced to Buck Holth (from North Carolina—"wah you all frum?") who attempted to teach me the art of "riding the surf" on a small stomach surfboard. With a little practice and his engineering shove-off, I had a number of fast thrills over the surf—riding it up onto the beach. Lots of fun.

August 22.

We were in Williamsburg, Virginia, most of the day. This little colonial town has been restored at Rockefeller's expense—very dignified and refined looking—lots of white picket fences, gardens, trees, shuttered windows, red brick buildings, unpaved streets without curbs, and lots of hitching posts.

Had chow mein for dinner. Saw the movie "China Seas" with Gable, Berry, and Harlow.

August 23.

Hay fever has me for sure today. Spent all morning in Richmond. This part of the South looks much like Northern Minnesota. No extreme heat so far. Lots of red soil and mulberry trees. Came onto the pretty little city of Charlottesville. There are a great many Negroes in what we've seen of the South.

August 24.

Drove out to Ashlawn—James Monroe's home. It was too well hidden by green hedges to be seen (without paying an admission.) Spent an hour or more at Monticello—the beautiful estate of Thomas Jefferson a few miles southeast of Charlottesville. He was a most ingenious man—a host of self-made inventions all through his house. Jefferson died a poor man—heavy in debt—spent too much of his money entertaining guests. Some of his furniture had to be sold to pay his bills. He was the writer of the Declaration of Independence, ambassador to France, and third president of the United States.

Garneth and Annette on a bench in Williamsburg, Virginia

The Virginia Wonders

There were yet more natural wonders for us to experience—the hazy Blue Ridge Mountains, deep dark caverns, and the most amazing—"The Natural Bridge" of Virginia. Annette beautifully described it in her journal as "towering, sheer, majestic cliffs vibrating with music."

August 25.

We spent last night in our tourist home in Luray, Virginia. The grandmother of the house must chew tobacco according to the amount of it displayed around the corners of her mouth! Betty fastened the name "little dynamo" onto her granddaughter because of her very energetically carrying our baggage from the garage all the way upstairs.

Beginning to count the days until we get home—a grand trip—but just can't help missing some dear people that were left behind.

We saw much of the Blue Ridge Mountains today. One marvelous hour and a half in the "Endless Caverns" of Virginia. The

"The Natural Bridge" of Virginia

cave is over 9 million years old. It was discovered on October 1, 1879, by two boys who, with their dogs, were chasing a rabbit and thus discovered the entrance. No end to the caverns has been found, although explorers have penetrated 2 1/4 miles farther than the ordinary visitor is allowed.

Came onto our second "world wonder" for today— "The Natural Bridge" of Virginia. Supremely wondrous! It's 215 feet high, 90-foot suspension, 100 feet wide, and 40 feet thick. George Washington surveyed it at one time—later owned by Thomas Jefferson. Towering, sheer, majestic cliffs vibrating with music.

We took a tourist home in Buchanan, Virginia. It was dark before 8 p.m. Read "Rip Van Winkle" yesterday and "Legend of Sleepy Hollow" today.

The Beauty of North Carolina

The lush countryside was beautiful as we wound our way toward Asheville and the Great Smoky Mountains, but we were also amazed at the poor white farmers living in dilapidated shacks on the mountainside next to their little tobacco patches. They appeared to live in such poverty. We also encountered some very challenging driving conditions up those narrow winding roads.

To relax our minds and add laughter to lighten our souls while driving, we made good use of our imaginations. After so many weeks out on the open road, the Studebaker had become our little home. We created a "family situation"—Annette was Pa, I was Ma, and Betty and Garneth were the kids. We also played made-up games along the way to entertain ourselves, such as the "good grammar game."

Burma Shave was a well-known men's shaving cream at this time. We enjoyed poetry, so we got a bit silly and began creating Burma Shave jingles.

August 26.

Up and on our way before 9:30 a.m. Another cool night. Had a fried egg sandwich and two fresh hot raised doughnuts for breakfast.

The Virginia Alleghenies are beautiful—thickly wooded, green soft peaks, rugged in parts, steep slopes, rocky and red soil. We saw our first tobacco fields today—drying racks, too. Took an awful detour on a dirt mountain road, narrow, winding, with numerous blind curves—unceasing. Real mountain huts in this part of North Carolina—one-roomed scantily furnished shacks. Poor white farmers living in them. Abundance of dull-looking children. A very small plot of land cultivated behind or alongside their mountain hut—mostly corn, tobacco, and vegetables. Yes, very dilapidated shacks—one story with open porch in front.

Really difficult driving—narrow road giving away at the edges. Garneth almost hit one oncoming car in rounding a curve. We were an hour and a half on this mountain detour and then in Asheville, North Carolina, by 6:30 p.m. We have a cabin in the foothills of the Great Smoky Mountains tonight. The sound of crickets, the stars out . . . the quiet.

I have won 25 cents on our "good grammar game." The jolly travelers also spent the time concocting a number of Burma Shave jingles today.

> *A whiskered face is yours, I see.*
> *So call it the end for you and me.*

> *A good clean shave is what you'll find,*
> *If you keep Burma Shave in mind.*

August 27.

Another cool night in the southern mountains—foothills of the Smoky Mountains. An especially clear, starry sky last night. Betty conveyed a greeting from Mr. Bridgman! Left our tourist cabin and on our way by 7 a.m. We had to drive through a lot of mountain mist and fog—hard on the eyes. Most beautiful scenery in these southern mountains—unsurpassable. Green, heavily wooded, so close to one. High as the White Mountains, too. Gurgling, soft, charming streams—fine highways—nothing more picturesque.

Tennessee and Kentucky

It was always a thrill to get our mail at various designated cities along the way. (We had addresses with us and spent time writing letters almost every day.) We were grateful to each of our family members and friends who faithfully wrote to us. Just as Annette had written in her journal, "We would slowly drink in each word." It warmed our hearts and connected us to the other world that we called home.

Yet adventure called. There were more caves to discover in this part of the country. I can't believe we were able to sleep at all after our experience in Floyd Collins' Crystal Cave.

August 28.

Up at 7 a.m. Apples and grapes for breakfast in Chattanooga, Tennessee. Cloudy morning. We called for our mail at the Chattanooga post office. Hurrah for family and friends who write! I received eight letters. It took me more than an hour to read all my mail. What deep satisfaction reading it all—slowly drinking in each word.

We drove to Nashville (the capital city of Tennessee). Had lunch there. Bought a strap for my wrist. Looked at the Parthenon (art museum modeled after the Greek.) Drove steadily until reaching the Kentucky Cave region. Supper at an old-fashioned farmhouse. We took a large first-floor room there with very few modern conveniences—no running water, electricity, etc. Had a kerosene lamp, huge pitcher and wash bowl, an outside "sanitary" (an Eastern term for it).

We bought tickets for Floyd Collins' Crystal Cave—discovered by Floyd Collins in 1917. He met a tragic death—caught in a sand

**Chatting over a split-rail fence near Hodgenville, Kentucky.
Women in the south have their pipes, you know.**

trap in 1925. Lived for eight days—finally died of pneumonia. (His father wouldn't allow them to cut off his leg in order to get him out.) His body remained in the cave for 83 days, was removed and buried in a cemetery for two years, then put back down in the Crystal Cave. We saw him inside the coffin. His body was as hard as stone. The temperature was 59 degrees.

August 29.

The cold woke me up this morning. No bad dreams after the weird tromp through Crystal Cave last night. Hearing about Floyd Collins' death with a highly uncanny atmosphere about us—bats whizzing by and an irregularly lighted cave—also having actually seen his body when our guide opened the coffin.

Drove down to Mammoth Cave and hiked down to the old entrance as far as the barred door. Then to Hidden River Cave. There were 250 steps down into the entrance and the muddy, strange, hidden river that flows through it. The cave was discovered by Daniel Boone in 1784 and opened in 1908.

Went on to Hodgenville. We had lunch there and then went to see Lincoln's birthplace. It's a huge pillared memorial building with a cabin inside. At Louisville, Kentucky, I saw my first large race-track—Churchill Downs.

Indiana and Illinois

After covering 7,000 miles, our journey was leading us ever closer toward home. Betty celebrated her twentieth birthday while on our trip. (Does that ever seem young to all of us now!) Of course, we wanted to make it a special day. We recalled our little surprise dinner that we had for her at the end of the day, complete with angel food cake, candles, and gifts.

We crossed the Ohio River into Indiana. Southern Indiana is much prettier than the northern part; more country, open green hills, and woods. Have a large room in a tourist home in Vincennes, Indiana, tonight. We have traveled 7,000 miles to date. Home soon.

August 30.

It's Betty's birthday—20 years old. We greeted her upon arising in our tourist home in Vincennes. Apples and powdered doughnuts for breakfast. It's a fine sunny day. We made Springfield, Illinois, by 1 p.m.

We put the car in a garage for new gaskets to be put in while we ate lunch. Lunch was at a very attractive, but expensive, place. Then went through Lincoln's Springfield home where he lived from 1844-1861. He left it upon going to the White House as president. His Springfield home was a large white house with green shutters, five windows in front downstairs, small white fence around it, and set up off the sidewalk by a red brick wall. Only the downstairs is furnished and open to visitors. The large clock in the dining room was stopped on April 15 at 7:22 a.m.—the time of Lincoln's death in 1865.

We took a tourist cabin just north of Industry, Illinois. Had a little surprise dinner for Betty on her birthday—two large cans of vegetable soup, beans, crackers, cheese, peanut butter, and angel food cake (candles lit, too). Our gift to her was a very lovely copy of "The Rubaiyat." We drove 11 miles to Macomb, Illinois, to see a Wild West picture, "Danger Trails." Hopelessly a waste of time— poor acting, etc. Cold drinks and to bed.

August 31.

Our tourist cabin is a few miles outside of Industry, Illinois. Had a large double cabin—two rooms, one with a blue light. A ton of blankets kept us warm. I drove for the first couple of hours this morning as usual. We crossed the Mississippi River out of Illinois into Iowa (our last new state of our trip) at Burlington. This makes the 20th state. Bought doughnuts here—big, fresh, delicious raised ones.

Iowa

We could never forget our first sight of a sign for Minneapolis upon our driving into Des Moines. We were so excited that we had to have a snapshot taken next to the sign.

We saw the University of Iowa at Iowa City and, at Des Moines, viewed the capitol. Have a nice cabin tonight outside of Hubbard, Iowa—two beds. Our last cabin meal—salmon salad, potato chips, bread, peaches, peanut butter, and cheese.

We saw our first Minneapolis sign today at Des Moines—287 miles to home! We have covered 8,000 miles in nine weeks.

Our first Minneapolis sign. Irene, Annette, and Garneth

Home from our journey. Betty and Garneth

September 1.

I was awakened by the others at 4 a.m.—not quite light. A very cool morning. We were on our way before 6 o'clock. We watched the sun rise like a big ball of fire. (This is the second sunrise that we have seen on our trip. The other was while climbing Mt. Washington on July 17.)

Our last day together. A shout and cheer as we cross the boundary line into our home state of Minnesota. Back again after nine weeks and two days and 8,500 miles without one flat tire during the entire trip.

The Journey's End

We were very happy to be back home, yet we were not without tears. It was sad to separate after spending over nine weeks together as a little family. Once again, Annette's journal captured the feelings in our hearts as the journey ended for The Fortunate Four—or The Four Young Ladies.

Farewell to my three traveling chums. Our wonderful summer has come to an end. A leave-taking snapshot and several goodbyes.

I followed the first impulse of throwing myself on the bed giving expression to an emotion of loneliness—tears, too, but only for a few brief moments until I caught hold of myself. Got busy with unpacking.

Annette (left) saying goodbye to the other "Young Ladies"

❧

Annette closed her journal and we returned to the present moment—it was no longer 1935, but 1996 once again. In these 61 years, the country had changed, our bodies had certainly changed, and we had developed into the women we were destined to become. Our dreams about the future as four young women were now individual memories of the past.

What had we learned from this journey? Betty had reflected on three experiences that she felt had helped her grow up and take responsibility for her actions:

The first experience was when we stayed at a lovely home in New Hampshire. We slept in the host's bedroom with their marriage license framed and hung above the bed. We enjoyed breakfast with them and then packed the car. When Irene started the car, smoke poured from the hood. As Annette mentioned in her journal, out of my limited experience, I called out, "Take off the brake!" Well, the car rolled down a gentle slope and broke the trunk off a young apple tree. Our host calmly opened the hood and threw a couple handfuls of sand on the flames and ended the emergency. The car started, and he wouldn't accept any money for the loss of his tree.

The second episode happened in Salem, where we had a beautiful room in a fine tourist house. We wanted to iron a dress. With no ironing board, I suggested we use a tabletop. Well, we ruined the finish of a small mahogany end table. I said, "There's no way we could pay for restoring that table." Irene said, "We have to report it to our hostess." She did, and she said that we wanted to pay for the damage. The woman said, "Can you afford fifteen dollars? I know I can get it fixed for that." Among us we came up with the money.

The third experience was at the train station in Philadelphia. We were saying goodbye to my sister Amy who had joined us in New York for four days. We had a few hours yet to walk around the historic city, so we checked Amy's bags. Checking cost 10 cents per piece. I opened my sister's small carry-on case and stuffed it with another bag. When I closed it, the carry-on case burst—it was probably cardboard. Here I was trying to save just 10 cents.

Before this summer trip, we were so ignorant. We didn't know what to expect. Our experiences on this journey together had spanned a wide gamut—from walking through the ghetto of New York to dining with the wealthy families that we met in the Catskills and Martha's Vineyard. We had climbed to the top of mountains and explored deep underground caverns. We were in awe of the Great Lakes and the surging waves of the ocean. This journey gave us a lasting appreciation for the beauty and history of our great country.

We had very different personalities. Surprisingly, we all got along well, thanks primarily to my sister Garneth, I believe. She does have a soothing effect on people. (We never took a vote, but I think she deserves a lot of credit.)

Throughout the trip, we always behaved as young ladies. No one got into any trouble, and there was no hanky panky.

Our hearts were grateful for our safe passage and for the kindness of strangers. We only hoped that they had been sufficiently thanked. This experience also gave each of us a feeling of personal strength and confidence that would continue throughout the rest of our lives.

There were no tears this time as we said our goodbyes—only laughter and warm hugs—and of course, leave-taking snapshots. We all agreed, "Let's do this again soon—we can't wait another 61 years!"

THE REST OF THE JOURNEY

You may think this is the end of the story, but in 1935 the personal journeys of Irene and the other three young women were just beginning. At the ages of 19 and 20, their hearts were filled with individual hopes and dreams. Upon returning from their trip together, they all graduated (Garneth, one year later) and got busy making plans for the future. There was little time to reflect on their summer journey at this point in their lives.

What happened to each of these women after the summer of 1935? It was now the year 2000 when I caught up with two of these intriguing women—Irene and Annette. Did their hopes and dreams come to pass? This is what I learned about the lives of The Fortunate Four.

Irene Holth Hoebel

Irene became a war bride about five years following graduation from Hamline University. Unfortunately, the marriage was unsuccessful. She said with a subtle smile, "The marriage didn't last as long as the war." Her second marriage to Victor Williams in 1947 seemed like a perfect match. They met through friends. She described him as "very literary and terribly bright." Tragedy struck, however, only two months into their marriage. Victor died suddenly of a ruptured appendix at the age of 31.

At this point, Irene found herself a widow with a young daughter named Sue. She went on with life and earned a master's degree in social work. She enjoyed a successful career, including a job as administrative assistant to Mayor Naftalin. After 16 years as a widow and career woman, love struck again, thanks to a matchmaker who invited both of them to a party. Here she met E. Adamson Hoebel, who was a Regent's Professor of Anthropology at the University of Minnesota. They were married just two and a half months later. Why so soon? Irene says, "We were both mature and had the same values. What was the point of waiting around?" In August of 1963, they were united in marriage beneath the apple tree in their backyard.

Her life has been filled with travel and adventure, a reflection of the summer of 1935. Irene and Adamson traveled together to far-off lands such as Fiji and the Trobian Islands. (Irene said, "I thought Europe would be nice, too, but my husband always had projects relating to his work in anthropology and people to look up in these exotic places.")

Ad (as he as called) also wrote a collection of books on the subject of anthropology. He and Irene worked together on these projects, and she enjoyed the role of editor. They shared 30 wonderful years until his death in 1993.

Irene is now living in Kenwood, a luxury residence for seniors in Minneapolis. Anthropology books fill the bookshelf in her small apartment, a reflection of their life together. A broken hip has confined her to a wheelchair, but she still has her same wit and humor. Commenting on her journey, Irene said, "When I think about my life, it has been rich, but also damn sad." (She experienced sorrow once again when her beautiful daughter Sue died suddenly of an unexplainable heart attack at the age of 33. Sue left behind a husband, a five-year-old son, and a two-month-old daughter.)

Irene said, "I can't think of anything worse than losing a child. Thanks to a brilliant and sensitive father plus a helpful extended family, both children are bright, healthy, and emotionally secure—perfect grandchildren. They are a delight. At this stage in my life [85 years old], they have become my best friends, giving suggestions for books, movies, and social events. I feel blessed. We're inclined to take all the credit for everything that goes right in our lives. I think there's always something larger—something beyond ourselves."

Garneth Holth Buchanan

Irene had this to say about her sister: "Everyone loves Garneth. I happened to look in her high school annual years later after our trip. Under her name it was written that she gets along with everybody—even the teachers."

Garneth met the love of her life in quite a unique way. Following graduation from Hamline in 1936, Garneth met John Buchanan while out in a strawberry patch, of all places. They were both picking strawberries for a farmer in Excelsior, Minnesota. Garneth and John were married a year later. Their family grew as they had three children—two boys and a girl.

Throughout her life, Garneth enjoyed hiking, camping, and reading. They may not have had an abundance of financial wealth, but she described her life as "fun, happy, and eventful." Her sister Irene added, "Their priorities were remarkable. John did not have the opportunity for a higher education and had to physically work very hard. However, they always had the best reference books and encyclopedias for their children. They also saw to it that all their children went to college."

After retirement, Garneth and John moved into a senior residence in Waconia, Minnesota. John passed away recently. They apparently shared a deep love and respect for one another. It was said by many that there was never a cross word between them. Garneth is now living in a retirement home in Forest Lake.

While sorting through some of his mother's things recently, Garneth's son Peter discovered 14 postcards and a letter that she had written to her mother, Hazel Holth, during the trip of 1935. He was surprised at how often she used the word "keen" in her postcards. Apparently, it was a popular slang word for teenagers at the time. (While Peter was growing up, he had never once heard her use that word.)

The following is a letter that Garneth wrote to her mother from Connecticut on August 1, 1935.

Southport, Conn.
August 1, 1935
4:10 p.m.

Dearest Mom,

We've just arrived here in Southport amidst an awful rain, lightening, and thundershower. We took this place in great haste to get out of the rain because we have some people here to visit. The car is in the garage. This is the first time we've had a place where the people were not nice. It costs $1.00 each and then we'd have to pay 50 cents apiece extra for a bath. To safeguard against anyone taking even a cold bath, they have unscrewed all the faucets, etc., in the bathtub. It's really funny! Tomorrow we get to N.Y. We're only 40 some miles away now.

The last day we were in Woods Hole, Mass., the others took a boat trip to an island—Martha's Vineyard—but I stayed behind. I met Bob [her boyfriend, the scientist] and had lunch at the mess hall with him. (We met a lot of crazy scientists that we'll have to tell you about later.) Afterwards I put on shorts, and we went canoeing across to a small island—Nonamesset. It's fun canoeing there in the saltwater bay. The waves tip the canoe, and many came right in on top of us.

After we had come back and dressed, we drove in our car down to the post office. On the way there (after we'd gone 4,000 miles and through big cities), a policeman stopped us for having the license covered. Bob took the spare tire off and put it in the back seat. When we returned, we had to spend the rest of the afternoon fixing it. He moved the license plate higher and put the tire back the same way—even padded the bumper with cardboard and a sack to protect the tire more. Oh well, it's on good and tight now, and the policemen in large cities aren't fussy about things like that anyway. It was kind of fun. We barely got it fixed when we had to meet the others at the boat at 5:30. Then we started right on to New Bedford.

The rain is all over now, so we shall get ready pretty soon to eat and then visit the Perrys—friends of a friend of Mr. Bridgman's. They have a gorgeous big house—the prettiest in town—right on the ocean. We drove by it earlier.

Last night we were in R.I., tonight Conn., tomorrow N.Y. We get through these states fast.

We buy quite a few peaches, etc., but it's very different from having everything right when and where you want it. Irene and I have a hard time to keep from picking up and tasting things in the stores we go into. We'll probably be "picked up" for shoplifting soon.

Today we drove straight through from Charlestown, R.I. We saw Yale University at New Haven. Had the car greased this noon.

I hope you are well now. Please write to us at N.Y. and Washington as often as you want to because we like to hear from you. Say "hello" to Vincent and anyone else I know and take care of yourself and Terry. The cats will take care of themselves. I must get ready now.

Much, much love—

Garneth

Annette Strand Scherer Robbins

Annette experienced loss at the early age of three when her mother died. She was raised primarily by her two Swedish grandparents and two Swedish maiden aunts.

Annette's lifelong friendship with Betty began back at West High School in Minneapolis. Having the same grades, it was declared that they were both valedictorians of their class. Betty could write beautifully even back then, and Annette had the loudest voice; therefore, Annette gave the valedictorian's speech that Betty had written.

Following graduation from Hamline University, Annette followed her advisor's encouragement to go on to graduate studies in social work at the University of Minnesota. She also spent summers teaching tennis. Remember, this was during the Great Depression when, as Annette says, "You were lucky to have a tennis racket."

The love for tennis led her to a new love in her life—Paul Scherer—another avid tennis player. Annette first noticed this "fine specimen of a man" out on the tennis court. She asked her friend Liz, "Who is that fellow?" Liz replied, "That's Paul Scherer. Now that's the kind of man you should date."

Paul later called and asked if she would be his mixed-doubles partner. She laughs when thinking about their first date, "He included everything you could possibly think of—tennis, swimming, dinner, and a movie—about four dates in one." Then he wanted to kiss me and I said, "I can't kiss on the first date." "Oh, yes, you can," he said. (So . . . we did.)

Well, they went from being partners on the tennis court to also being partners in life. They were married on June 14, 1940, a year and a half after they had met and just two weeks after the marriage of his twin brother. Paul "proposed" while she was at a conference. She received his telegram that said, "School is out June 14." She said, "That was a secret message. I knew what it meant, but nobody else could interpret the message." They had a simple wedding ceremony at the Hennepin Avenue Methodist Church in Minneapolis. Their honeymoon was a five-day cruise on a steamship. (She laughed, "We couldn't afford much. The cabin was so tiny we had to take turns dressing.")

Annette and Paul had three sons. Tennis always remained an important part of their lives. They later joined the Minneapolis Senior Tennis Club. They had been married 42 years when Paul died in 1982.

Annette's continued connections with Hamline led to her meeting the man who would become her second husband. While touring the campus during a college reunion, she noticed a brand-new building—the Orem Robbins Science Center. She commented to her friends, "I know who he is. He was in my high school." She discovered he was a lifetime member of the board of trustees. He wasn't an alumnus of Hamline University but was helping the college by being a board member and raising funds. (This was similar to the role that Mr. Drew had played many years earlier.)

One month after her reunion, Annette received a call from Naples, Florida. It was Orem Robbins asking if she would have dinner with him when he returned to Minnesota. They went to the Officers' Club, and she discovered he was a really good dancer. (Annette still loved to dance.) He then returned to his home in Florida. The next month he called again asking for a second date, on which they went to the Minikahda Club, where he is a member.

She recalled, "Our third date was in December, right after Christmas. We were up at the top of the IDS building for dinner. It was still daylight, so you could see the Mississippi River and the beauty of Minneapolis. We were just relaxing and talking, and he asked me what kind of wine I wanted." I said, "I'm half French, so I'll have French wine." I had a glass and he proceeded with, "You know, I think you and I could make sweet music together."

When Annette's relationship with Orem developed to this point, she knew she had to end a friendship with another gentleman caller. When this man heard Annette was dating Orem, he said, "You better watch out—he'll sweep you off your feet." (Annette said with a smile, "I did get roses for quite awhile.")

Annette and Orem were married on her birthday on May 17, 1992. She said, "Robbie asked me what kind of wedding I wanted—a simple one?" "No," I said, "I had a simple one—I want a big one." Well, he hired a 12-piece orchestra! They had a lovely church wedding that she enjoyed planning, followed by a reception of dinner and dancing at the Minikahda Club. It was the culmination of quite a fairy-tale romance.

Irene described Annette as "a very beautiful woman and avid sportswoman." She added, "Annette has been involved in so many sports over her lifetime—tennis, golf, hiking, and even field hockey." Today, Annette and Orem spend time among their three homes and continue to enjoy an active lifestyle. Together they have nine children. Yes, I believe many of Annette's dreams have come true.

Elizabeth (Betty) Klein Bridgman

Following graduation from Hamline, Betty went to the University of London to study for a year. This was probably due in large part to Mr. Bridgman's encouragement, as he continued to want to add culture to each of their lives.

By the way, what happened to Mr. Bridgman, the wealthy bachelor and the trip's benefactor whom you heard about at the beginning of the story? Upon Betty's return from London, the other young ladies were surprised to be invited to a wedding—Betty Klein and Donald Bridgman were getting married. He was thirty years her senior, but as Irene put it, "Who knows exactly how any romance develops. Perhaps it was the letters that they wrote to each other while we were on our summer trip or while she was studying in London that fueled their romance." Betty and Donald were happily married for 39 years until his death in 1976. They had six children—five boys and one girl.

Irene described Betty as "a very energetic and efficient woman who loved life. Besides her intellectual accomplishments, she was a wonderful camper. She spent a lot of time in the Boundary Waters and arranging camping trips for her children and grandchildren. We shared a love for poetry, but she was an excellent poet with two published poetry books."

At the age of 80, Betty moved into Kenwood, the retirement community where Irene lived. Unfortunately, the promise in 1996 for another joyful reunion was never fulfilled. Betty died suddenly on August 2, 1999. As a friend said, "She died with her boots on—while taking another class."

Annette and Betty's friendship that had begun in high school continued while they were roommates for two years at Hamline. They remained close friends throughout their lives.

Annette spoke of her dear friend at a memorial service for Betty.

> *Remembering Betty is no easy task—when I think of the full, generous, and exemplary life that she lived for 83 years. I knew her for 68 years. . . . Legacy comes with the life she lived and the many people she befriended. She achieved fulfillment, and she shared her good fortune with many. I remember Betty Bridgman in so many ways: her wisdom, her humor, her creative ability (poetry and prose), her compassion, her love of nature, her generosity, and her unselfish sharing of her many talents and her friendship."*

It was difficult for Annette to say goodbye to such a dear friend. They had shared so much throughout the years.

Yes, it has been quite a journey. Four young women—Irene, Garneth, Annette, and Betty—each from families of modest means, experienced much of what life had to offer. Their numerous mountain-climbing adventures during the summer of 1935 were followed up by a lifelong interest in hiking. (Betty and Annette remained active in the Minneapolis Hiking Club.) A desire for learning and growing also followed them throughout their lives. It was no surprise that Betty spent her last day on earth attending a class.

None of their lives were without the loss of a love—the death of a child or a husband. Irene said months after Betty's death, "Betty and I didn't have a close friendship where you share intimate feelings, such as Betty's friendship with Annette. However, since her death, not a day goes by when I don't think of her and wish I could talk with her."

Together, the lives of these "four young ladies" were also filled with romance, travels to exotic places, love for the outdoors, culture, and poetry. When given the choice of whether to sit it out or to dance, they most certainly danced. Their lives were woven together forever by the experiences shared on their 1935 journey. They may have begun as four young, naïve college students; however, along the way, they each learned lessons about the kindness of strangers and about taking responsibility for their actions that couldn't have been learned in a textbook.

As it turns out, the summer of 1935 was merely a dress rehearsal for the rest of the journey.

They went on to live lives of abundance—which included, best of all, the richness of lifelong friendships. As reflected in the summer of 1935, they shared their good fortune with others and maintained their love for life. Irene, Garneth, Annette, and Betty truly were The Fortunate Four.

Now That the Play Has Run for Years

I think they handed me a script
and said, "You get the goose-girl part."
I said, "I need it—I accept."
They said, "The play's about to start."

They had already named the cast,
yet had I shared in the selection,
I would have picked these as they passed,
so pleasant is our interaction.

A playwright had laid out the plot,
and had I known from rise of curtain,
how it unfolded, I could not
have changed one episode, I'm certain.

And when I walked out on the stage,
I liked the blue backdrop of hills,
the weathered boards, canary cage,
and clay pots on the windowsills.

Now that the play has run for years,
the goose-girl part, so long rehearsed,
has been re-written. It appears
she was a princess from the first.

I am surprised I was assigned
to stardom, contract still renewed,
with every curtain-rise I find
I speak new lines of gratitude.

By Betty Bridgman

2
A BRUSH
WITH DESTINY

Experience the incredible magic that comes when two people
are destined to become the best of friends and lovers.
Experience the magic of love.

JOY KUBY

A BRUSH WITH DESTINY

People come into your life for a reason, a season, or
a lifetime.   —Elanda Vanzant

Have you ever pondered the age-old question regarding life being a journey of destiny versus a series of random experiences? In other words, does life unfold randomly, by fate, or through a mysterious combination of the two? Some people have a great impact on our lives. Do we meet them by chance, or are they brought along our path at the time when we are ready to learn from them or to appreciate the joy of their spirit?

Whatever the answer, you will have a hard time convincing each of the following women that she was anything other than destined to meet her partner—the love of her life—her husband. Their destinies seemed fated to intersect.

The first wonderful lady you will meet is Jeanette. I met her "by accident" . . . or so it may seem. I had just begun my search for heirloom stories. I took some time off to search out a second passion of mine—estate sales. These interests are quite intertwined; with both, I'm in search of those forgotten little gems or treasures.

On this particular day, I found the correct location for a sale according to the ad in the paper. Unfortunately, I arrived too late, for the sale had ended early. However, I found something more valuable. I discovered a little retirement community that led to my meeting Jeanette. I had driven by it many times before but had never noticed it. A coincidence? You decide.

LET'S HAVE A PICNIC

Jeanette Naftalin Scherling

This is a love story about how a chance meeting at a summer picnic altered and enriched the lives of two families. Jeanette was born into a Jewish family in Buffalo, North Dakota, in 1912 but spent most of her childhood in Fargo. Her father had immigrated to America when he was 30 and initially made a living walking from farm to farm as a peddler. Her mother had arrived in America as a young child of six years old. Jeanette had three siblings and later became the mother of three children.

In her seventies, Jeanette sent her children a priceless treasure—a series of three letters telling them about her life, how she fell in love with their father Sidney, and the life they had shared. Jeanette had lived a rich life filled with many blessings, and she wanted to share her fascinating story—a story that intertwined several generations in surprising ways.

The following is a portion of the first letter to her children. I hope you enjoy this remarkable story as much as I have.

February 11, 1985

Dear Beth, Bruce, and Carol:

I have decided to write you a series of letters about my life, marriage, and some of the ideas that have been cir-culating in my heart for a long time. For many years, it has been my inten-tion to write the story of how your mother and father met, for it is a coincidence by definition. The dic-tionary gives the definition of "a coincidence" as an accidental and remarkable occurrence. This really characterizes the meeting of your father and me. Now, in the 50th year of our marriage, I want to put the story in writing.

This story begins in the summer of 1933 when I met a second cousin, Harold. At this time I was 22 and in my last year of college to become a dietitian. Well, he told me I had a cousin, Marion Berman, living in Minneapolis, and he thought she and I would really like each other. (Growing up in Fargo, I had not met any of my Minneapolis cousins.) Harold told Marion about me, and she invited me to visit her, which I did that Labor Day weekend. Marion and I hit it off right away, and this was the beginning of a wonderful friendship that would last for years. In addition, it put me in touch with the Berman fam-ily, who have played an important part in my life and about whom I will write on later. Now back to my story . . .

On a lovely summer Sunday in 1933 while I was visiting Marion, she and I decided to plan a picnic for that very afternoon. Marion had several young men in mind to invite, one which was to become my husband and your father. (Your daddy said later that because of the short notice in the invitation, he almost refused. For some reason, he decided to accept.)

I helped Marion by making the sandwiches . . . and then at the picnic proceeded to eat a good share of them. (Daddy always tells the story that he was attracted to me because he thought anyone with such a healthy appetite would make a strong, healthy wife.) Well . . . he was attracted to me, and I also thought he was very nice.

He had been invited to attend a wedding that very evening at the Radisson Hotel and asked if I would accompany him. I had never been to a

Jeanette sitting on the fence next to her friend Marion.

fancy "big city" wedding, and I was very excited about going—especially with such a nice date. We both parted to dress for the evening.

When Sidney returned home, he told his mother and visiting aunt that he had met a young lady that afternoon to which he was attracted. They asked her name. When he said my name was Jeanette Naftalin, they asked him to find out if my father's name was by any chance Zundel or Mendel. (They had known people by that name in Telz, Lithuania, where the Sherling family had lived until coming to America in 1920.) Your daddy laughed and said that the possibility of my being from that family was very remote. However, he did ask me. To his amazement, my father's name was Zundel and the story began to unfold.

We discovered that both of our families—the Scherlings and the Naftalins—had lived in Telz. In fact, at one time they even shared a house in Telz, and my father, Zundel, and Sidney's mother, Shifra, had played together when they were children. The time frame of this story is very important. In 1894 when your grandfather Zundel Naftalin was about 16 years of age, he left with his father and older brother Mendel and came to America. They originally came to Minneapolis and later settled in North Dakota. The Scherlings left Lithuania twenty-six years later in time to escape from Hitler. (Most of the Jews who remained in Telz perished in the Holocaust.) Neither of these two families knew the whereabouts of each other for all of these years . . . until now.

So, after Sidney and I met, the two families were very eager to see each other again. And they did reunite. I remember my father asking Sidney if there was a certain big church still standing on a certain corner in Telz when he left. The fact that our families knew each other in Lithuania created a strong bond for us. Our romance developed in large part through letters, since we lived apart throughout our courtship. Our love grew and we longed to get married, but Sidney was in his internship to become a doctor, and finances didn't allow it. We had to wait until he was offered his first job. We then set the date for September 15, 1935.

I had spent the early weeks that September shopping for the wedding. I spent a couple of days in Minneapolis on my way back to Fargo and believe I purchased my wedding dress at Young Quinlan. My dress was an eggshell, pan velvet, long, backless dress that was worn with a long-sleeved jacket that buttoned up the back with small covered buttons. A headband was made from the material that was cut off when the gown was shortened. This held a fingertip veil.

It had become the custom that when one married she brought a sort of dowry with her. This included necessary things for starting a home. It used to be said that a bride should not need to buy any clothes for a year; of course, this all depended on the financial state of the bride's family. Money was scarce for my family, but my mother had grown up in Minneapolis, and she knew the customs of America (more than her contemporaries in Fargo did.) My mother was always a good manager, and she saw to it that I went into my marriage very well supplied with what I needed for my home and myself. I remember all of these nuptial preparations as being very exciting . . . but back to the wedding day.

Of course, we had a lovely Sabbath meal Friday night and Saturday noon. On Sunday morning all of the furniture was removed from my parent's downstairs bedroom, and wooden planks were used with wood horses to make long tables for the wedding meal. The ceremony took place under a chupa in our living room. After the Shiva Brochas (blessings), which followed the ceremony, we all sat down for the wedding dinner. I remember the great pleasure of this meal. One of Sid's brothers commented in his toast about the coincidence of our meeting and marrying. He said that it would have seemed impossible to the people of Telz, Lithuania, that Shifra Brody's son would meet and marry Zundel Naftalin's daughter in America in the distant year of 1935!

This is what I mean when they say it was bashert (destiny) that we should meet. Can you believe that your daddy and I would meet on our own, fall in love with each other, and marry? Everyone had a feeling of astonishment that this could happen. If only our great grandparents could have seen this happen in America.

After the ceremony and wedding meal, Sid and I went down-town to have our pictures taken. After coming back home to say goodbye to everyone, we drove to Detroit Lakes where we spent the night. The next day we drove to St. Paul, where Sid had made reservations at the Lowry Hotel. We had an enjoyable evening of dinner and dancing.

The following day we started off to our home in Taylors Falls, Minnesota. It was such a glorious September afternoon. I am sure you remember the beautiful view one gets when you come down the hill into Taylors Falls. In the fall when the leaves are turning all shades of gold, orange, and red, the view is magnificent! This is the way it was that September morning. It was as if it was setting the scene for our 50 years of marriage.

After one week into our marriage, I had the great responsibil-ity of selecting all the furniture for our home. Sheboygan, Wisconsin, was a place well-known for furniture manufacturing. My cousin, George Abramson, lived there. So I took the train to Sheboygan, where he met me at the station and took me to the fac-tory. Being a Home Economics graduate, I was somewhat informed on what was required to furnish a home tastefully. Early American Maple was in vogue, and I liked its simplicity. Luckily it was not as costly as some furniture and was very durable. For $350, I ordered furniture and rugs that completely furnished our home. (This furniture stayed with us for many years, moving with us as we moved around the country in the Army and back again after Sid was discharged from the Army and we returned to Minneapolis in 1945. Many memories are brought to the surface when I think of the furniture that I selected that day.)

Now our life began a new phase. Sid started his life as a doctor in Taylors Falls. Since the whole country was in a deep depression, generally people had very little money. Many people were out of work, so there were not many patients seeking care.

Sid would work through the hospital in nearby St. Croix Falls, but his office was in one section of our house. Often I would forget that patients sitting in the office could easily overhear our conversations in the house. One day I made lunch for Sid and called out to him very cheerfully, "Your lunch is ready, honey bunny." There was no question the patient in the waiting room overheard. (I decided to be more careful after that.)

Some people came to the hospital to have their babies delivered, but many had them at home. That meant deliveries out on the farms, and sometimes these turned into crisis situations. It often meant long and lonely hours for me when Sid was called out on a delivery, for he would be gone for hours on these cases. So when the weather was nice, I would sometimes ride along with Sid. I continued going on house calls with Sid until after you, Beth, were born. When your date of arrival was later than calculated, your daddy took me on a call that was miles out in the country. The patient was a man with pneumonia, and he needed to be taken back to the hospital in St. Croix Falls. At that time, doctors carried a sling that could be put in the car to make a bed so that the patient could be taken to the hospital. Of course, this meant there was no room for a passenger, and one of the family members had to drive me back in their truck. It was not a very smooth ride. This was probably responsible for the fact that that evening I went into labor, and you were born the next afternoon on August 1, 1937. We were thrilled with our baby daughter! We named you Paula Beth but very soon changed it to Beth Paula (after my dear childhood friend Beth).

Living in a small town, my whole life revolved around you, my husband, and my home. I missed my family and old friends, but those years were mostly happy ones for me. There was a social life in St. Croix Falls, but it was very different from anything I had experienced. It was centered mostly around the hospital staff, and they were much older than I was. Being a young mother, I wanted to talk about my baby. I recall Sid telling me that perhaps I should refrain from talking about my baby so much, as these people were long past this stage in life and would be quite bored with that.

Since there wasn't much medical work to do, Sid had a lot of free time, and we did have wonderful times together. We were living in the midst of a beautiful countryside with many beautiful hiking trails and picnic grounds. We spent a lot of leisure time taking advantage of these things in our early years of marriage. Our paths intersected at a picnic, and picnics continued to be such a joy later as husband and wife.

I am so happy to have told you this story about the uniqueness of our meeting and our early years together. I feel I have been fortunate in having lived a life that has been most satisfying to me. I must say that I have always wanted more fun and something different than was available for me in Fargo. Having met Sid and *marrying him, my life has always been interesting and challenging. In reliving my life, I realize it has really been pretty much the way I had wished it to be. First, I wanted to fall in love with a nice Jewish fellow. My friends say I had always wanted to marry a doctor . . . and I think this must be true. You see, I always had quite a clear idea of the way I would like to live my life. I can honestly say my dreams have pretty much come true. Life has mostly been great for me. I have been married to a wonderful human being for the past 50 years. I have had you three wonderful, bright, and handsome children. You are now all married and have given us nine lovely grandchildren. I have never had to worry about not having enough money. There has been a wonderful opportunity to study and grow intellectually—to develop interesting and loving friendships—and good health has been a good fortune for all of us. Certainly there have been some rough spots, but they were always smoothed out. I am very happy, thankful, and my heart is filled with gratitude for all of this.*

This is the end of my first letter to you. My plan is to write you several letters in which I will write about my life, in the hope that it is something you will enjoy knowing. For now, I will say goodbye. Lots of love to you all! Mother

Jeanette and Sydney spent about five years in Arkansas during the war where he was the Post Surgeon. She enjoyed the life of a colonel's wife and was thankful that he never had to go overseas. Returning to Minneapolis after the war, he established a long career as a pediatrician. Life became busy raising three children. He continued in his practice until the age of 79. When I met Jeanette in the early days of 1999, she was trying to adjust to life without her beloved Sydney. He had died just months earlier at the age of 88, living his final years with the challenge of Alzheimer's disease.

She missed his gentle soul and the special love they had shared. She said, "Everyone loved him!" Her only regret is that early into their marriage she had destroyed his beautiful love letters. She remembers thinking at the time, "We have each other now—what do I need with these letters?" However, now that he is gone she would have cherished these letters. She said, "He wrote the most beautiful love letters!"

Theirs was truly a special love story.

Oh . . . just one more "coincidence." Many years before, a woman named Tilly Berman had introduced Jeanette's parents to each other. Unbeknownst to anyone, years later it was Tilly's daughter Marion who introduced Jeanette to Sidney . . . and this wonderful love story began.

BOUQUETS OF DAISIES AND WILD ASPARAGUS FERN

Dorathy Lysne

This love story relates how a poem, a photograph on a bulletin board, and a little help from their guardian angels drew a young woman and young man together. It will touch your heart.

I was born Dorathy Jensen on October 17, 1907, in a small town in Wisconsin called Janesville. I was one of those gals who wanted to get into everything in high school. My folks said, "You better go to college and . . . grow up." So I went to St. Olaf in Northfield, Minnesota, on a scholarship. We girls were often kidded that we only wanted to go to college to meet somebody and get married.

It turned out that I did meet someone special—through a strange twist of fate and, I believe . . . a little help from our guardian angels. The year was 1925, and I was beginning my freshman year of college. There were no sororities on campus. Instead, we had what were called "Societies." I belonged to the Nu Sig's society. That's short for Nu Sigma Rho, which was the Greek word for our society. Our "brother" society was the Pi Sig's, which was short for Pi Sigma Rho.

These societies were a great way to get acquainted with other students, particularly other freshmen. We planned a "get acquainted" Christmas party during my freshman year and pooled the names of the freshman boys in the Pi Sig society. Each of the girls was supposed to get a 50-cent present for the boy's name she had drawn. Well, when we drew names we had one more boy than girl, so somebody had to take two names. Of course, no one wanted this extra name because that would mean the expense of buying an additional gift. After arguing back and forth, I said, "Oh heck, I'll take it." So I did. For both boys I bought a little model car and wrote a poem to go along with it as part of the fun.

This "extra" boy's name was Reuben Lysne. I attended the Christmas party with two dates, and at the end of the Christmas party Reuben asked if he could walk me to the dorm. Since he had asked me first, I felt duty-bound . . . but he was really cute! He was a slim, tall, blond Norwegian. (I'm Danish.) So, that's the way that started.

We began dating, and every Sunday Reuben would take me to an organ concert at Carleton, which was the other college in Northfield. He had grown up in this beautiful college town.

Near the campus was a grocery store where one could sit and have a cup of coffee and a roll. A bulletin board posted in the store became a place where the grocer would hang pictures of various students from campus. It became a popular spot for students, and one student or another would stop by there every day and check out the pictures that were on the bulletin board.

This bulletin board turned out to have great significance for Reuben and me. After we became acquainted, I learned from his best friend of a startling "coincidence." He said, "Do you know that Reuben previously picked you out of a group of pictures on the bulletin board at the grocery store?"

(I was in a ballet costume because we were putting on a play that was a satire of ballet.) There I was in a little "fru fru" standing on my tiptoes. He looked at this crazy picture and said, "I'm going to marry that gal!" He had never seen me or met me at that time! (If the Lord's hand wasn't in that . . .)

Reuben's declaration came true, and we were married on August 9, 1932, after a seven-year engagement. This was towards the end of the Depression. We had decided to wait until he finished his dental training and we could afford to get married. Reuben took pre-dental courses at St. Olaf and then went on the University of Minnesota. I had graduated by this time, in 1929. I taught high school English to help pay for his tuition in dental school. I just loved it and could have made a career out of it.

We had a small wedding with just family and close friends. I couldn't afford to buy a wedding dress, so I wore my prom dress from high school. (Luckily, it happened to be white.) I borrowed my sister's veil. We couldn't afford any pictures either, so the images of that day could only be preserved in my mind. I didn't even get a Kodak picture of my wedding! No one could afford to travel, so I had only one attendant. Since there was no money to purchase flowers, we went out in the fields and picked daisies and wild asparagus ferns for our bouquets and to decorate the church. We created beauty with what we could borrow from nature.

After we were married we moved to Minneapolis, where we lived for a time in a converted garage. We lived around Broadway and Lyndale at a time when it was a thriving business area. Reuben had started his dental business nearby. We didn't own a car for the first six years of our marriage, so he walked to his dental office. (In fact, we had to borrow a car to go on our honeymoon to my parents' cabin on Dardis Lake in northern Wisconsin.)

They were very hard times, for the Depression lasted a long time. There was a great deal of unemployment. You learned to make do with what you had. Our motto was, "Eat it up, wear it out, make it do, or do without." Reuben was such a good and caring dentist. During that time, he never once turned away anyone who was in pain, even though he might get a chicken or two in place of payment. We didn't suffer too much, though, because we were young, in love, and had the outlook that things would eventually get better. We created our own entertainment, because we couldn't afford to do things such as going to movies.

Reuben and I were happily married for 63 years and had three children. Our son Dick became a doctor; Paul, a dentist; and Barbara, a pastor's wife. Five of our twelve grandchildren have earned their master's or doctoral degrees. We also have seventeen great grandchildren. All are healthy, happy, and in careers of service—social work, the ministry, or related careers where they are helping people.

We really were a team. We built our own cabin by a lake in Minnesota, our children working as hard as we did. We just had a ball. It was a wonderful marriage and journey together.

My loving husband Reuben died around Easter time in 1995. He was 91 years old at the time of his death. When I went through his personal things, I found a worn and faded piece of paper folded in his billfold. I was surprised to discover that it was the little poem I had written for him the night of the Christmas party—the night we had met so many years before. Tears rolled down my cheeks as I read the poem. I was so touched that he had carried it with him all of these years! I felt it was a special connection between the two of us and too personal to share with anyone else, so I threw the poem away. The words and memory of what it represented would always remain in my heart.

I have so many special memories. Even though Reuben is gone, I can still clearly see this handsome, tall, blond Norwegian. What attracted me to him? Oh . . . I don't know. It wasn't that he had money. He didn't—we started out really poor. My instincts told me he was an honest fellow, and I was drawn to his kind and caring spirit. I had never before believed in love at first sight, but it came true for us.

Life certainly contains many mysteries. I can't help but wonder what path my life would have taken if I hadn't volunteered to take his name for the Christmas drawing, and why was he so drawn to my picture on the bulletin board? Both of our journeys would have been quite different had it not been for the little nudges from our guardian angels orchestrating this unique way for Reuben and me to meet and fall in love. Our life together was indeed a beautiful love story.

When I interviewed Dorathy in July of 1999, I was amazed to discover that she was now 92 years old. She is a very active woman with a wonderful sense of humor. Her loving and positive spirit keeps her young at heart.

She still enjoys writing poems and recently joined a poetry-writing group. She said about her love for writing, "I always thought I'd write a book about Reuben's dental practice. I was planning to call it *Open Wider, Please.* He had some very interesting . . . and some very strange . . . patients over the years."

While sharing her story with me, tears filled her eyes as she told of the discovery that Reuben had continued to carry her little poem throughout his life. Yes, I like to think there truly were guardian angels at work orchestrating this unique way for Dorathy and Reuben to meet and fall in love. Who's to say?

DESTINY THROUGH TIME

Ruth Evelyn Tillman Swanson

This story tells how the love and friendship between two men—Andrew Swanson and Daniel Danielson—two generations before shaped Ruth's journey and led her to the love of her life.

Now retired, Ruth is a petite woman with an ever-present smile and love for life. I was happy that Ruth was willing to look back over her life and share the following love story.

My story actually begins many years ago and far away in Sweden. It all started with a friendship formed between two classmates—Andrew Swanson and Daniel Danielson. Andrew and Daniel were both born in 1852 in a little Swedish community called Varmland. Their friendship began when they were schoolmates and continued throughout their lives.

This was during the time when a lot of Swedes were immigrating to America in search of a better life. Daniel came to America in 1875 as a young man in his twenties. He later married Clara, a widow with a four-year-old daughter. Clara's first husband, a gentleman named Eric, had come to America, and after finding work had sent for her in Sweden and asked for her hand in marriage. Unfortunately, this union had a tragic ending. While working in the mills, he died in a work-related accident. Daniel and Clara then met, married, settled in Iowa, and later moved to a farm in Rush City, Minnesota. They had four children together. One of the children was my mother, Minnie. So you see, I have a heartfelt connection with this man, for Daniel was my grandfather.

Meanwhile, his friend Andrew was still living in Sweden. He married a woman named Carolina. They had also grown up together in Varmland. They were married on April 22, 1882, and a short time later traveled to America on their honeymoon.

Their journey first led them to Chicago where Andrew found work on a farm in Illinois for sixteen dollars a month. While there, he contracted typhoid fever and was ill for about a month. Andrew and Carolina then decided to leave Illinois and arrived in St. Paul, Minnesota, with about 10 cents in their pockets. They lived in St. Paul for 13 years where he worked in a foundry and for the railroad. Their journey then led them to a small Swedish farming community in Minnesota called Maple Ridge. They lived around this area for most of their remaining years. Andrew and Carolina had four sons and two daughters. Andrew also holds a special connection for me, for he was a grandfather to Kenneth—the man I would later meet and marry.

In America, every few years the two families would locate each other in spite of the moves to various neighborhood farms. They always enjoyed the opportunity to reconnect. This meant that Andrew's children grew up playing with Daniel's children. I also learned that as teenagers, some of them even dated each other. One generation later, the love bug bit for Ken and me. Let me tell you how this transpired.

How We Met

I met Ken's siblings one day while both of our families were visiting my grandmother, Clara Danielson. Ken spent the day downtown with my brother, so I didn't see him that day. Another Sunday afternoon at a later time, I went with my parents to Maple Ridge to visit the Swansons. I remember Ken came driving up in the car after a baseball game. (My mother thought he looked kind of wild.) Just as we were to leave at the end of the visit, I realized I had forgotten my purse inside. When I went back in the house, Ken was there, and he suggested going to Rush City to go roller-skating together sometime. (I was later teased that I forgot my purse inside on purpose.)

Well, we did go roller-skating. Our first date was on September 14, 1940. While driving to the roller-skating pavilion, we saw a sign that said, "Watch out for children." Ken said, "Oh—we'd better be careful!" I then gave him a little tap on the cheek, which he later called a "love-tap!" I remember on this first date they played "crack the whip" at the roller rink. It can get pretty crazy. I slid into a bench and got a huge sliver in my thigh. (I didn't say anything about this until much later, though.)

What initially attracted us to each other? I thought he was a nice-looking guy with sparkling eyes. He said he liked my big brown eyes and smile.

The Long Engagement

Our love continued to grow, and we were engaged on May 4, 1941. Then the war started, and Ken went into the service the following spring. He was a combat engineer of the 43rd Infantry Division of the Army. As with many others, our engagement period was greatly affected by the war. Many couples rushed off to get married before the men left for war.

Ken had one furlough three months after going into the service, and then we were apart for three and half years! My, it seemed like an awfully long time, and it was hard to wait all this time to be together.

Our daily love letters helped to sustain us during this long separation. He was stationed on many different islands in the South Pacific. He would try to drop subtle hints as to where he was at the time; however, the Service censored the letters I received from him. I remember his letters would arrive cut into strips of paper with anything revealing his possible location removed.

Of course there was the constant concern over when the war would end. One particularly anxious episode was when Ken had a long hospitalization in New Zealand due to a great deal of back pain. It was determined that he had three kidneys! A specialist removed one and one-half kidneys leaving him with one and one-half good ones.

Thankfully, Ken returned safely from the war. After our four and a half year engagement and a three and a half year separation, we could finally set our wedding date.

Wedding Bells . . . Finally

The day we dreamed about for so many years and wrote of in our many love letters had finally arrived. I was 23 years old at this time. We were married in Rush City on October 6, 1945. It was a nice sunny day and quite mild . . . but, I remember . . . a really busy day. Every wedding seems to have some little mishap. For mine, it was that the flowers didn't get delivered. So, Ken made a flying run to town to get them. We also picked fall chrysanthemums from our garden to decorate the little church.

I have another memory of that day, which now seems rather strange. My parents' home seemed quite unorganized on my wedding day. They were putting new linoleum on the kitchen floor. Why they waited until that day, I don't know. I believe guests were coming from the Minneapolis/St. Paul area and would be congregating at our home before going to the church. Knowing my mother's deep concern for having things look nice, she must have felt the need to improve the kitchen. It just happened to be done on my wedding day of all days.

After our wedding and reception, the wedding party went in three cars to Cambridge, a neighboring town, to have pictures taken. We were in my sister and brother-in-law's car. My brother had our other sister in a second car, along with her daughter Julie, our flower girl. On the way to Cambridge, they had a minor accident with another car. Apparently, both cars were going quite fast on this gravel road. As the two cars met, they got scraped—but luckily neither car went out of control. It was quite unnerving to hear about this, and we were thankful for their safety. I trust that prayers had been said earlier. There were many people that were grateful for Ken's safe return from the war and that our long-awaited day ended happily.

The Honeymoon

We began our honeymoon by driving to Taylors Falls and spending our wedding night in a cabin. The next day we traveled on to Pine City and then to a cabin on Lake Pokegama for fishing. We didn't stay for very long. Since Ken had been gone from the States for such a long time, he was very eager to get back home to the farm. I didn't want to leave . . . but we did. We then began our life together.

So this is our love story, and like characters in a play the cast began to form for Ken and me to meet two generations before our time. It seems like a miracle to me that the friendship of Andrew Swanson and Daniel Danielson endured over the years. They could have easily lost contact with each other amidst the many moves throughout their lifetimes—moves that even spanned across the ocean. I wonder what path my life would have taken if our two grandfathers had not made that little extra effort to look up an old school chum and maintain this lifelong friendship. I am thankful for this legacy of love and friendship that was left to us by our grandfathers. I truly believe that Ken and I were destined to be together.

The Rest of the Story

You may be wondering what happened to Andrew and Daniel. Ken's grandfather, Andrew, lived a long life and died at the age of 88. As aging grandparents, Andrew and Carolina made their home with Ken's family during the last five years of their lives. Ken, his parents, and his siblings were living on the "home place" during this time.

Ruth's grandfather, Daniel, loved to fish and spent many hours out on the lake. He had a stroke one day while out in his boat. He was rescued and grateful that he survived, but he was never able to speak after that. He created his own version of sign language to communicate.

Apparently, Daniel had struggled with a fiery temper throughout his life. He thought the Lord allowed this stroke and loss of speech to happen to help him learn how to control his temper. Ruth was only two years old when her grandfather died at the age of 72, so unfortunately she never got a chance to really know him. She learned about him from stories passed down through her grandmother.

As a young married couple, life was busy for Kenneth and Ruth raising four children and "making the money stretch." But it was also a good time. As Ruth said, "I enjoyed this time. I loved my kids, and I knew it would go so fast."

What happened to all of the love letters from their three and a half year distant romance? Ruth said, "Ken and I sat down together and read through all of them one day and then destroyed them. They were too mushy for our kids to read!"

Amazingly, the love bug struck once more between the Swanson and Danielson families. Ruth's sister Jeanette and Ken's brother Bill were each six years younger than Ruth and Ken. When Bill got out of the service, he purchased a new car. Jeanette heard about this new car and told Ken, "Well, tell him to make use of it." This one simple comment resulted in their first date, and they never stopped. Jeanette and Bill were married on her 18th birthday, and they've had a nice life together ever since.

Kenneth and Ruth have now been married over 50 years. They are enjoying retirement even though there have been some ongoing medical issues for both of them. They have eight grandchildren and four great grandchildren. Life is good!

As you can see, the patterns of life often unfold in mysterious ways. A decision we make today can truly affect the generations that follow.

Lost Love

Eva Gerdin Olson

Who can forget the warm blush and excitement of a first love? Unfortunately, these feelings are often followed by the heartache and sorrow of the loss of that love. They are timeless emotions that can quickly bring back vivid memories in each of our own lives.

Eva had three older sisters—Arvida, Lydia, and Hilda. (You will read more about Eva in an upcoming story called "The Little Girls.") She watched as all three sisters experienced the emotions of young love. Hilda met her husband in the church choir at the age of 15; however, because of their age difference Hilda and Charlie kept their relationship a secret from her parents for a few years.

Many years later, Eva shared her memories of Arvida's and Lydia's love stories in a personal journal. She reflected on the lost love experienced by both Arvida and Lydia while they were young women in the early 1900s. Here are her stories.

Lydia's Lost Love

My older sister Lydia and my brother Eric worked for a time in a town in northern Minnesota called Sparta. While Lydia was there, she met a young man by the name of Paul Hertrich. She liked him a great deal and was quite taken by him. He wrote such sweet love letters, which my sister Hilda and I proceeded to secretly read.

After Lydia moved back home from Sparta, Paul desperately wanted to come to see her, but he had such a difficult time getting here. Something always seemed to prevent him from coming. Before one planned visit, for instance, he had been picking straw-berries in Kansas and was stung by a bee. He had a severe reaction and had to spend time in the hospital instead.

However, luck was finally with him and he did manage to come up to visit Lydia for a short time. My dad met him on a Saturday in our neighboring town of Braham and brought him home, although he could only stay one day. On Sunday afternoon, Lydia drove the buggy to take him back to Braham to catch the train. However, when they got to Rice Lake, which was just part of the way, he wouldn't let her go any farther. He insisted that he would walk to town across the fields and woods from there. (We felt later that this was probably to hide in the woods, which I'll explain in a moment.)

It just so happened that later that evening the bank in Braham was robbed. When mother had made his bed that morning before he left, she had moved his suitcase. Thinking back on it later, she said that it was so heavy—it had to have had more that just clothes in it. Perhaps it also contained tools or guns in preparation for a bank robbery.

Some time after this "strange" visit, Paul wrote to Lydia and said they would be married. However, then his love letters stopped coming. In search for an answer to his whereabouts, my brother Eric wrote to someone in Clara City, Minnesota, where Paul had said he worked one summer. Eric later received a response to his letter, and we learned that Paul had died on the streets of Minneapolis on Christmas Eve. So . . . that was the end of that. Love is blind.

It will always remain a mystery if this young man, Paul Hertrich, actually was the one who robbed the bank that night so long ago or if it was just a coincidence in timing. Much of his life remains a mystery. How did he happen to die at such a young age on the streets of Minneapolis on Christmas Eve? Was his death caused by an illness, or did he come into harm's way? Was he really planning to come back to Lydia for her hand in marriage? What was Lydia's reaction to his marriage proposal and then later to the news of his untimely death? Unfortunately, all of the answers to these questions were buried along with the two of them. Perhaps, though, she was spared a lifetime of heartaches.

I was a bit surprised by Eva's matter-of-fact reflection in her journal about this whole episode. She said, "So . . . that was the end of that. Love is blind." True . . . so true. Perhaps because of all that the family had experienced together over the years, this was viewed as just another part of life's journey.

Eva's second love story recorded in her journal reflects on the loss of a love experienced by her sister Arvida.

Arvida's First Love

My older sister Arvida was keeping company with a young man from the Nordell family. The Nordells were a family in our little Swedish neighborhood. She was very fond of him. This was during a time when tuberculosis was a real scare for many people. Unfortunately, he was a part of a family that had a lot of tubercu-

losis, so father didn't want her to continue to be with him. He was afraid that she would come in contact with this awful disease; therefore, they were forced to end their relationship.

This young man later moved to California and married someone else. Arvida, too, later married a man by the name of Otto Thornberg in 1905. They had four children.

As it turned out, her first love never did contract tuberculosis. I guess it's best to leave love alone and not interfere.

How would the journeys of these two young people—Arvida and her beau whose name is unknown—been different had it not been for the parental forced ending of their relationship? I can't help but wonder how Arvida reacted when her father's strong feelings of fear ended this relationship. Did she keep all of her feelings stored in her heart and cry silent tears or just accept her father's wishes? What dreams died that day? Did she tuck those dreams away and make new dreams?

Arvida was apparently a survivor. She was a strong, healthy, and determined woman who will always be remembered for her courage to make the journey from the old country (Sweden) as a young child of ten years old. She lived to the age of 102 after an adventure-filled life, and she left her family a rich heritage. (I wonder how the rest of the journey fared for the young man in this story.)

During this period in history, I also wonder how many other love stories were affected by the ravaging disease of tuberculosis . . . or the fear of it. Both fear and love can be equally strong forces.

How fortunate it is that Eva recorded these two little love stories in her journal. They would have otherwise silently slipped away into the forgotten chapters of family history.

THE "BRIDE AND GROOM" SHOW

Donna Woods Grinvalds

*I*first met Donna on a warm August day in 2002. She and her husband Emil share a home in Mound, Minnesota, near Jennings Bay—one of the bays on beautiful Lake Minnetonka. They have shared this nearly century-old house for the past 38 years. When I arrived, the long driveway was bordered with blooming day lilies, and mature trees provided an inviting canopy that shaded the house. A colorful garden and an expansive lawn completed the picture. Million dollar estates had begun to creep into the area, but their home still had the peaceful feeling of country days long past.

Donna greeted me at the door and invited me in for a visit. She was a slim woman in her 70s and still very blessed with physical beauty. She had incredibly creamy skin, long eyelashes, and soft silver hair. As we enjoyed the afternoon together and she told me her life story, I also discovered her inner beauty and very generous spirit.

Her journey through life includes a beautiful love story about how she and her husband met under very unusual circumstances, fell in love, and were married in an even more unconventional manner. There were a lot of pieces that needed to fall into place in order for them to meet. Donna feels they were destined to meet and that God definitely played a part in bringing them together. They took what could have been a very lonely time for both of them and turned it into a time of wonderful memories. To understand what led up to their meeting and learn the path they each had walked, let us have Donna tell her story starting at the very beginning.

My Childhood

I was born by a home birth on February 3, 1928, and given the name of Donna Jean Woods. This home was near Winthrop, Minnesota, and I was part of a rather large family. My mom had about 12 pregnancies, but sadly, only seven of us survived. When I was one year old, we moved to a thousand-acre farm near Clifford, North Dakota.

This farm included a number of horses, cattle, and sheep. One of my earliest childhood memories is the enjoyment of riding our horses. Of course, we would ride bareback with just a bridle from the time we were really young. I remember one time when my brother and I rode doubled up on one horse from our farm to the neighboring town of Clifford. We rode across a meadow that was filled with Russian thistles and tumbleweed. All we had was a bridle, and I started slipping off the horse's back. To keep from falling off, I held onto my brother so tight that we both fell off. We started rolling through the Russian thistle and tumbleweed. We didn't get hurt at all, but he was quite upset with his little sister.

Actually, I had two older brothers—Marion and Harold. As a little girl of five, I would often go along with them to school. The teacher would hold me on her lap while she was teaching. Can you imagine? This was a small town school. Finally, the teacher said to my mother, "Well, she is coming to school all the time anyway—she may as well begin first grade." So I did. I started first grade when I was five years old.

How well I remember the long country road going from our house to town. We kids would have to walk to school— there was no other way to get there unless we hooked a ride with the Norwegian milkman. He had a house on runners that he would use to haul his cream and milk to town. We would sometimes hook onto those runners and ride along.

The memory is a curious thing. There is one image that is vivid in my mind to this day. Like I said, we would have to walk to school every day—no matter what the weather. (Today there is a long border of trees that would have provided protection, but at that time there were no trees to help buffer the cold winter wind.) In the winter, the girls would wear long underwear, long brown stockings that pulled up, and dresses—there were no snow pants. A few times when it was so bitterly cold, my brother and I would stop at the village blacksmith on the edge of town to warm up. Well, this would cause us to get to school late, which started at 9 o'clock. If we did it two or three times. . . I don't know. This one time, the teacher had the whole room ready when we arrived (it was mixed grades) and they sang, "*A diller, a dollar . . .* (I'm going to cry if I talk about it.) *. . . a 10 o'clock scholar. You used to come at 9 o'clock, but now you come at noon.*" She humiliated us in front of the whole class! I can feel it as clearly as if it happened yesterday. One little incident like this from childhood can be burned in your heart forever.

On a brighter note, there was this boy, Bobby, who had a crush on me. We had a big round tank on our farm for all our cattle. (When you're little, everything looks big, but I'm sure it was quite big.) Bobby said, "Donna, if you swim across this tank five times—underwater—I'll marry you when we grow up." (I think he's still alive and living in the area. I wonder if he remembers that comment.)

We lived near the town of Clifford until 1936. The early '30s were well-remembered times for having a lot of severe weather. I have memories of the grasshopper invasion wrecking the crops, the dust storms where you couldn't breathe—the dust would come under our doors and through our windows—and the drought. I mean . . . I have memories of these things even as a young child of eight. This is about the time when my dad had to gave up farming in the area, and the family moved back to Minnesota.

Well, our move brought us back to Winthrop, and we were again about one mile from town. The winter of 1936 had very severe temperatures of about 40 degrees below zero. This was before anyone talked about the added wind-chill. I was only eight, but I was already in the fourth grade by this time. In contrast to the previous teacher, this teacher was so nice! How clearly I can remember her picking me up in her arms and saying, "You're such a brave little girl to walk in this bitter cold." Then she'd cuddle me and pet me.

We were temporarily living in an old house on the edge of town. Then my father got a farm the following spring. Because of our many moves, I went to three different schools in the fourth grade—Clifford, Winthrop, and finally a country school around the Lafayette area.

I finished eighth grade in another little country school out in the middle of farm country. It wasn't a very large school—in fact, I was the only student in the eighth grade. I had excellent teachers, though. I was blessed with good friends, many of which are still my friends. They were all farmers' kids. It's been sad to see some of them pass away.

The High School Years: The Moves Continue

I had lived in so many places by this time, and my high school years also involved several moves. My first year of high school—ninth grade—found me back in Winthrop. My brother and I went to stay with our uncle and aunt in order to get to school more easily. That's just the way it was. We kids accepted things—the way our parents set them up. Ironically, my uncle and aunt owned the same house and farm that my family had lived in when I was in the fourth grade. They also had two children of their own, in addition to a young hired man that was also in school. So it was a full house with all of us kids living under the same roof.

Tenth grade arrived, and I went to New Ulm High School. My oldest brother and I drove back and forth to school because Dad decided he wanted us home. So we came back to live at home. We were still about 12 miles from New Ulm. There were no buses, you know. Again, it was a terrible winter. We couldn't even get out of our driveway. I remember breaking down the transmission in several cars trying to get out of our driveway. Somehow we got through the year, but sometimes we'd be really cold. Thankfully, the principal and everyone were always so kind—they were so good to us.

During my last two years of high school, a friend and I boarded with two different widow women in New Ulm so that we would be closer to school. They were both very motherly and kind to us. We had a bedroom, and one place also had a spot in the basement for a hot plate and kitchen utensils to do our cooking. My friend, who was a year older and from a big family, usually did most of the cooking. We couldn't afford to buy hot lunches—our folks didn't have much money. Instead we would bring vegetables from our gardens at home.

Career Decisions

Following graduation in 1945, it was time to make some tough career decisions. I had dreams of becoming either a teacher or a nurse. (Of course, there weren't too many other occupations for women at that time.) Our counselors were very good. They would say, "You are so good in math and science—you should go into the medical field." They would encourage us like that.

I can see now that my career decision was affected by the times. This was during the war years. About this time, my brothers Marion and Harold enlisted in the service. They were big, strong, healthy farm boys. (I think the service actually chose the men by looking to see who were the strongest looking.) My brothers were both serving in the South Pacific. I also had three cousins in the service at once. It's just amazing to me that they all came back alive—not many in my brother's Third Division lived.

Many of the nurses were helping in the war effort, so this was a time when nurses were badly needed. Then the government started a program called the U.S. Cadet Nurse Corps. (The girlfriend that I had boarded with in high school went into nurses' training one year ahead of me. She went to Northwestern Hospital's School of Nursing so, of course, that's why I went there.)

I graduated from high school in May and then had to be at St. Olaf College in June to begin my major science courses. There was no time in between to enjoy the summer. My best friend and I were happy to be able to begin our training together.

Nurses' Training

I remember the day my dad drove the two of us to St. Olaf. When we got there, he saw there was a Marine program there, and a Naval V-12 program there . . . and here I was barely 17!

He almost turned around and took me back home. You can imagine how worried he was to leave his young daughter at a place surrounded by so many young men! No problem—we were nearly imprisoned—we really were. There were strict curfews, plus we had a very heavy schedule of study—areas like anatomy, college chemistry, and all that.

We took courses at St. Olaf for three months, and then we went to Northwestern Hospital to begin our clinical experience. The total training took three full years. It was really hard labor because they were short on help. However, I believe that we had excellent hands-on training. The patients got good care at that time. You would give them a morning bath, followed by a back rub with special cooling lotion, and then the same procedure would start all over at 4 o'clock. At bedtime you would give them another back rub. Yes, they got pretty nice treatment.

During my training for Communicable Diseases at the old General Hospital, I was a private duty nurse for a pregnant woman who was so sick with tuberculosis. Her death was imminent while I was with her. We were all set up to do a Caesarian. The resident and I did do the Caesarian, but the

Donna in her U.S. Cadet Nurse Corps uniform

baby didn't live. (The baby wasn't due for another three months.) That was very sad and difficult to see death firsthand.

Our psychiatric experience was at the old Rochester State Hospital. We got to go to the Mayo Clinic when they were doing lobotomies to observe this procedure.

My final experience was on a medical station, which was primarily for cancer and coronary patients—very ill people. During the last six months, they asked if I would take the position as assistant head nurse. So, I held that position in the last six months of my training. I wasn't even 20 years old yet when they asked me. Thinking back, this was a lot of responsibility at such a young age.

After each nursing experience, we were given Mantoux tests. Tuberculosis was very prevalent at this time—the sanatoriums were full of patients. I was looking forward to completing my training in June of 1948. Some time in the months before this, I developed a very large, positive, swollen red response to the Mantoux. At that time there wasn't all the medication that they have now, so nothing was done right away. I was just watched closely by the class doctors. I did finish training and then worked as an assistant head nurse. I took and passed my state boards at the University of Minnesota.

My Path Takes an Unexpected Turn

Soon after I finished my training, the head nurse went on vacation for a month. I took over and was actually acting as head nurse already at my young age. Soon after she returned, I was given a chest X ray. The doctors took me aside and said, "Donna, you have something on your lung. We think it may possibly be pneumonia." (They were trying to soften the news, I believe, rather than telling me they suspected that I had TB.)

Ironically, I was put to bed on my own station. Can you believe it? They put tubes down to wash out my stomach. I had to have four of these procedures. The doctors themselves were surprised when it took two months to determine that I did, indeed, have the TB germ. Then they immediately put me into isolation in the same room that I had been in during this time. (Somewhere between Rochester and elsewhere I had contracted TB. Three of us came back testing positive, but I was the only one who did develop the disease.)

Even though I was a patient in bed, I was put to work teaching the new nursing class how to do isolation techniques. Ironically, I taught and supervised the student nurses on their technique while they were taking care of me. They kept me busy, which also helped to keep my mind busy. During that time, I also read *War and Peace* and, I remember, a sexy novel that was big at the time. I was there in bed—in my own station—for six months following graduation.

Everyone at Northwestern was very supportive and kind during my six months as a patient, especially a telephone operator nicknamed "Petey." She would call me both in the morning and the evening with her chirpy, cherry voice, adding comfort to my days.

Some boys that I had previously dated also came and brought me a sex book by a famous doctor—I can't remember the name of it. They brought it to me to read—as a joke. They were farm boys from Rochester. (At the State Hospital, a lot of farm boys would just drop in. They knew there were a lot of student nurses there from different hospitals.

They'd say, "Anyone want to go out tonight?" That's how everyone met. It was a fun way to meet new friends.)

I was transferred to a sanatorium called Ah-Gwah-Ching near Walker. It was the first time in my life that I became homesick. All my family and friends were so far away. In 1949, it was a very long trip for my parents to make from their farm to come and visit me. I was in a women's nine-bed ward. The windows were kept open for fresh air. Since I was the youngest in the room, my bed was placed parallel to a wall of open windows. Sometimes I had four army blankets doubled over me to stay warm, but being young, I slept well.

Before I left Ah-Gwah-Ching and in the years following, I never again tested positive for TB, as far as I can remember. I did have to have many gastric lavages, however, and my lungs were very slow to clear.

It was now 1949, and my sister Carol was getting married. She wanted me to be her maid of honor. I was able to be up

The wedding party. (Donna is happily standing next to her sister, the bride.)

a little bit by this time. (You wouldn't believe how weak you get from being in bed all the time.) I had still not regained any weight, nor had my X rays changed much. The doctor didn't want me to go, but I just said, "I'm going." I so badly wanted to be in her wedding. He finally reluctantly discharged me.

Well, I went home for the wedding, and the doctor in New Ulm and the social workers there kept track of me. While I was at home, I was very cautious and slept on an army cot in our living room. I also boiled my dishes and silverware, to reduce any chance of infecting the rest of the family with the bacteria. When weeks had passed and I didn't appear to be improving, the doctor said, "Donna, you're going to have to go back in the sanatorium." So on February 3, 1950, on my birthday, I walked into Southwestern Minnesota Sanatorium in Worthington. I wanted to be closer to home this time for my parents to come and visit me. I spent the next ten months there recovering. After this time, I was at least able to get up, go outside, and take hikes out along the country road. (It seemed these TB sanatoriums were usually out in the country.) The day finally arrived when I was able to leave, return home, and begin picking up the pieces of my life once again.

Life After the Sanatorium

It was 1951, and I was so glad to be home again. I began the search for a nursing job and applied at several places. I would have to send my X rays, but after seeing them nobody wanted to hire me. My body wouldn't heal for some reason. Everyone was hesitant to hire a nurse with a history of TB.

The doctor in Worthington had wanted me to stay there, but you should have heard the language he used. I certainly didn't want to stay there and work around him. He was an excellent tuberculosis doctor; however, he was about 80 years old and would make the young nurses bawl. Nobody was going to make me cry—I was a tough nut.

I was a single woman during this whole experience. I did have a sweetheart during the war years—when I was first at Northwestern. His name was Ned. We met when I was still 19 and while I was in Rochester for the psychiatric training. He was working at the Mayo Clinic and going to Luther College at the time.

One day during my struggles with tuberculosis, I sat down and wrote him a letter and said goodbye. I thought, "Who would want someone with tuberculosis?" I later received a letter from his mother, who was a librarian in Decorah, Iowa. She said, "I hear you're laid on the shelf for awhile." She also wrote in her letter that Ned had joined the Navy. (I wonder if my "Dear John" letter had a part in his decision.) You know, I don't even know if he came back alive—hopefully so. I remember he had blond hair and brown eyes. If he's still alive, I try to envision what he would look like now and what he did with his life.

But . . . God had other plans for my life. I give God the credit. While I was lying in isolation, I read the *Bible* from cover to cover. My mother was having a difficult time with my illness, too. In her letters she would write, "Donna, put your faith in God."

I had been home from the sanatorium for about ten months by now, and I was still looking for a job. Nobody would hire me. Then in August of 1951, I wrote to Glen

Lake Sanatorium against my better wishes. I hadn't wanted to work there for personal reasons. Well, writing that letter turned out to be one of the best decisions in my life.

A New Chapter Begins

At Glen Lake Sanatorium, "Papa" Mattil reviewed my job request, took a chance, and hired me. (Well, his name wasn't really Papa, but everyone called him that. He was Dr. Mattil and the doctor for my future husband.) I was still trying to work up my strength, so I started working just four hours a day and then, over time, built up to six and eight hours per day. I was a medication and treatment nurse and also responsible for bedside care.

Glen Lake Sanatorium was on beautiful grounds and, at that time, out in the country. It was entirely for tuberculosis patients. There was the main hospital, separate buildings for men, women, and children, the "up" buildings for patients as they were recovering, the nurses' dorms, and others.

The ward I worked on was a post-operative station. This was an era when they were doing surgery for segmental resections or removing whole lobes or whole lungs, if necessary, for some difficult TB cases. It was very intensive-care nursing for the time. (Before I left Glen Lake, the University was beginning to do some open-heart surgery. The University sent students to our station, and I trained some University girls in the intensive care unit for lung surgery.) This is also the unit where I met my husband. His name was Emil Grinvalds. He was a patient on a six-bed ward that was located on the sun porch. It was a ward of all young men.

Emil was what was called a Latvian D.P.—a Latvian Displaced Person. He had come to the United States in 1949 and was about 23 or 24 years old when he arrived. He was proud of the fact that he had never been on any type of county assistance but had always worked since arriving in the United States.

Emil had developed tuberculosis in all five lobes of his lungs. He was on strict bed rest while he was recuperating at Glen Lake following lung surgery. He had been very ill and had had very extensive surgery at such a young age. They did surgery on four of his five lobes.

Well, I was the youngest nurse at Glen Lake and quite good-looking, so you can imagine how it was working with these six young men. One man on the ward was married. There was also a young priest on the ward by the name of Father Charlie McCarthy. When I took their vital signs, I had to stand and take the pulse of these young men. They would tease me that their pulse would go way up when I checked their heart rate.

Courtship at Glen Lake

Emil wasn't even out of bed yet at this time, but soon after this he was well enough to get up. The sanatorium had an auditorium where movies were regularly shown for the "up" patients. This is what they called recovering patients. So when he was allowed up, he asked me for a date to the movies. The other men on the porch teased me that Emil's pulse went "pitter-patter" whenever I checked his blood pressure and that he had a crush on me.

As I got to know Emil, I learned that he had had an incredible journey, himself, up to this point. He was here in the United States all by himself. He was born in Latvia, but his family later moved to Germany. Then so many people were getting sick from tuberculosis. His father was very frightened of this and wanted to protect his family. He wanted them to leave Germany and get to where they were going as soon as possible. Emil had been sent to this country all by himself, at his father's insistence. For some reason, his father wanted someone in the family to be here in America. Emil's parents, one brother, and two sisters moved to Australia. It must have been very difficult for him to see the rest of his family leave for Australia. (His older sister later became very ill with tuberculosis, also.)

Emil had been in World War II when he was eighteen, later fighting against the Communists because the Communists were overtaking Europe and his own country of Latvia. His parents escaped to Germany and, because he was a young man of enlistment age, he was conscripted into the German Army to fight against the Communists. (He felt that he would be safer with the Germans, and he wasn't going to allow himself to be captured by the Russians.) I probably don't know a fraction of what he went through. He tells stories of being in the forest all alone with no shoes, and it was freezing cold.

The United States and Russia were still allies at this time. At one point my husband ended up being a prisoner of war for 11 months somewhere in France and Belgium. There was inadequate food—the men were literally starving. They even tore grass from around the fence to eat. There's a picture of him where he looks like he came out of the concentration camps. (It's no wonder that he got tuberculosis, as did many others.)

I'm sure that many internal scars and memories remain with Emil over these dreadful experiences. To this day, he hates spaghetti. For his birthday one year during these hard times, he was given four sticks of dried spaghetti and some prunes. That was his birthday meal! If he got a slice of bread, it would have to last all day.

Emil had lived in Germany for three years before coming here. Ironically, he worked for the American Motor Pool fixing U.S. Army jeeps. So he came over here on a U.S. troopship. The troopships were transporting a lot of Latvians, Estonians, and others at this time.

But . . . back to life in the Glen Lake Sanatorium. The courtship between Emil and me was carried on mostly through notes and love letters. Of course, nurses weren't supposed to fraternize with the patients, but there were several—even women from the head office—who did. Emil's and my daily notes and love letters were secretly delivered with the help of little "cupids."

As Emil continued to heal, he was allowed to be up more. He gradually built up strength to go for walks. Glen Lake Sanatorium was also out in the country, so we would go for walks together along the peaceful and healing countryside.

There was an underground tunnel the nurses used in the winter to go from the nurses' dorm to the hospital so we didn't have to worry about having a coat. Well, one day we got in a smooch during our walk to the door of the tunnel. Our first kiss, and we knew it. Firecrackers went off, and we were very much in love!

Glen Lake also provided occupational therapy so those who were trying to work up their energy and were talented could do leatherwork. Emil began making beautiful hand-made purses—beautiful work—with tool-designed leather. They were expensive because the leather was very expensive.

People were lined up to buy them. A lot of people were also buying them to help him earn money. You see, he was trying to earn the money to buy me an engagement ring.

Emil surprised me one lovely May evening in 1952. He wanted me to come to the men's "up" dorm, and I didn't know why. Here it was such a nice spring evening—I wanted to go for a walk. He was quite persuasive, so I did finally go to his dorm room and then . . . what a surprise! He even got down on his knees and asked me to marry him. He gave me a lovely diamond engagement ring. A patient who was quite well off financially and from Jacobs Jewelry in downtown Minneapolis had helped him go down there and select the ring. I discovered Emil's parents had also been sending him money to help pay for the ring.

There had not been much of a chance to date away from the sanatorium. We were finally able to go back to my home where he met my family, but Mom had already passed away by then. My mom had died the previous February, so he was never able to meet her. Emil's family was far off in Australia, so I hadn't met any of them.

We were two lonely people, both living far away from our families. (Of course, I had no car. To get home to the Gibbon area where my family was now living, I took the Greyhound bus.) How delighted Emil and I were to have found each other. Yes, we were deeply in love. Even though we had been born in different countries, we discovered we had similar backgrounds. To begin with, both of us had walked to school during grade school, and we had both boarded with other families during high school. We discovered other similarities as well, as we opened our hearts to one another and talked of life experiences.

Emil and I were eager to get married, but we didn't know how we were going to do it without any money. Only one-third of my nursing class made it to graduation. There was one former classmate of mine living in California. I had written to her about Emil and how we were engaged and in love, but his folks were in Australia, my mother had died, and neither one of us had any money. I said, "I just don't know how we're going to get married." She wrote back with a very creative solution.

My friend knew of a television program, "Bride and Groom," that had just started in 1951 in California. She went to the TV station, got the application on how to get on it, and mailed it to me. I hadn't ever seen a TV—I didn't know there was such a thing as this program. Anyway, I filled out the application and then got busy with work and put it in the back of my mind. One fall morning while I was doing medications and treatments for the whole station, I got a called from Manhattan, New York. New York! Here it was 7 a.m.—I didn't know anybody from New York! It turned out to be Doris Beckman from Manhattan, New York, who organized all the weddings for the "Bride and Groom" show. She loved our story that I had submitted with the application and wanted us to be married on their show.

Wedding Bells Rang on the "Bride and Groom" Show

We were both thrilled! We didn't get to choose the month that the wedding would take place—Doris did. She chose the month of December for our wedding. The only reason I can think of that she picked December for our wedding date is that TB was often connected with December. They always sent Christmas seals home for the kids to sell, and Christmas seals were used to help fight tuberculosis. (Today Christmas seals are connected with the Lung Association.)

There was little time to make all the plans for our trip to New York—December was a short time away. It was an exciting time, but I was also still very heartbroken over my mother's death. Being the oldest daughter, I had been very close to her. I remember I was in the nurses' dorm when I was told of her death. She was only 45 years old. I literally got hysterical at the news—they thought I was laughing. She had her first heart attack at age 35, and I knew she could go at any time. Still . . . I was heartbroken at the news.

Emil and I were expected to arrange our own way out to New York for our wedding. A limousine was supposed to pick us up when we arrived in New York, but that's not how it turned out. We left Minnesota in a blizzard; in fact, it was a blizzard similar to the famous Armistice Day blizzard. Unable to fly because of the storm, we began our journey by Greyhound. We only got as far as Chicago that day and then had to sit all night in the bus depot waiting for the next bus to go. We were both eager to get to New York, but it took us into the third day to arrive there.

When we got to New York, we had to get blood tests, a marriage license, and all that. There wasn't much time left for anything else since our journey out there had taken so long. We didn't even get a chance to watch the televised "Bride and Groom" show until just a day before our own appearance on the show. An aspiring actor and his wife were getting married on the "Bride and Groom" show that day. You may have heard of him—Dick Van Dyke. He wasn't well-known at this time but just a budding actor at the beginning of his career.

Emil and I didn't get a chance to practice until just before we went on the air. I was able to select a wedding gown to wear from a rack of wedding dresses. I didn't get to keep my gown, but that was OK. I remember selecting one with tiny little buttons all the way down. Emil wore a nice tuxedo.

Donna and Emil posing for the cameras by one of their
gifts—a new stove.

We didn't have any attendants with us, so the show provided a budding actor and actress to be our attendants. (No, it wasn't Dick Van Dyke.) There weren't any people in the audience. It was filmed on a set made to look like a church.

I remember there was a rather large bridal assistant helping me with my gown before the show. I was so nervous—I was crying. She said, "You're going to be just terrible! Oh, you're going to be just terrible!" (She wasn't kidding—she was so mean to me. Of course, that only made me feel worse.) Emil was a little broken in his English, and when he gets nervous, his accent comes out more. We were there alone with no family members. However, the soloist, the minister, and the man interviewing us were all just wonderful. They really relaxed us. We exchanged wedding rings that we were able to keep as gifts from the program. (At the time, I did not notice that the minister had a beautiful Danish accent. It wasn't until 20 years later—when we saw the movie of our wedding for the first time—that I noticed his beautiful accent. I guess I was too nervous at the time.)

We also received a Westinghouse refrigerator, a Tappan gas stove, Cannon towels, linens, glassware, dishes, silverware, and a sound movie of our wedding to send to Emil's parents in Australia. After the show, this same bridal assistant said, "Oh, you did OK." I believe our wedding ceremony was shown over CBS on the "Bride and Groom" show at 11:00 a.m. on December 2, 1952.

On the day of our wedding, even the Gibbon school had a TV in the auditorium so that the students could watch us get married. (My younger brother and sister attended there at the time.)

Glen Lake Sanatorium also did the same so that our friends there and patients who were able to be up and around could watch our wedding ceremony.

An image taken from the TV screen during Donna and Emil's debut on the "Bride and Groom" show. Donna said, "We look pretty serious."

Doris had arranged for us to go to Boston following the wedding for our honeymoon. There was all this limousine business lined up. Well, wouldn't you know, it was very bad weather in New York, too. Working only part time since I was still recovering from TB, I hadn't built up much vacation time. Glen Lake Sanatorium did the best they could, and I think I had about nine days before I had to be back to work. With the time taken for getting out there and time needed to return, we didn't have that many days in between.

Usually the show sent the couple to Bermuda or some other exotic spot for their honeymoon, but we were sent to Boston due to the short amount of time we had. Again, it was bad weather so we took a taxi to the train station and had a lovely train ride from New York to Boston. I had never before had a train ride, so that was beautiful. The train had turquoise velvet seats, and the dining cars glittered with all the fancy lights.

We had a lovely wedding night dinner at the Sheraton Plaza Hotel in Boston. While we were eating our dinner, a girl came up to us and said, "You are the couple that were married on "Bride and Groom" this morning. You were beautiful!" Then after our dinner, Emil asked me to dance the Tango. (The Tango was a dance he had learned in his native country of Latvia, and it was his favorite dance.) Well, I knew how to do the Waltz, the Fox Trot, and several other types of dances, but I certainly didn't know how to dance the Tango. Emil just couldn't convince me to get up and try the Tango with him that night.

Emil and I had a few days to enjoy in Boston. I loved American history, so I was very interested in seeing the area. We had also toured New York. We went to Grand Central Station, and we saw the Statue of Liberty. In both Boston and New York, we took the Grey Line Bus Tour, which was a very inexpensive way to see the cities and their historical parts. We originally walked around the city, but I wore a hole right through the sole of the high-heeled shoes I was wearing. After that, we found that the Grey Line Bus Tour was a much better way to see the city. We took a taxi once, but it was so expensive. It was very easy to find our way around in Manhattan. (I'd like to go back and do the same tour again—and look at the "hotsy totsy" jewelry on Fifth Avenue in New York.)

During our brief honeymoon, we also went by train to Washington, D.C., and took another Grey Line tour of the capital city. A President—I believe it was Eisenhower—was soon to be inaugurated at that time. They had built the scaffolding in preparation for his inauguration.

Father Charlie McCarthy, who had had tuberculosis and been in Emil's ward at Glen Lake Sanatorium, was now living out there near the Capitol in Washington, D.C. We looked him up, and were we happy to see him again! He showed us around his quarters, even though he wasn't supposed to allow women in there. (I can't help but wonder what happened to him since then. He was a very nice man.)

It was thrilling for someone from the Midwest—who had never been anywhere other than North Dakota and Minnesota—to see all these things. Both Emil and I said we were "country bumpkins."

Married Life Begins Back Home

When we returned from our honeymoon, I continued working at Glen Lake Sanatorium, gradually building up to full-time hours. Emil had been in the Glen Lake Sanatorium for twenty-seven months prior to our wedding. They were very good to him—the staff had become like family. They were called Papa "so-and-so" and Mama "so-and-so." Yes, they were all like family to us—even the elevator man. The staff helped Emil enroll in the Tool and Die program at Dunwoody Institute. He also started classes to become a naturalized citizen. We lived in an apartment in Hopkins so that he could ride the bus to Dunwoody and I could also take a bus out to the Sanatorium to work.

We rented a basement apartment from a man whose wife had just died, and we lived there for two years. It was only $45 a month, and we didn't have to pay for any utilities. Well, I was getting along pretty well and I wanted a baby. I was working full time and have always been pretty good at saving money.

We had our first baby in 1956, and that's when I quit working at Glen Lake. Emil was now a naturalized citizen and was working. We planned the first baby, and then the next baby arrived in 1957. Our family was later complete with one boy and three girls.

Emil and I bought our first house at Acorn Ridge by Excelsior, paying about $10,000 for it. We lived there for eight years. By this time, we had four children and needed more room. We were both happy to find this big old house that we're living in now. This has been our home since 1964.

When we moved here, it was all open land around our house. It truly felt like you were way out in the country. There is a lovely woods behind us where neighbors would tap the trees for maple syrup, and we would go for walks with the animals. Fortunately, this area has been preserved. In spite of my childhood episode with horses and Russian thistle, I have always loved horses. We had horses here for years—three of our own, and one the druggist in town kept here. Our neighbor also had one. Yes, we had a lot of fun with horses while the children were growing up.

A Time of Service

Even though I had quit working at the Glen Lake Sanatorium to raise our children, my days remained very full. I became involved with the Welcome Wagon—called the Newcomer's Club at that time. I was with that organization for five years as the program chairman. I saw it grow from a small group of women to 250 women. I had to arrange for the guest speaker at our monthly meetings and then get up and introduce the speakers. I had been a very shy girl in high school. In fact, my senior yearbook used the saying "Silence is Golden" to describe me. That speaking experience was a wonderful growing experience. It cured me of my fears, and I am no longer afraid to speak up in a large group.

During the 1980s and '90s, I was very involved with helping those in need. Our organization was called Westonka Christian Service—now called the Westonka Community Action Network. I was nominated to be the director of emergency services, and I put over 100,000 miles on my little Volkswagen Rabbit. I would go and meet people who needed gas for trips to the clinic or even drive people to the hospital myself. I would also often meet people in my home around my kitchen table. Whoever was in need—there was help available for them.

I was the director for seven years and conducted business from my home in a little office off the kitchen. Our organization later became incorporated. There were paid employees, but mine was always volunteer work. It could become very stressful at times dealing with many victims of abuse. It was difficult trying not to get too involved in these people's lives.

A Lutheran church in Mound sponsored a Hmong family and wanted a local family to take them in, so we did. Lutheran Services had paid for my husband to come here, so this was our way of paying them back for what they had done for him.

We were enthralled by the story of this particular Hmong family. Gatua Ly, the father, had helped our downed U.S. pilots find their way to safety through the jungles when he was just a young man of 13. It was during the Vietnam War. This time in our country's history was a part of their family history.

I remember it was a bitter cold March day when we went to the airport to pick up our Hmong family. They arrived looking as though they had come straight from the jungle—wearing thongs on bare feet, their native clothes, and long black hair. Relatives of this family had been featured in a *National Geographic* article, where they had been photographed in their native village. I remember our new family arrived looking just like they had stepped out of a *National Geographic* magazine.

Because they had lived in Thailand for five years and Gatua Ly had worked as a medic, he knew some English. In fact, he had learned bits of four different languages. It was very rewarding to us that Gatua Ly had helped our American soldiers, and now we were able to help him and his family become established in their new country.

The mother, father, grandma, and three children came home from the airport with us and lived with us for two months. To make room for them, we got some bedroom furniture—a French provincial set—and turned the dining room into a bedroom for them. There was a crib for the baby, the little girl slept on the window seat, and grandma slept in the den. Another child was conceived in our house. (She was such a pretty little girl; however, she died at age four from leukemia. It was very sad.) Emil and I also had three kids of our own who had moved back home at this same time, so we were a full house.

At first we cooked separately. But out of respect to us, our houseguests would not eat unless we sat down and joined them. So we would usually have combined meals. That's how I learned some creative oriental cooking using ginger root and different greens that they liked to use.

We are still involved with the lives of this family. Luckily, the parents were able to get jobs when they arrived, and they later got a home of their own in St. Paul. Chor, their little girl, turned six in our house. I fondly remember putting her on the Kindergarten bus every morning to go to school from here. She graduated with honors and is now a prosecuting criminal attorney. Two other boys are in college now. We are so happy and proud!

Looking Toward Retirement

After training at Dunwoody Institute, Emil worked for a company that became Control Data. Later he worked for Lake Engineering for over 40 years. He retired at 67 and stayed home for two years. When he was 69, they called him back, and he worked until this year when he was 76 years old.

He had a heart attack in 1988, which was really scary. We were sitting watching TV, and he was very quiet. Then he said, "Donna, I think we better go to the hospital." He was clammy and had some pain. I took his blood pressure and pulse. He had just had an angiogram at Abbott Northwestern. A woman resident was on call. When I called and explained the situation, she said, "It doesn't sound like a heart attack." From my nursing background, I knew it was. So I drove him to Waconia's emergency room. There we discovered some surprising connections to a previous chapter in our lives. We learned that the doctor who met with us was the nephew of the doctor who had been at the Glen Lake Sanatorium when I was a nurse and Emil was a patient. I think this helped to calm our fears. What a coincidence—or was it? God has an interesting way of weaving people and events from the past and the present together.

I was able to ride in the ambulance with Emil to Abbott Northwestern. They redid the angiogram, and he had a quadruple-bypass surgery the next day. The second day he developed pneumococcal pneumonia, which is very serious after just having surgery. He kept developing pneumococcal and streptococcal pneumonia again after he returned home, which again is a very serious disease for someone his age combined with his lung problems that had resulted from tuberculosis.

During all these years, the rest of Emil's family were still living in Australia. We had never been there to see what they called home. Finally, in 1970 our entire family was able to make the trip to Australia. What a memorable trip that was!

Emil's father also came here all by himself when he was 70 years old and stayed with us for three months. We got along really great. Later, we learned that his father wanted to come and live here in Minnesota, but his children in Australia didn't think he could make the trip. (He later died in a nursing home in Australia.)

I never met Emil's mother. She died of a cerebral hemorrhage. As I mentioned, he never met my mother either. Ironically, both of our mothers died of cerebral hemorrhages. Our lives seemed to continue to parallel each other in so many ways.

A Connection with the "Bride and Groom" Show . . . After All These Years

Just recently, we were at the Excelsior Senior Center, and I won a quilt in a drawing. I've won a lot of things over my lifetime—I've been lucky that way. I said, "Oh, the best thing I ever won was my husband!" (He's a little shy and maybe didn't like that comment.) I continued, "Well, I've got more to that story. We were married on a national television show called "Bride and Groom" in the 1950s."

Well, it was time for one more coincidence. There was a couple, Mrs. and Mrs. Holde, who happened to be sitting at the table right next to me and overheard my comments. They said, "We were married on that program, too!" Here they were married just six months after us in June of 1953. Neither of us had ever known anyone else who had been married on that show. I never did see the show after we got back from our honeymoon because we didn't have a television.

These many years later, my sister and brother-in-law said, "Why didn't you ask us to go along and be your attendants? We would have gone along with you." As farmers at the time, I didn't think they would have been able to get away. Plus my mom had died—I was feeling sad about that. I just figured nobody would be able to go.

Now at this point in our lives, Emil and I are enjoying each day. We are filled with the peace that comes from working in the garden soil, caring for the stray animals that have found a path to our door, and housesitting a dog or two. Our children are busy planning our 50th wedding anniversary celebration. Our wedding ceremony on the "Bride and Groom" show has been put on video for the guests to see and enjoy. I don't want a big party—mainly family. Most of my friends have already died—mainly dying from cancer at a young age in their forties and fifties.

I am grateful for all the kind people who helped me along my journey. Many of my teachers and one principal, in particular, were wonderful. I made it through nurses' training with the help of Mom's prayers—and the home-baked cakes that she sent. The TB years were made better by God's love, family and friends, the staff at the sanatorium that became like family, and of course, my meeting Emil.

Later in my life, the many years of volunteer work were so rewarding. I'm still willing to work hard, but I no longer want to take the leadership role. It's a good opportunity for the next generation to give of themselves to the community. God has been so good. I know He is satisfied.

What a unique journey for Donna and Emil! How amazing it is that this young man who had traveled from distant Latvia should cross paths with this young woman in a TB sanatorium in Glen Lake, Minnesota.

They truly felt they were destined to meet. In fact, I learned that Emil wasn't even supposed to come to Minnesota. When emigrating from Germany, he was sponsored by a church in upstate New York. However, the process was taking so long that Lutheran Services sponsored him instead and brought him to Minnesota. The thread of destiny was already being pulled to draw these two people together.

When they met, they had both already endured so many dark days and hardships in life. How heartwarming to hear how their love for each other brought light and joy into their lives.

Donna's story about their being married on the "Bride and Groom" show was most fascinating. I had never even heard of this television show. What a creative way to get married when there were no funds for a wedding. It also provided a way for them to begin life together with unique memories all their own.

This wedding story was also a wonderful glimpse into the early days of black and white television. It's now difficult for us to imagine homes without a television—many today have several of them.

Donna was given a list of interesting instructions before appearing on the "Bride and Groom" program. One item said, "Because of the problem of colors on television, we prefer that the bride wears a gown selected from our stock of bridal gowns from leading fashion houses. We are not able to provide a dress for the maid of honor. Her dress should be a full-length, pastel-colored bridesmaid's dress."

It is easy to understand why Donna and Emil were photographed posing by their new stove and refrigerator. It was a reflection of the time—Americans' newfound love with the household appliance. This was the early '50s, and Americans were just discovering the convenience of "modern" appliances. I can just imagine the couple's excitement at getting a free stove and refrigerator.

Donna's story about their unique wedding was a remarkable one, but it didn't end there. Through the many years of her life, I believe she was blessed in so many ways because of her grateful spirit. Instead of turning angry and bitter over the many challenges she had faced early in life, she gave of herself to others.

Donna heard someone on a radio show recently talk about "Your Authentic Self" and the seven critical choices in one's life. She said she sat down to reflect on the path that her life had taken, and she wrote down the seven critical choices that she had made in her own life. This is what she wrote:

1. *I studied hard and did well in New Ulm High School, even receiving several honors.*

2. *I made the decision to enter the Cadet Nursing Corps to receive my nurses' training.*

3. *I made the commitment to "save myself" for my husband and to always remain faithful.*

4. *I made the difficult decision to work at Glen Lake Sanatorium.*

5. *I said "yes" to Emil's marriage proposal and got married on the "Bride and Groom" show.*

6. *I made the decision to have children.*

7. *Most important—I desired to live a Christian life.*

Few people take the time to review their life's journey and reflect on the important decisions that they made along the way. Donna's list proves to be an accurate summary of her life and how she lived it.

Emil also has a visual reminder of his past and how much he has to give thanks for. Underneath a shade tree in their yard are two chairs for relaxing from the heat of a summer day. Posted to the tree above them is a sign that reads, Grenadier's Pub. In English, grenadier means "someone who throws grenades." The sign represents a time in his life that he would not want to relive and one that he is most grateful to have survived.

As Donna and I neared the end of our visit, we found ourselves sitting cross-legged on the floor peering through a box of secret love letters she had lovingly stored from their courtship at Glen Lake Sanatorium. Meanwhile, beautiful Tango music filled the room as Emil played his favorite CD for us. Donna said, "Over the years, Emil was always such a romantic, buying me lingerie and bouquets of flowers. Being the practical one, I would say that a single rose would be just fine."

The young love between Donna and Emil that was just beginning to bud in those first love letters had come full circle. Their circle was now filled with years of memories and the love for each other, their children, and grandchildren.

By the way, Donna and Emil are still working on the Tango together.

3

A CELEBRATION
OF THE JOURNEY

May the light of your soul guide you.
May the light of your soul bless
the work you do
with the secret love
and warmth of your heart.
May you see in what you do
the beauty of your own soul.

A CELTIC BLESSING

A CELEBRATION OF THE JOURNEY

*E*veryone has a story. Even though many of the following women may have experienced similar events, such
as the Great Depression, the tapestry of their lives
became woven in a very unique pattern unlike any other. As
I interviewed these women, themes would often emerge as to
what their lives were really about. They each had gifts to
bring to the table. You will meet Charlotte, whose entire life
revolved around her love for music. For Chris, it became a
journey expressed by a rainbow of colors as an artist. For
many, events or opportunities were brought to them that
altered the course of their lives forever.

For all of the women you are about to meet, it was a time
of reflecting on memories gathered over a lifetime. Verdi
will remind you in "The Master Storyteller," "Remember,
all you ever get out of this life is memories. That's all you
ever get. You can't take your money with you."

So we will celebrate the uniqueness of each of their journeys. Perhaps they will cause you to ponder—even if only for a
brief moment—on the gifts that you are bringing or the memories that will lighten your heart at the end of the journey.

⁂

HILDA AND EVA—THE LITTLE GIRLS

Eva Gerdin Olson

*E*va's story portrays the special bond between two sisters and the wonderful opportunity they were given to reflect on memories of long ago that were lovingly stored in their hearts.

I remember it was a summer day in 1996 when my sister Hilda surprised me with a telephone call. Normally this wouldn't surprise me, for we had had many phone visits over the years. However, I wasn't expecting a call from her today. At 103 years old, she had been in and out of consciousness for a couple of weeks. Her family had gathered around her bed to be with her as the end drew near. Hilda had even had a visit from our older sister Arvida, who had passed away several years ago. No one else could see her, but she was apparently there to help prepare Hilda for her final journey. (As any good Swede would do, Hilda said, "Shouldn't we offer Arvida some coffee?")

Now my dear sister Hilda was talking to me on the other end of the line. Apparently she had become alert, had a full meal, and then wanted to have a talk with her sister. So we got a wonderful gift—the opportunity to say goodbye and to reminisce about the 100 plus years of memories that we shared. Being the youngest siblings in the family, we were always known as the "little girls." We were now the last direct link to our original family of eleven.

We shared so many memories . . .

❧

Family Roots

Our family lineage actually began from what may have been a chance meeting. Our grandfather's great grandfather came to Sweden from Germany as a young man. His name was Sivert VonDress. We were told he had been walking through the woods on his journey to Sweden and hadn't seen a single soul for quite some time. Then he heard a cowbell in the distance, so he decided to walk toward that sound. He came upon a girl tending the cows in their summer pasture. Well, they became acquainted and were eventually married. So from this line came our grandpa, Sivert Knutson. He in turn married a girl named Dorthea, and they had two children—our Uncle Knut and our mother, Sigrid Amelia. Our mother married John Gerdin, and they eventually had nine children.

Memories of our Childhood

Hilda was born in 1893, and I was born a little later in 1895. We grew up in a Swedish community in Minnesota called Maple

Ridge. This beautiful little community was made up of our school, a church, a store, a blacksmith shop, and neighboring farms. We lived in a white colonial farmhouse with green shutters and an expansive front porch. We could still clearly see in our minds that white picket fence around the front of the yard with two large gates to drive the horses through.

I remember, I remember
The house where I was born
The little window
Where the sun came peeping in at morn.

As children we spent a lot of time in the woods and pasture, where there was always something interesting to see and do. We would climb young trees and as they would bend, we would just hang on with our hands and drop down until we almost touched the ground. Then we would let go and the trees would spring back up again. What a feeling of freedom! We would also lie on the cool grass, gaze at the blue sky, and watch the fluffy clouds float by . . . just dreaming.

There was always a lot of work to do, but we "little girls" would love to go for walks in the evening after the day's chores—always singing as we went.

Of course, in the spring or summer, we had to pick potato bugs or mustard in the fields. But then there was also berry-picking time. We would go to the neighbor's pasture (with his permission, of course) and pick raspberries. Sometimes we would meet other girls there and have a fun time, but of course then we'd come home with fewer berries.

Since television hadn't yet been invented, we used our own imaginations. We would spend hours playing underneath the granary. It had high posts and was built on a hillside, so there was room under the backside of the building. We made farms, windmills out of sticks, and the doghouse became the store. Our brother Jonas would be the storekeeper. We put little shelves in there, got little pieces of cloth from Mother, and made little baskets to hold white beans (which were the eggs). There was a weed that had brown seeds on top. We'd take the seeds off and that would be coffee beans. We would also catch little fish—tiny minnows—in the creek in back of the farm, put them in a little keg that carpet tacks originally came in, and that would be herring.

All the boys in the neighborhood quickly learned how to swim in the creek. We girls didn't go along because the boys didn't have bathing suits—they just swam in the nude. Sometimes we girls would put on old dresses, tie red bandanas on our heads, and go down to wade in the creek by ourselves. One time we took clothesline along because the creek was quite deep—about 10 feet in one place. (The "Deep Hole," they called it.) Well, we'd tie one end of the line around our waist and wade out into the water. If it got too deep, the other girls would pull us in. There were bloodsuckers in the creek, too. Hilda recalled how we used to let the bloodsuckers get on our legs, and then we'd watch them fill up. Oh . . . what memories.

The Sisters

We were originally six sisters in all; however, Agnes Virginia died from the measles when she was nine, and Ina died from TB when she was 13. These were some very sad times for our family. Ina and Arvida went to stay overnight at the neighbor's house when Agnes was born in 1901. Ina slept by an open window and got a cold from the draft, which then developed into tuberculosis. It is sad to think about how our sister Ina was alone a lot of the time before she died. Mother was worried that the rest of us would get sick also, so she kept Ina apart.

Then years later all us kids were really sick with the measles. It was a terrible time! Agnes just wasn't able to recover. We had funeral services for both sisters at the North Church. We created bouquets of flowers for the services from whatever the neighbors had in their gardens. No one bought flowers at that time.

I always had a special bond with my sister Arvida. She took care of me as a baby. She would wash my baby clothes and then hang them out on the line with the arms all stretched out so it would look like a big wash and like she really did a lot of work. However, she told me she was so glad to get another little sister. (Many, many years later, Arvida died on my 90th birthday. I always had special thoughts of her on my birthday after that.)

Our Sister Lydia

Now Lydia, she was our mysterious sister. We had heard about her for years but didn't get to meet her until she was a young woman. This was another family story that we had heard repeated many times throughout the years. Hilda and I were born in America, but Mother and Dad had been married and started a family in Sweden. Dad wanted to come to America. He felt there was no future for a family in Sweden at that time. It was terribly difficult for mother to leave Sweden, but she went along with his decision. When their train was leaving to take them to the boat that would take them to America, Lydia (a little girl at the time) had her arms clenched around her grandfather's neck and refused to let go. Lydia's grandparents had fears that the whole family might perish on their journey to America and perhaps they would never be able to see any of them again. So the grand-parents said, "Leave her with us so that someone will be left." The train had already been held up for twenty minutes and emotions were running high, so they finally threw some clothes out the train window and let her stay with her grand-parents. She lived with them until she was about seventeen.

Hilda and I could both remember our excitement on the day Lydia came from Sweden. We had a difficult time sitting still in school. We hurried home after school to meet our grown sister whom we had never seen. The memory of this day was still clearly etched in our minds. Dad, Mother, and Lydia were having coffee in the summer kitchen. Lydia looked so very grown up. She wore a white blouse with a brown knit vest with a pretty pattern and some red on it. She had brown curly hair and was very pretty with a light complexion and rosy cheeks. (She thought we looked pretty wild with our tanned faces.) We did eventually become acquainted, and Lydia became best of friends with her four American sisters.

Young Ladies

As we got older, we had so much fun in our teenage years. On Sundays, we would often go with a bunch of young people for a picnic to a nearby lake called Lewis Lake. Our brother Jonas or one of the Swanson boys would take a team of horses and the hayrack. We would all ride on the back of the hayrack. We would stay all afternoon and sometimes not get home until maybe midnight. Some of us girls would go out in the boat, which probably wasn't the safest since we couldn't swim. One of the boys, Alvin Swanson, was a real scamp. He'd get in the

A relaxing picnic with friends—Eva and Herman in front.

boat with us and then rock it back and forth out in the middle of the lake. It's funny none of us drowned!

Hilda and I had a lot in common, but we also had our differences. We did have our spats, of course, but we basically got along fine. Hilda liked to help at home with the cooking and sewing, and I preferred to work outside. In school, I loved to read and memorize poetry, and Hilda preferred arithmetic. Yet we still had a strong bond that only sisters can understand.

We wore handmade clothes to school. Mother made a lot of our clothes out of flour sacks. Talking about that really brought back a lot of memories. We didn't have underwear until we were old enough to know about it—store bought underwear, that is. Ours were made from flour sacks, of course. And black stockings—how we hated them! We had to wear long underwear inside of our stockings, and our legs looked SO BIG. So sometimes when we got out of range of anyone seeing us, we would pull our stockings down and turn our underwear up above our knees so that the stockings fit better. (The lady next door to us knit the stockings from yarn that mother had previously died black and spun.)

Those stockings were so tight we could hardly breathe. We would swear we had caps on our legs—especially as we got older and starting getting some shape to our legs.

After we finished school (8th grade) and before we got married, both Hilda and I spent some time working up in Duluth. We chose Duluth because Lydia had been working there before us. Hilda reminisced about her experiences up there and oh . . . how we laughed.

She worked for a widow who had one son. This woman had funny ideas. Hilda had to get up at five o'clock in the morning and have all the white clothes washed before breakfast. There were no washers or dryers at that time, so of course this meant washing everything by hand in the basement and hanging the clothes outside to dry. To make matters worse, this woman burned coal for heat. She had a big bedspread that was some type of a family heirloom. She insisted Hilda spread it out in the snow and freeze it to make it whiter. Hilda said she could hardly bend it to get it down into the basement later. She couldn't help but touch something, and then she'd get black soot on it and have to try to wash off the black spots. It was the same way with the sheets. "Oh God," Hilda said, "that lady had funny ideas." Hilda lasted there for three months. That was long enough.

Boys Enter the Picture

We both married boys from the neighborhood. I had just finished school when Herman's family moved down here from Duluth. Teddy Falk had been my boyfriend and was so much fun, but then Herman came along and well . . . he won my heart! I thought he was pretty cute! He was a quiet, steady sort of guy. We were friends for several years before we got married.

We all loved to hang May baskets in the neighborhood. This tradition involved making a handmade basket filled with candy or other treats. You would go to a neighbor's house and hang it on their front door, yell "May Basket," and then run and hide. They would have to come out of the house, find you, and tag you. We had just hung one on Herman's family, and I was chasing him. He fell down a couple of feet into an old well that had been partially filled. After we were married, Herman would tease me that the well is where I caught him.

Hilda met Charlie at choir practice one evening when she was 15. Both Hilda and I were good friends with his sisters. Charlie was eight years older than Hilda and had been working in the Cities (Minneapolis and St. Paul). Then he came home to work on the farm so that his brother could go to the Cities. Well, he took Hilda home from choir practice one night, and that's how it started. They "kept company" for the next ten years (although our parents didn't know about it for the first few years.)

Charlie was nice and quite patient. Well, he did like to tease. Hilda talked about when they were first married and she would be washing dishes. He would take a towel and help out by wiping the dishes. Hilda always wore an apron with long ties on it and the first thing she knew, she would be tied to a chair. He was always doing tricks like that.

❧

Reflections

We could have talked for hours as the memories came flooding back. Our journeys had each been filled with many blessings. I had three daughters, and Hilda had three sons and a daughter. Both of our families had survived the Depression without losing our farms. We did have to take clothes back out of the "rag bin," and wouldn't you know—they didn't look so bad after all. There was always food on the table because we planted large gardens every year.

Our lives had also gone down individual paths. I had lived my entire life in the country within a 10-mile radius of our home place. Hilda had spent the last half of her life in the big city of Minneapolis. Herman and I had been able to enjoy our years together well into our 90s. Unfortunately, Hilda had lost Charlie due to a heart attack over 30 years ago. She had never remarried.

As we were daydreaming and watching the clouds float by as children, we could never have imagined that we would be having this conversation over 100 years later. Our hearts and spirits were still young—it was just our bodies that had played tricks on us by aging. We would always be the "little girls."

⚘

The End of the Journey

My sister Hilda passed away a short time after this special conversation in June of 1996. I can just imagine the rest of our family greeting her as she arrived in heaven: "Hilda! You're finally here! We've been waiting for you." Well, I'm glad she stayed on earth just a little bit longer, so we could have this last conversation and say goodbye. What a wonderful gift! For me, this was one of life's special moments!

Eva surpassed her sister's longevity by living on this earth to the age of 106 years and one month. She died in September of 2001, after having lived life to the fullest. At her passing, there was truly a celebration for the rich life she had lived. (I'm sure there was quite the celebration in heaven, also, as she was reunited with her family.)

Eva had touched many lives with her love, humor, and quick wit. She always had a tender heart and a tear for someone's misfortune. She passed down her appreciation for art, the beauty of flowers, birds, and all of nature. Those who knew her were truly blessed by her love, laughter, and passion for life.

She had touched my life also, for she was my grandmother. I loved her as a child, but cherish the special moments within these last ten years that we spent woman to woman. I gained a much better understanding of her life and my family history by the experiences that she shared with me. We shared laughter and tears.

I can also understand the strong bond that she had with her sisters because I am fortunate to go through my own journey with the rich blessings of my sisters. I can only imagine the conversations that we three sisters will be having when we are over one hundred years old. It brings a smile to my heart.

Caught Between Two Worlds

Winifred (Mann) Miller

*L*ife's journey is often similar to a rolling landscape of hills and valleys and can be mixed with abundance and hardship. So it has been with Winifred's path. Her story tells about her experience with both worlds. She had a carefree childhood and received anything her heart desired. Then she had a head-on collision with the other side of reality as she experienced the struggles of being a young wife and mother during the Depression.

My Childhood

I was born Winifred Mann in 1906 in a very small town in the western part of the state, in Lake Benton, Minnesota. (This is where they now have all the windmills generating electricity on Buffalo Hill.) I had a wonderful and very care-free childhood! If I wanted something, my father would go to the Cities and get it for me. For example, in those days we had little push cars where you go back and forth, and you could make them run all over the place. I really wanted one of those. Wouldn't you know, he went up to Minneapolis and bought it for me. Then I wanted ice skates—he went up to the Cities and got them for me, too. Oh, yeah, I was such a spoiled brat!

We have laughed so many times over one of my childhood escapades when I was about six. I was always taking off out of the yard. I wanted to play with someone—I just didn't want to be left playing around home. My mother finally resorted to tying me to a line in the backyard just so she could keep track of me. We had clotheslines out in back, you know. Our house had running water in the bathroom and everything, but we also had an outhouse. In order to keep me home, she would give me my lunch and tie me up to the clothesline with a rope. I could have the freedom of the backyard but not the entire town. Yes, that's all I could go . . . up and down the backyard. There were trees so I wasn't hot, and I could get to the toilet. One day I went to work on the rope, untied it, and went up the road with the rope dragging behind me. (Mother wasn't too happy about that.)

To better understand my background, I must tell you about my mother and father. My mother and father came up to Minnesota from Iowa and started a bank. My mother owned the bank, and my father was the cashier. It was a Federal bank. Then during the war, Roosevelt closed all the banks. Then they sent in what they call "Receivers."

However, before this happened, my folks had sold the bank. We had a lot of farms at that time. My mother sold them but she made good on all the bank losses. It was such a hard time, for so many people were losing their farms.

This was also the time when we had the drought. It wasn't bad enough that we had a Depression, but everything dried up and farmers didn't even have seed. Mother had to buy the seeds for some of the farmers so that they could plant. So my mother was a strong businesswoman with a lot of drive and vision. (I believe she got these strengths from my grandfather.)

My grandfather was a wealthy man. He had been born in Germany before coming to the United States. He became a farmer down around Davenport, Iowa. He also had a fine china company, and he had also invested in several other things. So you can imagine this was where my mother got the money to invest in a bank and her drive to achieve. (Unfortunately, my grandfather died when I was four, so I never really knew him.) As I said, he had a china company and one of his lines was Haviland china. Therefore, my mother eventually had a set of Haviland china that came from France, and I also had an aunt, Minnie (my mother's sister), who had a set. Now today my three girls each have eight-place settings of Haviland china. This special part of my grandfather's history has been passed down for several generations of our family to enjoy.

College Days

Well, in 1923, I went off to college. I attended a girls' college in Rockford, Illinois, for one year and then went to Carleton College in Northfield, Minnesota. One of my girlfriends was going to college there, too. One time she had a date with a man and her mother wouldn't let her keep it, so I took the date instead. That's the man I married in 1926 before I graduated. (His name was Theodore William, but we all called him Ted.)

The Bet is On

I thought it would be better to wait to get married until after I graduated, but Ted was eager to get married right away. There was a football game coming up between St. Olaf and Carleton. I guess you could say we got married on a bet. We decided if St. Olaf won, we would get married right away. If Carleton won, we would wait for two years. Well . . . St. Olaf won the game, and so the wedding was on!

We made arrangements to be married by a Congregational minister in the nearby town of Cannon Falls. It was just Ted and I and two witnesses that had been arranged by the minister. After the wedding, I remember we stopped at a little restaurant and had sardines and crackers. We were married on Tuesday, November 23, 1926, and then I wasn't able to see him again until Thanksgiving. You see, our marriage had to be kept a secret! If the college had known about it, they would have kicked me out. They didn't want any married students!

Our Secret Marriage

Our marriage was still a secret a month later, so I went home alone for the Christmas holiday. Ted wrote me a letter and said he thought I ought to come back since I was married now. Well, somehow my sister got a hold of that letter and read it. Then the story about our secret marriage came out. My parents didn't like it, but they took the news pretty well. They were good parents.

Days on the Farm

After I graduated, we started our married life on his parents' farm in Randolph, Minnesota. His older brothers and sisters had each been given a farm, and the understanding was that we were to have the next farm—his parents' farm. What a reality adjustment! I had been brought up in a home where I never had to do any work or have any financial worries. Now I had to learn how to milk cows and so on. I didn't even know how to bake bread when I was first married. (I don't know why I didn't even know how to do that.)

I remember my first batch of bread. Ted came in from the field about three times to see how the bread was coming along. I think it was the best batch of bread I've ever baked. He picked up a warm loaf of bread and ran down the road to show it to his mother. He was so proud.

The Depression Years

Ted's parents lost the family farm during the Depression, so we had to move a few times to other houses that had been vacated. As a way to earn some income, we bought a truck to deliver cattle to South St. Paul. Then the prices became so low that the farmers couldn't even get enough money to pay Ted for the deliveries, and we lost the truck.

Parents normally want a better life for their children. I remember thinking how difficult life was for my children compared to my own childhood. To this day, I have such a vivid memory of one particular time when the children next door were enjoying some store-bought apples. This was quite a luxury. (Their father worked for the railroad, so they had money.) Of course my own children wanted some apples, too. I cried realizing that I couldn't even buy my children apples.

Since times were so tough with the Depression, my sister sent money for me to come home. So I packed up our three small children and went back to my home place. (My father had died in the meantime.) Our stay stretched out to 13 months. Ted came down to see us several times when he could catch a ride with someone. This was quite a difficult time for our family.

Better Times Ahead

Then Roosevelt was elected, and he started the WPA (Work Progress Association) to get people working and get things going again. My husband could get a job for $25 a month, and we could rent a cottage for $10 a month. That would give us $15 on which to live. Then the WPA found out that I had a college education, so they said I had to go to work, also. My salary would be $60 a month! Later the people in Randolph complained that we were getting too much money, so the WPA said we better move to St. Paul.

From there, my career evolved over the years. Initially, I worked in a factory embroidering mittens. (You had to embroider five flowers with two leaves and a center in three minutes to make any money.) Now that was work. I worked so hard that I decided I had to get a better job. Next I worked for DuPont in Rosemount where I made sulfuric acid and measured other powders. Then for 20 years until my retirement, I was in charge of the chemistry laboratories at the University of Minnesota.

Our Retirement Years

Ted and I enjoyed our retirement years, spending several winters in Arizona. I've always said they should have given Texas away. It's the most terrible state I've ever experienced—it was so cold! We went down there one winter, took some lawn chairs with us, and rented a mobile home for the winter. We stayed in it for only one month and moved back to Arizona. I loved Arizona, but it's so dry—I couldn't take the dryness after awhile. So we retired in Florida for 19 winters until Ted's health started to fail. Then we moved back to Minnesota to be near the children. We were married for 65 years until his heart gave out. He died on March 26, 1991, within a few weeks of our moving to this retirement community in Minnesota where I am living now. It has been an interesting journey.

When I met Winifred, I had a difficult time believing she was now 93 years old. Her four "children" are all retired themselves. She seemed to have the mind and body of "a young woman of 80." She still has the strong spirited personality that got her into trouble as a child but also helped her survive the Depression years. (In fact, she was leading the exercises the next morning at North Ridge, the retirement community where she now lived.)

She truly had lived in two contrasting worlds. I'm amazed to think that she had a childhood where all her dreams were fulfilled but later experienced more hardships and sacrifices than most baby boomers have ever known. (We were fortunate enough to be born when "life was good"; that is, after the Depression.)

A lot of her strength came from these challenging experiences. I am thankful for the sacrifices that Winifred and others like her made for my generation of women. I believe we are benefiting from that strength. (My college friends didn't have to lie about being married to remain in school. I didn't have to be separated from my husband for over a year as she did because of the Depression.) Thank you, Winifred!

THE JOURNEY FROM HOLLYWOOD

Clarice Alberts Matteson, Ph.D.

"The powerful magnificence of mountains represents, to me, life's currents and rhythms. And flowers? I see flowers as the creative outcropping of mankind's strivings."

—Chris Matteson

*O*ver the years, many have journeyed to Hollywood with dreams of fame, fortune, and creative expression. However, Dr. Chris Matteson's journey began in Hollywood as the child of a well-known portrait artist. Her dreams as an artist were realized in her own unique way on a journey that led her away from Hollywood.

The circumstances leading up to my meeting Dr. Matteson—or Chris, as she prefers to be called—held a series of "unique coincidences." We both quickly realized that they were more than mere coincidences and that our paths were meant to intersect in that brief moment. This meeting developed into a wonderful friendship that has nourished both of our creative souls.

Upon meeting Chris, one cannot help but see a vibrant, lively woman—both in her outgoing personality and the creative blending of colors in her clothing, jewelry, and long, red, manicured fingernails. This is not a woman who quietly fades into the woodwork. She draws you into her excitement about life and its creative possibilities.

As I learned about the life of this remarkable woman through her many colorful stories, I was amazed by the artistic contributions she had made to this world. Where does one begin? In 1986, she was honored by the Minnesota Historical Society Arts Committee, with her work shown in the Rotunda of the State Capitol. Her painting "My True Love Gave to Me" was created for the Courage Center and printed for their Christmas cards. The original is now owned by Dr. Reatha Clark King, retired president of the General Mills Foundation. Chris was honored by Metro State University in 1997 as one of its most outstanding graduates in the past 25 years. Her work has been displayed at the Minneapolis Institute of Arts, the Minnesota Museum of Art, Hamline University, and the Governor's official residence, to name a few. Her work is also on display in private and public collections throughout the Midwest.

Many of her paintings seem to reflect her intense love of nature and Minnesota landscapes. Art curator Roslye Ultan described Chris's paintings by saying, "In the Fauve-like paintings of artist Chris Matteson, the landscape serves as the metaphor for her ideas about the natural rhythms of life. The work is charged with a sense of raw energy. There is a sense of joy or pleasure in Matteson's work that others yearn to find."

However, recognition for Chris's accomplishments does not end here. She is a member of the International Alliance for Women in Music. Showing versatility in her creativity, she has also composed theme songs for five television shows. Subsequently, she received awards from ASCAP for the original theme songs used in these shows. She has also written several motion picture scripts. One is called "Journey to Joy." Chris is in Who's Who in American Education (1996/97), Who's Who in the Midwest (1996/97), Who's Who of America (1997), Who's Who in the World (2002), and Who's Who in American Women (2003), which were honors for "outstanding achievement in her field and for contributing significantly to the betterment of contemporary society."

When I met Chris, she had just concluded a whirlwind series of events and recognition awards. While many of her peers were retired and coasting through life, she was on a creative high. These recent events included a trip to Cambridge University in England where she was invited by the International Congress of Arts and Communications to speak on the topic of "Spirituality and Art" and to show her art. Next it was on to California where she was selected as the recipient of the 2002 Distinguished Alumni Award by the alumni association of John Marshall High School. As you will learn later in Chris's story, John Marshall was the high school that she had attended many decades earlier. Her travels then took her to Canada. There she was honored by the International Biographical Centre at the 28th International Congress on Arts and Communications and inducted as Vice Consul in honor of her outstanding contribution to art.

The list goes on. I was in awe of her accomplishments in a field that has remained a passion throughout her life. She displayed an internal spark and joy of life that created a desire for me to learn about her personal journey. Her exuberant spirit and unstoppable creative energy were infectious. I knew this was a woman with spirit and that her story would be a fascinating one to discover.

Here is the story that Chris shared with me—the journey from Hollywood to the many crossroads in her life. She openly shares her story about the struggles to discover where she fit into this world, the journey that led her to Minnesota, and how she blossomed from a shy young girl into a well-known lyrical impressionist artist.

Growing Up in the Hollywood Hills

Hollywood wasn't a vacation spot or a destination for me, but a place I called home. I grew up in a beautiful and spacious home in Los Feliz Hills, which was up in the Hollywood hills of California. My parents named me Clarice, but my name later became shortened to Chris. I guess it was easier for people to pronounce, and it also seemed much less formal.

I was only a couple of months old when I arrived in Hollywood. Actually, I had been born in Winnipeg, Canada. As a young man, my father had studied photography in Europe and had subsequently become a successful portraiturist for royalty and celebrities. He later moved to Canada where he married my mother and started a family. Then after hearing of the great opportunities in Hollywood, he moved the entire family there. He did indeed ultimately discover many opportunities in this new land.

Let me tell you a little bit about my mother and father, for they were both unique individuals. My parents were Nina and Sargis Alberts. My mother had been a beauty contest winner, and like I said, my father was a successful portrait artist. Since I came from such an artistic, successful family, I felt humbled by the other members in my family. I was the only girl in a family with three older brothers—Keith, Maxwell, and Cecil. Keith was fourteen years older than I. I was still a young girl when my older brothers began dating—often young rising actresses. I thought, "Oh God. I don't have a chance around here." They hardly had time for me. My mother was very busy also. It wasn't the thing for women to work in those days, but she was active in various philanthropic programs.

In his heyday, my father had a portrait studio on the northwest corner of Hollywood and Vine. He created portraits for many well-known families such as the Duponts, members of the Ford Corporation, Jean Harlow, and Mary Pickford and Douglas Fairbanks. Of course, there wasn't such a thing as Proex in those days for family portraits. Families who could afford to do so would hire my father to create portraits of family members to adorn their walls.

I have memories of walking around his studio amidst tall marble statues and larger-than-life images of Mrs. Roosevelt, Hoover, the Duponts, and many famous actors and actresses that he had photographed. It could be a bit intimidating for a young girl.

My mother entertained many prominent figures in our home from the movie industry. There would often be artists, writers, actors, musicians, and motion picture people at our house. I remember one particular time. Somehow

I happened to get poison ivy, and it had spread all over my face. It was not a pretty sight. I came downstairs from my bedroom, and a young actress happened to be at the house. You should have seen the shocked look on her face when she saw me. My mother said to her, "Oh, she's got poison ivy." This actress went, "Ah! Oh!" (She left the house soon after that.) You can be sure she didn't want to catch my poison ivy. I didn't know how contagious it might be, and nobody else knew either.

As a child and even through high school, I was a modest person—very shy—in fact, extremely shy. I hardly talked to anybody. I was also introspective. My mother and father were social people. It seemed they were always going to elegant parties. They were invited here and invited there all the time. Cecil, the youngest brother, was quite devoted to me, however. Wherever he went, he made sure I went with him. So I was never left alone.

I often think that my father must have hobnobbed around royalty when he was growing up. He acted just like royalty. He was impeccably dressed and an elegant gentleman—all the time. He wore leather spats that slipped down over his shoes, which were the style at the time. I remember he smoked these long cigarettes and the way he stood up—so straight and tall. He never slouched. Both his posture and his dignity were just like he was royalty. He was just impeccable—yes, like royalty. My mother was the same way. Just as he had in Europe, Father also hobnobbed with royalty in Hollywood. In addition to movie stars, kings and queens would come to his Hollywood studio from all over the world.

Yes, Father was in the midst of all the glamour in these early days of Hollywood. It was an exciting time for him.

Sometimes he would be invited to be a cinematographer—to look into the camera—when they were shooting scenes for a movie. I remember it may have included scenes such as groups of women dancing in big circles. He didn't do that often, but once in a while he was asked to participate in the movie production.

The sad part of this is that I never felt like I knew my father very well—or that he knew me. At Christmas, my father would give me a Christmas gift and a kiss on the cheek. Then it seemed he never talked to me the rest of the year. Not a word. Father would talk to my older brothers a mile a minute. He didn't know what to say to a young girl, I guess. My mother wasn't much better.

The Mystery of My Family History

My parents were both born in Moldavia, which was in the southeastern part of Europe. They met each other over there. I do know that my father and his brother went to England first, and then they heard about the opportunities in Canada. However, I don't know how they got to Canada. Nobody has ever told me the story, and my father never talked about it.

I didn't learn many details about previous chapters in my mother's life either. About all I know is that she arrived in Canada a couple of years after my father. In fact, she was very quiet about her whole family. Unfortunately, I never met either set of grandparents—they didn't make any trips here to the United States.

There is so much that I would have loved to have known. You don't think to ask questions about your family history when you're young. Then when you become interested . . . the family is gone. It would be nice to know the real story. I had cousins who would say, "Where do you get your blond hair?" I would say, "How do I know?" Or they would say, "Where did you get your blue eyes?" (Nobody else in the family had blond hair and blue eyes.) I would say, "How do I know?" As far as I can tell, I look more like I came from some Scandinavian country. (Just perhaps . . . someone in the family from a previous generation traveled across the Balkan Sea and met up with a Scandinavian. Who knows? It's fun to ponder.) Maybe my family forgot to tell me something. I don't know. Since everyone is gone, the details about my family history will just have to remain a mystery.

Hiking in the Hollywood Hills

We lived out in the open country, but there was a winding road that led above our house to where some homes had already been built. Walt Disney, for one, lived in one of the houses up on the hill above us. He had to go right by our house to get to his studio, which was on Hyperion Avenue. Sometimes he would wave to me as he went by.

Since I was extremely shy and introspective, I didn't have a large circle of friends. Instead of spending time with others, I would spend time by myself hiking in these hills above our house. (I wouldn't do that today, however, for love or money.) Here I was a young girl between 14 to 18 years old when I would go on these long hikes. It never occurred to me then that anyone would bother me. Never. It was very peaceful up there, and I felt completely safe.

How I enjoyed being surrounded by all the beauty of nature—the music of birds singing, the warm sun kissing my hair and tanned skin, and the soft breezes blowing through the leaves of the trees, wild flowers, and grasses. Thinking back, it was a healthy way to live. I probably built up muscles in my growing legs and body by hiking up and down those hills. At the same time, it was a time for reflecting on the dreams that young girls hold in their hearts.

Career Battle on the Home Front

I spent my high school years at John Marshall High School, which was located near my home. After graduating in 1937, I enrolled at Los Angeles State College to study journalism, but my father intervened. He wanted me to pursue a more "practical" career. He sent me to a secretarial school, which I hated with a passion. He said, "Oh, you'll learn to love it." I said, "I could go to school to become a teacher, or I could become a nurse. If you send me to secretarial school, I think I'll flunk out." He said, "No you won't, because I'll pay for it in advance." Well, I did go through the training, but I had a terrible time with it. I can't remember how long it lasted because I'd like to forget it. Surprisingly, I did finally become pretty good at it, though.

I moved to Washington, D.C., for about a year and had a brief stint as a civil service employee and then returned to LA. Fortunately, I quickly found a position with RKO Studios in Hollywood. Not long after, I was given the opportunity to work as a personal secretary for Orson Welles, and I jumped at the chance. It would provide a wonderful opportunity to enter into a career filled with exciting possibilities. This job offer brought me into a new chapter along my journey.

"Hello, Orson Welles' Office"

The year was about 1945, during the very glamorous days of Hollywood. Orson Welles was married to Rita Hayworth at

that time. I don't quite know when he had time to see her, because I quickly learned that he was a workaholic. He worked day and night!

He had a production company in Beverly Hills called Mercury Productions. I worked both at the studio and in his home. I would often type and deliver scripts to him just moments before he went on the air with the CBS Radio Theatre show. (Walking around the motion picture lot and seeing all the famous movie stars from all over the world—you sure could get an inferiority com-plex in a hurry.) Orson

Chris, as a young lady in Hollywood standing near her brother's home.

Welles didn't drive a car, so I would also chauffeur him around to where he needed to go.

When I went to his home, I would work downstairs in the library. Mr. Welles was always nice and friendly to me. At times I would come into his house and hear "boogie woogie" music flowing through the air. I would find him playing the piano in the library. No one else was around, so he'd give me a bright smile and say, "Hi, Clarice." I didn't say much to him—I was still quite shy. Or sometimes I would come in, and he'd be painting in watercolor. I'd look at the painting and smile pleasantly. (If it were now I would speak up and say, "Oh, what a beautiful painting.") Sometimes he would say to me, "What can I get you?" He'd bring down some coffee or tea to where I was working in the library. I remember one time he said, "Go upstairs and make yourself some coffee." Well, I went all over the kitchen trying to find a coffee pot. Finally I gave up in disgust and went back downstairs without the coffee.

I didn't work for him that long—less than a year—because I realized something was happening to my health. I didn't know what it was at the time. I hadn't gone to a doctor, but I knew I was worn out. Not only was Mr. Welles working day and night, but I was also working with him day and night—at least 70 hours a week. I don't know how he did it. I couldn't keep up with him. It finally became clear to me that I couldn't go on like this. As much as I loved this job, I would have to resign as his personal secretary. I went to him one day and said, "I just can't keep up this pace." He was nice to write a letter of recommendation, which I still have today. It was dated November 13, 1945. It is an interesting remembrance from this chapter in my life. A little excerpt from his letter reads,

> *"I should like to recommend Clarice's ability as a secretary, which role she fulfilled while in my employ. Her knowledge of typing and shorthand should be an asset to any future employer."*
>
> —*Orson Welles*

I still didn't quite know what was the matter with me. I hadn't even discussed it with my mother, I'm sure. I finally went into a nearby drugstore and said to the pharmacist, "Boy, am I sick!" He said, "Well, what's the trouble?" I said,

"I feel so exhausted! I feel like I have to lie down and stay in bed for three months!" The pharmacist gave me some B12 pills. When I found this was helping, I finally went to a doctor. He started giving me shots of B12, and that seemed to pull me out of it.

About that time, Orson Welles and Rita Hayworth completed a successful motion picture together. Sometime later I heard that Mr. Welles went to Spain and his wife Rita went to France. Not long after this, I believe, they got divorced. (There were all kinds of stories while I worked for him that he was making passes at other women, but I never saw anything that confirmed these rumors.)

She's Into What? Plastics?

After I ended my position as secretary to Orson Welles, I was at a crossroads in my life. I said to myself, "There must be a place for me in this world." I dreamed of a career where I could be creative and less dependent on my family. Somehow this dream led to my designing things out of polyvinyl chloride. (How this happened, I'm still not quite sure. Friends would say to my brothers, "God's sake! This is your sister?") I was making plastic toys with the help of the BF Goodrich Company. I designed an elephant with a trunk that would move up and down, a skunk containing sweet smelling powder for women, and several other little animals. This was about 1953. My family said, "Look at her. She's into plastics? And she has her own business?"

An entrepreneurial spirit just came out from within me. I also developed, patented, and marketed a product called "Hilde-Gardes." It was like a glove that fit over the back of heels to protect women's high-heeled shoes. (I chose the name "Hilde-Gardes" as a takeoff on the name of a popular nightclub singer by the name of Hildegard.) These heel guards were sold in department stores and all over the country by mail order. I even got a copyright for the name.

To start this business, I had borrowed quite a large sum of money from my mother. The business had grown to where I had a plant and employees helping me make these plastic shoe guards. In 1952, it was exciting to see the business section of the *LA Times* feature me as a businesswoman with patents and copyrights. This was a very unusual accomplishment for a woman at that time. I didn't realize that I was a forerunner in the feminist movement.

My business was growing, and I was still living with my mother up in the Hollywood hills. My father had died by this time. Sadly, he died in a sanitarium in 1941 of a heart condition. He was only 54 years old when he died. After his death, my brother Maxwell took over his studio. He also became very successful with the studio and hobnobbed with lots of royalty.

I thought I'd better begin paying back my mother. So in addition to developing my company, I took a part-time secretarial job in an engineering company. This turned out to be a life-altering decision.

An Adorable Man Named Dan Matteson

Life often brings you little surprises when you are open to receiving them. What began as just a part-time job to pay back my debts to my mother ultimately altered my journey down quite a different path. Into my life walked a man by the name of Dan Matteson. When I saw him I thought, "Isn't he adorable." He looked kind of like the actor Van Johnson.

Dan asked me, "What are you doing working here on a part-time basis?" I told him about my plastics shop. He said, "May I come around and take a took at it sometime?" I said, "Yes, of course; you do that," not really expecting him to actually do so.

Well, the next weekend there was a knock at the door. There he was. I said, "Boy, I'm surprised to see you." He said, "May I come in?" I said, "Sure." I showed him all my ovens and the things I was making. He said, "You really have some beautiful big old ovens here." I said, "Well, they do the trick." He said, "I bet you could bake pies in them." (It's funny how you remember certain silly conversations.) I said, "Oh, yes—I'm a good cook." He said, "Well, let's go to dinner later today and talk about this." So we did and I thought, "Oh, boy! How lucky can I get."

He was from Minnesota, and I had always held Minnesotans in high regard. Experiences from childhood can often make a lasting impression. There was a girl who lived across the road from me when I was growing up in Hollywood. Although she was born in Shanghai, China, the family came from Minnesota heritage. (Her father had several businesses in Shanghai.) They were such a lovely family, and they were always so nice to me. I thought anyone from Minnesota was perfect. I still feel that way.

Dan and I started dating from that point on, and we went together about a year and a half. The day he asked me to marry him, he came over to the house with a bottle of champagne—not for me—but for my mother. He said, "For you, madam." I thought this was a pretty nice way of softening up my mother about his upcoming proposal.

We became engaged to be married, and then he said, "Let's move back to Minnesota." I said, "What would I do with my business?" Again, I found myself at a crossroads in my life. You can be sure my relatives had a lot to say about my pending decision. They said, "Forget your business. Go ahead and marry him. This is your golden boy that you're so crazy about. You're going to continue on with your business? Marry him!"

I knew I wanted to marry him more than anything. I also thought about my business and other aspects of my life. I realized that my business had become so big, and it had grown to the point where I would need to change it over to an assembly-line business. I said to myself, "I don't think I'm ready for all that." I thought, "Should I marry the man I love and forget the business?" So that is what I decided to do. I just closed up shop. I didn't even take the time to try to sell it. My mother was adamantly against my decision to move so far away. She had always lived an active life, so I knew she would be just fine.

A New Life and a New Family

Dan and I were married in 1956 on Thanksgiving Day. I wore a white wedding gown and carried a beautiful bouquet of white flowers.

I had met Dan's grandparents and his mother already, and I was very eager to meet the rest of his family. I soon discovered that his father was a real joker. When he met us at the plane upon our arrival to Minnesota, he was wearing a big mask over his face with a crazy wig. It was hysterical! (You can imagine that this was quite a contrast to my father, ever the elegant gentleman.) I thought, "Oh God, who did I marry? What am I getting into?" Dan's family was always very nice to me. Since my family history was such a mystery, it was fascinating to learn of Dan's deep roots in Minnesota. Members of his family were early settlers of Eyota, Minnesota, arriving around 1836. We took a drive there one day so that Dan could show me the land of his heritage.

Dan's father was one of the pioneers in auto parts and supplies, and his job took him to several states. One of the areas that the company sent him to was Sioux Falls, South Dakota. Soon after we arrived as newlyweds, they held a lot of big parties for us in Sioux Falls, also. I was welcomed into his family and his world with open arms.

Of course, living my entire life up to this point in California, I wasn't accustomed to cold and snow. I had to buy boots and warm clothes to handle the chill of the winter months. I was grateful that everyone in Minnesota was so nice to me and helped me get acclimated.

Dan and I settled into life as a newly married couple. Dan was a sales manager for Gould Battery. They had their main office in St. Paul, which is how we happened to move to Minnesota. We were later transferred to Chaumberg, Illinois, an area in the northern part of Chicago. By this time, we had two young children—a boy and a girl.

While living in Chaumberg, I began working with the Board of Education as a volunteer. They didn't have any lunch program there at the time, so I initiated one with the approval of the Board of Education. I thought it was terrible for these young children to have to go home for lunch and come back in an hour. What could they have for lunch in that short time? In the cold weather of winter, they would gulp down a cup of soup, and then be rushing back again. So

I said, "They have to have a lunch program right in the school." It was rewarding to see that dream develop to completion. Dan was made a vice president, and we were later transferred back to the home office in St. Paul. He soon learned the company had been sold, and we entered into a stressful time.

Dan began developing some health problems. He was only about 45 when he learned that he had diabetes. He was extremely upset by this news. It must have been something that he inherited. Then he developed a heart condition. We did everything we could. He even had open-heart surgery, but his diabetes prevented him from healing. It was a terrible combination.

I remember it was the 4th of July in 1976, and we had gone to his parents' lake home on Lake Madison. He was throwing fireworks from the pier. The next morning, he said, "I don't feel well." I thought, "Oh, my God, not again." I said, "Lie in bed until you feel better." So he lay down and then he got up to have dinner. He said, "I still feel very tired." He went back to bed, and the next day—on July 5—he died in bed.

A New Role—Sole Parent and Breadwinner

Dan's death was such a shock! We had been married for 20 years when he died. I had gone back to school part time and received a Liberal Arts degree from Metropolitan State University shortly before his death. In fact, the graduation ceremony had been only one week before my husband died. He had attended the graduation ceremony, proud of my accomplishment. We had been through so much with his health, and I thought he was doing just fine. His sudden death just about drove me crazy—I had a very hard time with it. We all did.

After Dan died, my family said, "Move back home—come back to California. Don't stay there in Minnesota." Well, my son was just going into college at the University of Minnesota, and my daughter was in high school. They were both very upset at their father's death as well. The children were established in their lives here, and I felt that I was also more comfortable here than I would be back in California. Minnesota had become my home.

There is a period of about five years after my husband died that is all a blur. I don't even know what happened to those years. I don't have the slightest idea what I did with myself. It was simply survival. I'd think, "Well, I'm awake today. I'm alive today." It was such a hard time.

Then in 1982 my in-laws sent me on a trip to Europe. They could see I was in bad shape over my grief and huge loss. I traveled to Europe with some girlfriends. That trip kind of perked me up and helped me return to the land of the living.

I came back from Europe, and I said to myself, "What do I really want to do with my life now?" (Here I was, facing another crossroads.) I thought, "I'd like to go back to school." Then I said, "Well, do it!" So I contacted Hamline and entered their MALS program (Master of Art in Liberal Studies). I was in studio arts and also studied the history of art down through the ages—especially how it is connected with religion. Every religion has its own art. It also gave me an overall perspective of art. I got going on it and said to myself, "This is a challenge. I love it!" I'd get up at 2, 3 o'clock in the morning to do my coursework.

A professor who was overseeing my work said in the first week, "I want you to read this book, *The History of Art*, and put it in one sentence." My son was home at the time and he said, "Mom, nobody in the world can take a big book like that and put it in one sentence." I said, "Watch me." So I read the whole book. Then I wrote a series of long sentences, dashes, parentheses, and quotes to summarize it.

I called my professor and said, "I now have the book on *The History of Art* in one sentence." She said, "Read it to me." I read it to her. She said, "Very well. You pass." I said, "Don't you want me to mail it to you?" She said, "No. You pass. Goodbye."

In 1986, I received my MALS from Hamline University, and I was so excited. I had one of my paintings up on an easel at the graduation ceremony. After the ceremony, President Graham, the president of Hamline, said to me, "I love your painting." I said, "Well, thank you. I'm really honored, sir." He said, "Would you allow me to hang it in my office?" I said, "I'd be honored to have it in your office." He said, "Take the painting and let's go to my office now." So we walked up to his private office right then and there and hung it on the wall. I said, "Thank you. You have given me a great honor." He said, "The honor is mine."

Things like that—that are great honors—you remember. Things like . . . getting married is a great honor or having a child is a great honor. Having someone like that select your painting is a great honor. Later, it was an honor having the Minnesota State Arts Board, Governor Ventura, and his wife select one of my paintings that is now in the Governor's mansion as part of the permanent collection.

The chosen painting is called *Zydeco Flowers*, which means exuberant, flamboyant, or colorful. It's a New Orleans term, actually. The painting is hanging on the wall in the solarium. It nicely complements the colors and feeling of the room.

You may be wondering when this interest in art began. It is surprising that I didn't draw or paint at all as a little girl. With my father being such a famous artist, I was so overshadowed by him. There was no way I would have dared attempt painting back then.

Actually, I didn't start expressing myself through my art until my children were in grade school. They weren't home during the day, and I thought maybe I could look into some art classes. I started by taking a class at St. Catherine's, and then—lo and behold—I won an award from the Dakota County Art Society. The creativity was there—just waiting to come out. Once I let it out, it just started flowing out of me. Here it had been waiting to come out all those years.

I started small and then my career in art kept building from there. I began by teaching one art class in St. Paul. I thought it would be a fun thing to do. By this time, I was already winning several awards in art. I had won an award from the Courage Center because I had donated a painting for one of the Christmas cards. They reprinted additional cards several times.

One memorable experience was the time I was invited to create a painting of the flowers outside the Governor's mansion a number of years ago. The woman who had invited me said, "There is an abundance of beautiful flowers in the garden. You'll have a great opportunity to paint whatever you like there." She said, "Wear a fun cap and gown befitting an artist." So I arrived wearing a painter's smock and a funny little artist's tam on my head.

I brought a card table, easel, and my tubes of paint. Actually, I encountered quite a surprise when I got there—the gardeners had torn up the whole garden. There wasn't a flower in the place! There were about 65 women (including the wives of three previous governors) sitting out in the courtyard watching me and waiting for me to create a painting. I sat there for a short time and thought, "My God, what am I going to do now?"

I had said to myself beforehand, "Suppose you don't like the flowers? Be prepared—have another scene. Be calm. Be calm." I did have another scene there that I had visualized already. I started painting in the sky and then I painted in the trees. Then I began putting in steps. There weren't any steps there, but I put them in anyway. That's how the painting, *White Tulips*, was born. (This painting was later donated to the 1006 Committee—a fundraiser committee for the Governor's residence—where it was sold to a member.)

A Career in TV Production—Are You Kidding?

Going back a bit—around 1980, my friends said, "You've worked with motion picture studios, and you know a lot about cameras. Why don't you do a TV show?" I said, "Oh, I don't know anything about that." They said, "Well, you can learn." So I took classes in TV production, and after I finished the courses I felt pretty good about them. I said to the head of the television station, "How would you like me to do a TV show on interviewing famous artists of Minnesota?" He said, "Can you do it?" I said, "I think so." Since I had grown up around a lot of famous actors and writers, I was comfortable talking with famous people.

As a result, I started interviewing artists from all over the state and later, people from other parts of the world. They would come to the TV station, and I really had great luck in interviewing them. Then I would send tapes all over the country from Los Angeles to Manhattan. I subsequently went to different TV stations throughout the years. I have produced 161 TV programs since that initial idea was born in 1980. It has been fascinating to meet a lot of top artists from this area and also from places like China, Japan, Korea, the Netherlands, and England.

My first program was called *Senior Citizens and Art*. It was later renamed *Accent on Art*. This eventually led to other topics. I created one called *Kids' Art*, where I honored young kids winning awards in art. *Punt, Pass, or Pie* was a football program to educate women on the "ins" and "outs" of football. The things I got involved in! Then I did another program called *International Café—Internet Arts*, where I interviewed the heads of art galleries in Europe. I would interview them over the phone, and they would send me prints of their favorite artists. The TV show would also include pictures of the gallery owner. Here I made up a whole TV show without having to go to Europe. I didn't even have to leave the TV studio.

My latest program was called *Men Aware*. It was about physical and mental health. Like myself, I saw there were millions of other widows in the United States. It seems so many of the men simply don't take care of themselves. They don't feel they have to go to doctors. So I've done two programs having to do with men's health issues, and these programs have gone all over the country. As a matter of fact, I had a funny thing happen. I interviewed one doctor who is here in the area. His son called him from Manhattan and said, "Dad, you're on TV in Manhattan. I can't believe it! My father is on national TV!" So I learned one of my TV programs was being shown as far away as Manhattan.

Dr. Matteson

About 1993, I began thinking, "Wouldn't it be fun to have a Ph.D.? Gee, wouldn't that be exciting?" I said to myself, "What would you do with it?" I thought, "I don't know. Just look at the education you would get." So I went back to Hamline, but they didn't have a Ph.D. program. They said, "Why don't you do it as an independent study?" They wanted me to focus on visual studies and religions down through the ages as they pertain to art. I continued to be fascinated with this topic.

My Hamline professors told me about a university in Louisiana. I said, "What do you mean? I'm not going to Louisiana." They said, "Well, check out this place in New Orleans that specializes in TV production and art." I flew out there to meet with them and to discuss what was possible. They were certified by the state of Louisiana and the federal government, so I knew that it was a reputable school. I discovered that I would be able to complete my doctorate from home. They had an 800 number. Anytime I had a question, I could call and say, "Would you put the professor on?" I thought, "Boy, this is a different way of doing it." The Hamline professors reassured me by saying, "This is the best avenue for you because they are concentrating on people like you who have worked within this field for years and years." So, I guess I was a pioneer of distance learning.

I got my Ph.D. in 1995—another exciting moment in my life. (How I wished that my husband could have been there for this graduation ceremony, too.) The actual graduation ceremony was held around Christmas of 1996, so I flew back to Louisiana again for that.

The Current Chapter

Since beginning my career as an artist, I have taught at the University of Minnesota, North Hennepin Community College, Lakewood Community College, and have given talks on art at various civic and women's organizations. I continue to teach art classes and create artwork and TV productions. I also enjoy tennis and ballroom dancing and do a lot of creative writing. So my life today is filled with the excitement of creative projects. Some people say, "Where do you get all that creativity?" I say, "It's in you . . . it's in me. It's in everybody. The creative spark is within us—we are born with it."

Creativity can come out in many different ways. (I believe our guardian angels are also hovering over each of us helping us create.) I started out in a small way, and the creativity grew from there. God knows I've experienced sadness, but what a creative journey this has been.

There are many different kinds of adventures in life. For me, one of the most exciting adventures has been delving deeply into education. It has been a challenge that I went after with vigor. Achieving the goal is like hiking up Mount Everest and breathing in the fresh crystal air and saying, "I'm here! What a joy!"

I'm still amazed at how my personality has changed from that shy, introverted girl hiking in the Hollywood hills to an outgoing woman who loves people and embraces all the positive adventures of life. Perhaps who I am now is my real personality—maybe it was just patiently waiting for me to grow into it from the start.

After forging through the many crossroads in her life, Chris has now been reaping the rewards of her lifelong work in art and film production. Her work is shown in galleries coast to coast, and she is enjoying the recognition and awards that keep coming her way. Her two children are grown and have successfully established lives of their own. It was been over 25 years now since her husband Dan died. The heartache of this loss took many years to heal, but now her life is filled with joy.

Chris says, "People ask me how old I am." I say, "Who in the heck cares? I ignore age. Age is a matter of mind over matter. If you don't mind, it doesn't matter."

This past summer in 2002, Chris returned to where her journey began so many decades ago when she was elected as an honored alumnus of John Marshall High School in Los Angeles. The graduation was held in an outdoor Greek amphitheatre holding 5,000 people. Ironically, this out-door theater was not far from the Hollywood hills where she had walked as a shy, introverted young girl.

What a journey of growth and self-discovery has tran-spired since that time in her life. She is like a cocoon that has evolved into a beautiful butterfly. It has not been without sadness over the death of her husband. Through persever-ance she has come through the dark tunnel of grief to the light on the other side and has continued to evolve intellec-tually, spiritually, and creatively.

Chris returned and spoke to the students that day as a confident, outgoing woman who loved life and all that it had to offer. Her life was now rich with experiences and friends. She said that her talk on creativity was from deep within her heart and that she felt so honored to speak to them. She knew of what she spoke as she looked out into the filled amphitheatre. This is a portion of what she had to say to these young people who were beginning their own journeys— perhaps with the same fears and apprehensions that she had faced at a similar point in her own life.

Good morning to all of you—and especially those of you who are graduating today. You can be sure I believe, as a live artist, in the joy of creativity. Creativity is in each of you, too. The creativity comes out of a divine spark in you—from birth. It's true. It may be dormant, but it's there—waiting for you to encourage it—to bring it out.

After graduation, you will go into many channels of education and employment. Through all these channels of education, there is a divine spark of creativity radiating—and with that comes new energy! Enjoy what you do as you do it. That's the secret of life! Enjoy it! Love who you are and what you are, which in turn means loving others.

How can you know this divine spark of creativity? By simply believing in it. It's there for you. When you start thinking positively, the divine spark of creativity goes into action. The action you create becomes energy—not only in your body—but it effuses itself all around you. People will sense your positive energy!

This creative energy expands our love of others. Investing spiritually in others has its rewards in wisdom and contentment.

There are always new channels of energy waiting to be explored and insights into problem-solving to become more developed. Putting innovations of ideas into action helps to create new worlds for ourselves and for others. The divine spark of creativity is always there for you!

Teilhard De Chardin, a famous writer and philosopher, once wrote, "We are not human beings on a spiritual journey. We are spiritual beings on a human journey."

As we achieve new energy through creative thinking and the arts, we find ourselves practicing love, justice, forgiveness, and patience. Thank you! Enjoy your new lives!

What beautiful words of truth. I'm sure that she was an inspiration to people of all ages who filled the amphitheater that day.

Chris, I thank you for your never-ending creative spark that brings color and beauty to this world. Long after your journey here on earth has ended, your spirit will continue to shine through the paintings that adorn the walls of many homes, businesses, colleges, and the governor's mansion.

You draw others to you by your enthusiasm for life and your curiosity about what may be around the next bend. You are filled with hope. Yes, indeed, the road from Hollywood has been well traveled. You may have been humbled by the accomplishments and talents of your family, but I, in turn, am humbled by your abundant creativity and the grace and excitement with which you have shared it with others.

Viola Gets a School

Viola Ording Daetz

Anytime one has to make a choice, any choice, there is an opportunity to be creative and therefore the possibility to make more of one's life.

—Richard Stine

At 83, Viola is a very articulate woman. She spent her entire life educating children. Even as a young child, she had dreams of becoming a teacher. Her story is not about the fact that she did become a teacher. Instead, her story is about the unique way in which she got her first teaching position and the ripple effect that it had for years to come.

Viola grew up as a middle child in Gibson, Wisconsin, a predominately German-Lutheran community in Manitowoc County. (The area was called the car ferry slip, where people could take the ferry across Lake Michigan.) She loved school and seemed to excel over her two sisters.

As a child, Viola always wanted to "play school" with the other children, and she was always the teacher. Her mother had her skip a couple of grades because school came so easy for her. She graduated as salutatorian from her eighth-grade class. Because of this, her parents felt she should continue on with high school. She graduated in 1933 when she was 16 as valedictorian of her high school class. ("However," Viola quickly added, "there were only 18 students in my graduating class, so I didn't have a lot of competition.") She still had the strong desire to become a teacher, so her parents sent her to one year of "County Normal" for teachers' training. This is Viola's story.

It was the summer after I had finished County Normal School in 1935 and my parents said, "Now if only Viola *gets a school.*" That's what they called getting a teaching job. Well, the summer was going along, and my father came home one day all excited. He had been running errands in town. He often stopped at the town pub on the way home, much to my mother's disapproval. He said, "Hey, Viola, you know what I heard? They're going to be hiring a new teacher at the Holmes school." This was a school in the same county where we lived. The current teacher was getting married and, of course, would no longer be teaching. (I think she "had" to get married.) So we rushed over and talked to the superintendent. I didn't hear anything for a while. Then my folks got a call announcing, "We're going to give the job to your daughter."

My cousin, Alice Plank, had also applied. I didn't find out how they happened to hire me until much later when I was teaching. One of the farmers that I was boarding with said, "You know how you got that job, don't you?" I said, "Well, I often wondered since my cousin Alice lived so much closer, and you already knew her." He said, "The school board got together and discussed it. They thought they should give it to the Plank girl since she did live near here, but they thought you were pretty good, too. Then one member reminded us that she was Fred Plank's daughter. When we had the last cheese-factory meeting, we were wondering how often the cheese makers should pay the farmers—every two weeks or once a month. Fred Plank had said, 'I don't care if they pay once a year—that would be all right with me.' This was at the height of the Depression. So the board decided if Fred Plank has got that kind of money, then his daughter doesn't need a teaching job, and they should hire you."

Amazingly, one little remark had affected my whole path. I taught at that school for ten years. I started out with a salary of $65 per month, which was the minimum wage for teachers at that time. I was so pleased to get the job. Out of the 17 who went to the County Normal School, only 3 of us got teaching jobs. (Alice didn't find a teaching job that year, but she did get one the next year farther away from home. The economy was beginning to improve a little by that time. I often wondered if she ever heard this story.)

One day the superintendent came into my classroom and said, "You do such a wonderful job. It's not fair to the other children that aren't fortunate enough to have you as their teacher. You can do more than this." (At that point there were only nine school-age children living in the area, so I had a very small class.) But I said, "Mr. Miller, what if I couldn't find another job?" He said, "We already have one picked out for you." The parents at another school, called Maribel Graded School, had come and asked the superintendent if they could get me to be their teacher. Apparently, they had heard good things about me from other parents. Maribel School had one room for grades 1 through 4 and another room for grades 5 through 8. The teacher for the higher grades was also the principal. So I was hired as both the new teacher and the principal.

My father thought that with my new salary it was time for me to buy my own car. He wouldn't always have the time to take me to work. But I said, "I don't know how to drive." He said, "Well, I'll teach you." So we practiced up and down the cow lane in an old 1936 Plymouth. Then someone from the county took me for a trial run, and I was given a license. (Years later, my husband would often tease me about my driving skills and say he didn't think I could pass the driver's test now.)

I met my husband Paul while I was at this second job. I met him through my younger sister Ruth. Like so many others in town, she worked at Mirro Aluminum, which manufactured Mirro Cookware. Her boyfriend also worked there. She was a tomboy and really liked to have fun. They would often go to these country dances.

Well, you didn't have to have a date to attend these dances—you just needed transportation. Often on the way to the dance, a girl would say, "Would you pick up 'so and so'?" That third person would then become part of the date. So I tagged along to the dance with my sister and her boyfriend and met Paul, the man I later married.

Paul had such big ears—boy how they stuck out. It was a family trait. However, I fell in love with him for his wonderful sense of humor.

What a match we were. While I had just loved school, Paul hated school. It was during the Depression, and he was in his second year of high school. He had always loved working with meat, so he would sneak out of school and go to work at the nearest meat market. One day his mother called in a meat order. (The meat market would deliver and put it on your bill.) Well, she heard someone come into the kitchen and put the meat on the table. Then she saw a "head" run past the window. It was her son Paul! Later that day she said to her husband,

"Bruno, we've got a problem. Do you know who delivered meat today?" Well, they had a meeting with the principal. To their surprise, the principal suggested that they let Paul stay at what he loved doing—working at the meat market.

Paul and I were married in 1947 when I was 32 years old. Unfortunately, we didn't get any wedding pictures other than one snapshot. This was just following World War II, and there was a shortage of film. After our wedding, we continued living in this same community in Manitowoc where I had spent my childhood.

The principal came to me one day and said I would need to further my education to satisfy the state requirements. I said, "Do you mean I need to go on to college?" He said, "You have to at least give the pretense that you are working on a degree." Silver Lake Convent was nearby. Since the nuns regularly got an education, he thought that maybe we could see if they would let some of us teachers sit in on their classes. Well, I was a dyed-in-the-wool Lutheran. I said, "Do you think they will take us?" He said we should check. So we talked to the head sister, Sister Bernadine. This was a highly unusual request, but she said we could try it one evening if we rounded up enough other teachers for a class. Well, we rounded up about 22 students. This was the first class the nuns had ever taught. When the year was over, we asked if we could go on. Well, they had to have another meeting to decide, and they accepted our request. They said we would have to sit in on their religious class also, and we said that would be no problem.

Today Silver Lake Convent is spread out over several acres and known as beautiful Silver Lake College. It's amazing to see what has evolved from our request for that very first class. You know, I'm still a dyed-in-the-wool Lutheran, but I've always had a soft spot for Catholics ever since that experience. Years later, they would introduce me as the lady who helped start Silver Lake College.

Viola continued to live in this Manitowoc area where she was born until she was 80 years old. Her husband Paul died 24 years ago when he was only in his 60s. (By the way, his early passion for working with meat became a lifelong career.) Viola now lives in a retirement community in Minnesota near her daughter.

I find it fascinating to think how different Viola's path may have been if the father of her cousin Alice had not made his off-the-cuff remark. After talking with Viola, I knew in my heart that she had been a wonderful teacher. Some of her first students are now grandparents themselves, and she still

Viola's classroom

keeps in contact with many of them. She was the only teacher that some of them ever had. She said she learned early on that "if you could get the confidence of the parents, you had it made."

As we looked at a picture of Viola standing beside her students in that little country school, I was instantly transported back to my own childhood. I, too, had spent my first six years in a one-room school . . . with very similar wood desks, old wood floor, and large blackboards. It was also the school where my mother and grandmother had attended before me. I knew how fortunate Viola's students had been to have her nurturing spirit, for I had been blessed with a loving and supportive teacher just like her.

Viola made decisions as a young woman that may have seemed insignificant at the time. Little did she know that her first job teaching a handful of students in a little country school would lead to her making an unusual request to a group of nuns. This request would in turn lead to the creation of a beautiful new college campus.

It is a reminder to us all that God's plans for us are often much larger than we can see through our own eyes. We know not what is around the bend.

Sing from Your Heart

Charlotte Miller Sonnichsen

Music lifts the spirit of all who hear it. It has been said that music comes closest to anything on earth at showing what heaven may be like. It is truly a celebration for both body and soul.

Charlotte's love for music has lifted the spirits of many over the years. Music has been her life—her whole life. May you enjoy her story of how she and her husband Sidney met through music and how they wove music into their entire life together.

My father, Charles Miller, was a dentist in New Ulm, Minnesota. He had worked his way through the University of Minnesota and later married Verna Hanson. My sister Verna (named for my mother) was born first. Then I came along on May 21, 1911. I was supposed to be a boy—but I wasn't. I surprised everybody. They gave me the name of Charlotte Alpine. Lord knows where the name Alpine came from.

My sister and I grew up in New Ulm. One day after I had completed high school, my father said to me, "Now, what do you want to do? You're going to college, which is what you always wanted." I said, "I want to be a music teacher." He responded, "Then you're going to St. Olaf College. It's the finest school for music in the whole United States." And that was that. So I went to St. Olaf.

I am not a Lutheran, but my Sidney was. He grew up in Idaho where he was a good Lutheran because his parents were Lutheran. He went to church, sang in the choir, and did all the things that good boys do for their mothers. Their minister had been a member of the St. Olaf Choir. He talked Sidney into going to St. Olaf College in Northfield, Minnesota, because he had heard Sidney's low, beautiful bass voice. So Sidney took the train and went off to Minnesota to attend college.

He started paying his way through college by earning money working with the newspaper in Northfield. The first two years of college he was in the second choir. The third year he made THE St. Olaf Choir, which was quite an accomplishment. He had the same dream as I—to become a music teacher.

Their Paths Were Soon to Cross

I was taking all the music courses and so was Sidney. We ended up in a lot of the same classes, and we would always sit together. What I think was the funniest thing was that he just loved when we exchanged papers to correct in class. He always grabbed mine and corrected it with a red pen. I could have killed him! Then one day he asked, "Could I take you home from a game?" I believe it was a basketball game. That's how our relationship started.

Of course, then Sidney graduated. He was one year ahead of me in college. (He was older, but he had started late in order to earn some money first.) After graduation he did all kinds of jobs. There just weren't any teaching positions that year. This was about 1933, and it was the depths of the Depression. I finally helped get him a telephone labor job in New Ulm. It wasn't much. He stayed with my parents most of this time since they had a lovely home that could easily accommodate him.

After graduation, I got a teaching job in some little town for six months. It wasn't a very good job, but it gave me a little teaching experience. Then I came back to New Ulm. We had wanted to get married earlier, but we felt we needed to wait until one of us had a good job. Well, Sidney finally got a good teaching job, and we began plans for our marriage. There was just no question in either of our minds that we would be together. We were both so involved in music that we just worked together fine. I also liked his voice, his singing, and his sense of humor.

Wedding Plans

At the time I was married, people were usually married in a church. Everyone and his brother would be invited to the wedding. This is not what I wanted. I told my mother and father, "I will not be married in the church. I want a home wedding." They reluctantly agreed to my wishes.

I wore my mother's dress, but I really had to battle for it. She said, "I can give you a new wedding dress." I said, "I don't want a new one. I want to wear yours." We went round and round. She finally gave up and sent the dress down to the dry cleaners. They cleaned it very carefully, sent it back, and she presented it to me as part of my wedding present. A woman in Rochester, Minnesota, had made it. It was such a beautiful dress with imported Belgium lace.

We got married in the summer of 1935 at a noon wedding. This was a couple of years after I had graduated from St. Olaf. The weather was a little warm, but it was a wonderful day. After the wedding, we came to the Twin Cities and stayed at the Andrews Hotel for three days. I remember it cost us $3 per day. Then we spent our honeymoon camping near St. Peter for a week.

We're Making Music

Our life together began in the first of a series of many little rural towns in Minnesota. With two music teachers in one family, there would never be a job for both of us in the same school. Either Sidney or I would get a job in the neighboring town. So what if one of us had to drive 20 miles . . . it wasn't anything.

As a new teacher, you had to learn to play every single instrument. You wouldn't have to be really good at each one, but you would have to know how to handle the instrument. You just had to keep one jump ahead of the kids. The really good students would then go off to a nearby college, like we had in New Ulm, for additional lessons. (Before we were married, I had taken violin lessons at the college in New Ulm.) My main instruments were the piano and the violin. Sidney, of course, had his beautiful singing voice. He also played the clarinet, bass horn, and drums. We taught anyone from the little ones in first through sixth grade on up to high school band and choir. I really liked working with the younger children. I thought it was important for them to be exposed to music.

For years, Sidney also sang in a male quartet called the Troubadours. He had picked up that wonderful sound of the St. Olaf Choir. No other choir has quite the same sound. There were four men in this group, and I was their boss. I went to everything with them. Here I was in charge of four good-looking men with beautiful voices. I could tell them when to sing louder and when to sing quieter. It was a fun time!

We had an upright piano the first year of our marriage. We just had to have a piano. We couldn't live without one!

I've had a grand piano ever since. My mother said that she got a "baby grand" and a "grandbaby" about the same day. I have had her grand piano for years. It's a Mason-Hamline, and it's one of the finest pianos. They are no longer being made. I love all types of music but especially classical. Yes, I love it all! So do you see what our life was about? It revolved around music—the whole thing.

The Rest of the Story

Well, what happened to the lives of Charlotte and Sidney? By the end of their music careers, they had lived in seven small Minnesota towns. The last 22 years were spent in Princeton, Minnesota, where they had a beautiful place surrounded by lots of open land.

Then Sidney's health began to fail. A doctor friend next door originally misdiagnosed him. It was thought to be colon cancer, but it turned out to be prostate cancer instead. There were other health problems, too. Charlotte said, "Of course he also has that lovely disease. You know what I'm taking about . . . where you lose your memory. I can spell the dang thing but I can't say it—Alzheimer's. It's so hard on the family. Our same doctor friend discovered this. But it's the darnest thing about his sense of humor—he still has it. He laughs and sings."

Charlotte and Sidney have been married for 63 years and now share a two-bedroom apartment in a retirement community center. Sidney goes to Care Break each day from 9 a.m.—4 p.m., which gives Charlotte some relief from the responsibilities as caregiver.

The apartment reflects their journey that has been filled with music and laughter. A framed photograph from their 50th wedding anniversary in 1985 made me smile. Sidney was hugging Charlotte and expressing his goofy sense of humor. Of course, her grand piano took center stage in their small living room. (It had survived every move along the way.) Upon my request, she sat down and played a favorite Bach piece called "Well-Tempered Clavichord." She now needed the assistance of reading glasses, and a botched surgery on her left hand made for less flexible fingers. Yet, she filled the room with beautiful music, and the limitations of age seemed to melt away.

Whatever happened to her mother's beautiful wedding dress of imported Belgium lace . . . the dress that she fought so hard to wear? Well, it is being preserved in safe storage. The dress was also worn by both of her daughters, Cynthia and Donna, on their wedding days. A very large frame, which takes up the entire wall at the end of her hall, reflects the wedding portraits of her parents (Charles and Verna), Charlotte and Sidney, and her two daughters and their husbands. Many years have passed between the making of each portrait; however, this beautiful wedding dress is one symbol that ties them all together. For each of them, it represented a magical day of hope and anticipation over what the future might hold. Each couple went on to make their own musical journey.

THE JOURNEY ON THE TRAIN

Lee Anderson

None of us is spared the loss of a loved one at some point in our lives. Unfortunately, the largest loss in Lee's life occurred when she was not yet four years old. I am grateful that she was willing to share the following story during our visit one afternoon in 1999 of how one tragic event had an impact on the rest of her life. We often hear of family members dying from illnesses that today are not life-threatening. It's hard to understand the effect on the rest of the family until you hear a firsthand encounter of one such tragedy.

My Childhood

I was born on April 17, 1916, in Sioux Falls, South Dakota, as the oldest of three girls—Lee, Edith, and Emma. We were all less than a year apart. At the time that my baby sister Emma was born, there was a terrible flu epidemic. In one year, it killed more than one million people all over the world. It seemed everybody was sick with the flu. I don't think there was any medicine that would help. People were sick at home and even the hospitals and churches were full. I was going on four years old when my mother gave birth to her third child, Emma, in our house one evening. She had just given birth, and then my mother got very ill with pneumonia. Tragically, she died the very next morning—and the life I had known changed forever.

There was a lot of sadness for my entire family at this time. One of my mother's sisters had died from the same flu just two weeks before she was to get married. She and my mother died within a week or two of each other.

Following my mother's death, we were put on a train—my dad, us kids, and perhaps some relatives, too; I don't know. We headed 70 miles away to a little town called Sinai, where my grandparents lived. I believe my grandfather, who was an immigrant from Norway, named the town. It was just a wide-open space when he moved there. This is where we were going to bury my mother. I had so many questions. Why in the world can't mama come up and sit with us on the train? Why is mama in that box? I didn't get any help. Everybody else was brokenhearted, too. They just didn't know what to do about me. They didn't give me a chance to cry . . . they didn't. My father just kept saying, "It's my fault . . . it's my fault." (I didn't understand until years later that he felt if he hadn't made her pregnant a third time that she might not have died. I've always said that it was the flu and pneumonia that killed her so that I wouldn't be afraid of pregnancy.)

We buried my mother in a cemetery in this small town where my grandparents lived. When we arrived, the box sat in my grandma's living room, and people came by to pay their respects. I didn't ask questions and nobody thought to help me deal with it.

We stayed with my grandparents for a while. The house that had been my home up to this point in my short life was closed up, and we never went back there to live again.

Our family settled into this little town of Sinai, South Dakota. I started first grade soon after, but the teachers weren't quite sure what to do with me. You see, I was born a "lefty." They forced me to write with my right hand and would spank my wrists when I used my left hand. So for the fun of it—and I suppose to be a little mean—I would write with both hands and write all the letters of each word backwards from right to left. I'd let them decipher the code. (Today I write with my right hand, but if I'm going to draw or paint I use my left hand.)

We tried to create our new life in Sinai without Mother. We would periodically go the 70 miles by train back to Sioux Falls to see my baby sister, Emma. It was a big trip, but we thought it was wonderful. You see . . . my aunt took in the new baby. She was my father's sister, and he knew he could trust that she and her husband would care for his child. My father wanted to keep us acquainted and together as best he could, and these periodic train trips back home were his way of doing that.

My Father's Heritage

My father had an interesting family history. His parents had met in Lake Mills, Iowa. His mother was born en route from Ellis Island to Lake Mills. His father was then a little boy of three and already living in Lake Mills.

They met, married, and had a large family of eleven. When a neighbor lady died in childbirth, grandma and the neighbors went to help. The grieving husband said, "I can't take care of this baby. What am I going to do?" So my grandparents took in this baby girl and adopted her as their twelfth child. There were no rules or laws or anything like they have with adoption today.

One family story is that my grandma needed a nursemaid for all these kids that kept coming. Their oldest daughter (my aunt) was assigned this role. I heard that grandma would intercept her love letters so that her daughter, a very pretty woman, wouldn't run off and get married. We lived with this aunt and my grandparents until my father remarried.

My aunt never did marry, however. I remember seeing her many years later. She had a boyfriend whose last name was Johnson, but he turned ill and died before she could marry him. They were both quite old at this time. She said sadly, "If only I could have ironed Johnson's shirts." Poor woman . . . she had to make a lot of sacrifices for her mother. I think this happened a lot—an older girl would have to be the nursemaid for the family.

My grandfather's name was Oleg Stime. Someone made up the last name. (They couldn't pronounce Stahlheimer or whatever it had been in Norway.) Upon immigrating to the United States, my grandfather settled in this area and built a small earth home into the side of the hill. My grandmother had two children by the time she was 18.

One summer day when my grandfather was in town getting supplies, apparently a group of Indians came riding up on horseback. She came out of the earth home and said,

"Don't ride over my house and scare the daylights out of me! If you want a cup of coffee, you come and get it." So . . . she gave them coffee.

As the children were born, my grandparents added on different rooms to the home. (Years later, we grandchildren used to love to romp around in that house with the many rooms, chasing each other, and often getting lost.)

My Father Meets Mathilda

As I said, father did eventually remarry. He married a woman by the name of Mathilda whom he had known from our hometown. She wouldn't let you say her name with an "a" at the end. She wanted it pronounced Mathild-eh, with an "e." She thought that sounded more aristocratic. She came from a family that had also been hurt by the flu. She had taken care of some of them. I believe her mother and dad had both died, also.

Mathilda and her family were Jehovah's Witnesses. I remember my dad hesitated to let them come for a visit after my mother died. They had tried to convert us earlier. So he said, "You can come if you don't talk religion." There was another single woman who evidently wanted him in the first place. My stepmother won out, and a year and a half later he married her.

He said one day, "Well, I'm marrying Mathilda." (His older brother had married Mathilda's sister.) Mathilda and her sister were both very strong-willed women. My father said, "I'm not going to let Mathilda run my life like Emma has run my brother's life."

They got married out in my grandparents' yard. Unfortunately, Mathilda made a big mistake with me the day they got married. After the ceremony she said to me, "Now you call me Mother." I thought, "What is she talking about?" I couldn't figure out where my other mother went, except that there was a plot in the cemetery. I said, "No." That stuck with her. I didn't like her request, but I did always treat her fairly.

My Baby Sister's Destiny

When my father remarried, Mathilda wanted to have my baby sister Emma join us and make it a whole family. He had more wisdom than she did because it had been two years since my mother died, and Emma was accustomed to her new mother and father. He said, "No, you can't take her. Absolutely not!" However, she was determined she was going to bring this family back together. She wanted everything to fit her "norms," but she didn't get her way this time. He just wasn't going to take his daughter out of the only home she had known. My uncle and aunt were good parents, and they would have been brokenhearted. My uncle just worshipped this little girl, and their two older children loved her too. He said, "No, we just can't take her—that would hurt everybody." So . . . my sister Emma stayed where she was.

My father paid the mortgage on the house in Sioux Falls where my little sister Emma lived. He felt his sister and her husband were doing a nice thing for him by taking in his child, so he paid the rest of the mortgage on their house. This was a good thing, because then they didn't lose their home during the Depression. Emma grew up and got married in that house.

It's on to Chicago

My father was an inside finishing carpenter, working with cabinets. He was absolutely top-notch. He was so neat—everybody wanted to hire him because he also picked up after himself. Well, he thought he could do better in Chicago. (He had visited the city the year before.) So just before the Depression he announced to the family, "We're moving to Chicago."

By this time my father and stepmother had three more children, in addition to a new baby. This new little baby boy was not very healthy. He was skinny and didn't look well-nourished. When she was pregnant with this fourth one, she was quite angry. She didn't want to be pregnant, but I guess she didn't know how not to be. In those days, women didn't say "no."

It was not really good timing for a big move, but we took the sickly boy with us, and the entire family moved to Chicago. However, when we got there the unions had just started. My father didn't join the union, and I think he probably didn't know how to join. There were killings, and I think he was absolutely frightened. We said, "Dad, why don't you find some work?" (We became a little discouraged with him.) He would always say, "I don't want to be a scab." I believe he was afraid to go against the unions. He didn't dare say this, but I could tell he was afraid. He wasn't street smart enough for the ways of Chicago.

I also think he was so crushed with the loss of the woman he really loved—my mother. Fortunately, he did get support from the minister at the big Oak Park church that we attended in Chicago. This minister had also lost his wife during child-birth. He was very compassionate and understanding to my father because they shared the same experience. The minister had remarried a woman who wasn't so jealous of the first wife as, I believe, was my stepmother. My stepmother was better, however, after we moved to Chicago. I think her eyes were opened a lot.

My mother's family had had money and land. My father used money from her estate to live on when we moved to Chicago. When the banks crashed with the Depression, he lost the money and was brokenhearted over that too. He still had the land in South Dakota—I suspect that he lived off the rent that came in from farmers. (In later years, he gave guardianship of that land to me.)

Lefse, Lefse, and More Lefse

Since my father wasn't finding work, it was fortunate that my stepmother was a strong woman. She helped "put bread on the table." She made lefse for the delicatessens at Christmastime in Chicago. Every Christmas, there was a delicatessen that just begged for more. She made really good lefse, and we had to help her with that. We had to turn the darn stuff so much that we couldn't stand the sight of it.

My Hopes for College

When I finished high school, I stated that I was going to go off to college. I had a 96.4 average. I really liked literature, and I always had a book that I was reading ever since I was a kid. I had taken Latin, all the math I could find, and had even been in the Chicago paper for my scholastic achievements. However, college was not meant to be.

When the Depression hit, we girls had to stay around home and go to work as soon as we graduated from high school. Since I was the oldest, I had to stay with the family and "help with the cause." Later, my sister Edith was expected to do the same thing.

My stepmother found jobs for me initially. She originally tried to get me to do childcare for people in their homes. I just wasn't interested in that. I walked out of my first (and last) childcare job. I remember it was midnight and I left the job, walking through downtown Chicago by myself. I kept walking all the way home. (I walked the streets of Chicago at midnight many times . . . and this was during the Al Capone era.) My stepmother found me upstairs in my bedroom and said, "Oh, you quitter!" She was quite upset with me. I later found office work and worked my way up within the same company for ten years.

Romance in the Church

It was about 1941 when a young man by the name of Oscar Anderson came to our church. He was a third-year seminary student. Since he had lived in Minneapolis all his life, the professors at the seminary thought it would be good for him to go out of town for his internship. So they sent him to a one-year internship in Chicago. Well, we got acquainted. Oscar and I found out that we were exactly the same age. He was born just two days after me. (Of course, he has always teased me and said that I'm the oldest.)

When Oscar went back for his last year of seminary, we corresponded back and forth. The letters he sent were largely about God and his work. I did think, however, that this was an educated man and we could enjoy discussing books that we read. I looked forward to growing together. We became engaged and were married in 1943. We were both 27 years old at this time.

Lee and Oscar's Wedding Day

Life in the Ministry

We had many good times in the ministry. Early on in his career, Oscar was a minister in several different parishes. He later became president of Augsburg College in Minneapolis. We were both 47 years old at this point in his career. It was a busy time, for our kids were still in school. (I was 42 when my youngest daughter was born.) I was nervous about all the responsibilities as the college president's wife. There were many demands in the home, including a lot of entertaining. Sometimes I would get a few professors to help out with the entertaining. I did the best I could, and I even started doing some volunteer work in hospitals.

We were at Augsburg College for 17 years until Oscar's retirement. They named a building after him. The funny part of it is that the next president (whom he helped get the position) was also named Anderson. They didn't include "Oscar" on the building, so both of them could take credit for it.

The End of our Journey

We're now both retired. Over the years, I have challenged a lot of religious opinions. I suppose this is understandable when we come from very different backgrounds. As a Lutheran pastor, he was raised with a little bit of fundamentalist background. His upbringing was also much more straight-laced than mine had been by my growing up in Chicago. As an adult, I have been a great supporter of the work of Gloria Steinhem for women's issues. (I have every issue of her *Ms. Magazine* beginning with the first one.) Yes, Oscar and I have had some animated discussions over the years.

Well, it's been quite a journey since I was that little girl on the train. The strange thing is that after all these years I can still feel my mother's spirit. It is as if she is always with me. It took me years to understand why my father was feeling responsible for my mother's death. (It's not your fault, daddy. Yes, she might have lived if she hadn't had a third child, but not necessarily so. There's no reason to feel guilty.)

Throughout this journey, I have learned that God loves all of creation unconditionally, and I try to do the same. I am thankful for all my experiences—they have helped me grow.

⚜

An update from the family album:

- *Oleg Stime and his wife—Lee's grandparents—lived to the ages of 90 and 93.*

- *Both her father and her stepmother Mathilda lived long lives also, well into their 80s.*

- *Lee's sister Edith married a man who became quite wealthy. He died in 1999.*

- *Her sister Emma married a man who, ironically, died within 48 hours of Edith's husband. Both men were in their 80s.*

- *Lee's youngest stepbrother (the little baby who was sick when they moved to Chicago) dropped dead on the racquetball court as a very young man.*

❦

When each of us comes into this world, we know not what length our journey will be. However long or short our stay, we can deeply touch the lives of those around us—often beyond our knowledge. As with Lee, it's often a feeling that lasts a lifetime.

How I wish that the adults around her on the train those many years ago had been able to help her understand the loss of her mother. Perhaps it would have helped aid in the healing of this young girl's heart.

Lee never reached her dream of going to college; however, it is ironic that she spent seventeen years in the college environment as the wife of a college president. I admire her quest for learning, her strong support for women's issues, and her lifelong questioning of the truths in the world around her. It has been, indeed, quite a journey.

CLEAR BLUE SKIES
AND COOL DEEP WATERS

Arlene Johnson Graham

Trees, fields, rivers, and sky dance before me.

—J. Christie Kowalski

Many people dream courageous and adventurous dreams—and a few actually live them. One of these people is Arlene Graham.

Arlene is a high-energy person with an infectious laugh and a playful attitude. She is drawn to other people who also like to laugh and who have an enthusiasm for life.

Her deep passions in life have been many. They have ranged from competitive swimming and diving to camping and scouting to aeronautical engineering and so much more. She has always lived life to the limits. Her saying is, "If there isn't any confusion, I can create some."

Arlene's current passion is an heirloom project, that of recording her family history into her Macintosh. This personal journey to learn about her family history has led her as far back as 1589.

As we talked about her life and the lives of those who had gone before her, her entire dining room table became covered with priceless photographs spanning many generations. Many were rich, sepia-toned 8 x 10 photographs, with strong faces looking out from a time that I had never known. How I wished that I might have had a heart-to-heart talk with each one of them about their life experiences. Arlene is the only one who can now pass along remnants from her family's past.

I think you will enjoy this story that Arlene shared about her life. It is sprinkled with little gems from her family history.

I was born on January 20, 1927, and spent my childhood and teenage years growing up in Omaha, Nebraska. Since I grew up with a bunch of boys, I was quite the tomboy. I could pass a football better than they could. Even though we were close to the same age, I was bigger and had longer arms. I could also take care of myself if my brother or neighborhood boys picked a fight.

To this day, I still remember the poem that one boy made up and would always say to tease me:

Arleeny, she skeeny
She wanna be fat
so she can match her brand new hat.

My father was a humorous man himself and enjoyed creating little limericks. He often told the story of the time in

1927 when my parents were aboard a pleasure boat. My mother was on deck snoozing in a lounge chair, so he wrote this little poem about her.

> *Some people like to play baseball*
> *and some like to shoot craps,*
> *and more play football in the fall,*
> *but I like taking naps.*
> *A great variety of sports*
> *have lured me and impressed.*
> *But more than all the other sports,*
> *I love the game of rest.*

Swimming and Camping Were My Life

My great love for swimming, camping, and scouting began back in my early childhood. In fact, I began teaching swimming when I was only eight years old. (There was a young friend of mine who didn't dare go out to the deep end or use the diving board, so I taught her to swim so she could join me there.) Later in high school I was involved with the AAU swim team and the Red Cross. I also taught basic-survival swimming to soldiers at two army bases.

My mother was on the Omaha Girl Scout Council at a camp called Ma-Ha. I loved camping so much—I couldn't get my fill of it. I even called home from camp when I was fourteen years old to see if I could stay another two weeks. (Years later as a young mother, I trained my children to make and change their own beds by the first grade so they could do it when we were camping.) But I guess I'm getting a little ahead of myself. Let's get back to the story.

Days of Rationing

The war was going on while I was in high school, and it certainly affected our daily lives. I was a Senior Service Scout, and I have lots of memories of giving out doughnuts to the servicemen who were passing through the Union Station train depot. I was also on the sugar-rationing board in high school.

There was rationing for gas, also. During this time, gas stations had to close at 7 p.m. One afternoon I went to the office of a family friend who was a doctor—just for a visit. While I was there, the doctor got a call for an emergency appendectomy from out in rural Nebraska. He asked me if I wanted to ride along. Not being one to pass up a new experience, I said, "Sure!" We had to get there before 7 p.m. so that we could fill up with gas for the trip home. There wasn't much room on the return trip, so I was sitting close to the boy we were transporting back for the emergency appendectomy. Apparently, I was so close to the boy's head that I, too, got the effects of his anaesthetic. I was so out of it that I had to sit out in the hall during the operation. I missed the whole procedure except the stitching up at the end.

My summers were spent as a lifeguard. Any extra money I earned from being a lifeguard went into flying lessons. I loved the water, but those blue skies were also calling me.

Yet in high school, I was in the Civil Air Patrol Cadets taking classes in navigation, meteorology, and Morse code at the Marine Electronics School. I was just one year too young to get into the WASPs (Women Air Force Service Pilots). However, luck was with me during my senior year of high school. I had been out ill with the mumps, as had many others. The administration decided anyone who had missed more than two weeks of school because of the mumps didn't have to take their finals. I lucked out.

The Dreams of Youth

When it was time for me to go on to college, my parents asked me where I wanted to go. I replied, "How about Cornell College in New York?" "No, it's too far away," they said. I said, "How about my going to Stanford in California?" No, they also felt this was too far away. We finally agreed upon Iowa State College, which is now Iowa State University, in Ames.

I wanted to go to an engineering school, for I had dreams of becoming an aeronautical engineer. When I started college life at Ames, the Navy's V-12 engineering unit needed housing. So these young men were housed in the women's dorms while the men's dorms were being completed. That way the Navy could keep all those guys under their watch. During the war, the fraternity houses didn't have anybody to live in them since the boys were off to war; however, they still hired housemothers. So, we girls lived in the boys' fraternity houses. However, we had to walk across campus to one of the "non-V-12" women's dorms for our meals. I remember how we had to turn in our sugar coupons at registration to determine the amount of sugar needed in the kitchen for our meals for the year. When the war ended, my dreams of becoming an aeronautical engineer were suddenly cut short. The guys came back, and there was just too much competition getting into the program.

Love Struck

I had pledged Gamma Phi, and one of the active Gamma Phi members had a V-12 boyfriend. These two friends introduced me to my future sweetheart at a pledge dance. His name was John Robert Graham. (Since his grandfather's name was also John, his grandmother called him Johnny Bob. Later it was shortened to just Bob.)

I was incredibly attracted to Bob. He had curly blond hair. Of course, I was only 17 and he was only about 19. Bob eventually graduated from the V-12 program. As a young ensign, he was in charge of a landing ship for a year and a half and then came back to graduate in engineering from Ames. It just gives me goose bumps now to think of those young guys and the huge responsibilities they carried on their shoulders.

Wedding Bells

Our romance continued, and Bob and I were married in August of 1947 in my hometown of Omaha. I remember one of the other gals in my church had her wedding at noon on the same day. My wedding was at 8 p.m. that evening. The church was quite small and the fellowship hall was not very fancy, so we each had our receptions at the Athletic Club in downtown Omaha. They had to polish all the silver again between our two weddings.

My brother was in the service in Germany at the time. I so wished that he could have been here. He would have sung at our wedding. (He did manage to get a phone call through to me to wish us well. The call came in just two hours before the wedding.) We had a harpist play for the wedding instead.

There was so much excitement surrounding my wedding day! I had selected a beautiful pearl necklace to wear with my wedding dress. I remembered to wear it the day of the wedding portrait, but I completely forgot to put it on the day of the wedding. At the end of the ceremony, Bob and I happily walked down the aisle, our hearts filled with joy. I was so taken with the moment that I didn't realize until I got all the way down the aisle that I had forgotten to take my bouquet of flowers back from my matron of honor following our vows. She came down the aisle carrying both her bouquet and mine.

The Honeymoon

A cabin in upstate New York was the destination for our honeymoon. Along the way, we first stopped in Chicago to see the play Carousel and then stopped in New York City. (I had never been to New York before, so I was really excited.) We stayed in a cabin owned by friends of Bob's family, and we went swimming and canoeing. Our honeymoon cabin was by a little river where the water was so black that I was scared to death to put my face in it. Imagine that—I who had been teaching swimming ever since I was eight years old. It was so black— I just couldn't see the bottom. Who knows what was in that water. I skipped any diving and floated on my back instead.

My new in-laws arrived the next morning to check on Bob and me, which was a good thing. That morning we had decided to make a fire in the fireplace, and the room became entirely filled with smoke. Here we were crawling on the floor amidst all the smoke when his folks arrived. They said, "Did you take the squirrel cover off the chimney?" What squirrel cover? We learned the hard way that everybody in this area put covers on their chimneys. Otherwise, when the deep snow in upstate New York covered the houses, it became too easy for squirrels to get in.

Life as a Young Wife and Mother

My memories of our first year together bring up images of corrugated-metal barrack apartments. However, we were no different from everybody else. We were all in the same boat of finishing our education via the GI Bill. We were living in Iowa City where I was completing college and Bob was attending law school.

We had a portable washer that could wash four pounds of clothes at a time. In the winter, clothes had to be line-dried in the hall. It was quite a sight with four lines strung down the hall. You had to "part the way" to reach the bathroom.

Married life became busy as we started to raise a family. My heart still had a love for camping. Our family's camping experiences began when our first child was still in diapers. Our first camping trip was quite an unforgettable experience. My husband said he would wash all the diapers—bless his heart. He would also give our son his baths. For our son's baths, we used the same pan used for washing dishes. (It had formerly been the pan under the icebox in our kitchen.) Well, the skies opened up and it rained . . . and rained. It rained for 10 days out of our 14-day camping trip. Oh, well.

I guess my life continued to be surrounded by water. When synchronized swimming needed competition in the early 1950s, I helped launch it, hold meets, do the judging, and train other judges. Then there were swim meets at the Y that I helped to run. My family was growing, and one by one my children also became champion swimmers and Red Cross Water Safety instructors. We skin-dived in Florida's

Underwater National Park in 1963 the first year it opened. Our family's water experiences also extended to the Boundary Waters canoe trips. Those are all wonderful memories.

The Search for My Family History

My journey had led me through so many wonderful adventures to this point. Computers opened up another world to me when I purchased my first computer in the 1980s. Several years earlier, I had begun researching the family history of both Bob's and my families. Research findings for my family date back to 1589. Fortunately, I had genealogy charts ending in the 1960s that my father had started. My interest in this "heirloom project" had begun first with my great grandfather and was then passed on down to my father.

My great grandfather was a banker in upstate New York. One of his passions was collecting little picture postcards that were common at that time. He collected postcards of people he admired. He even had postcards of Queen Victoria and of opera singers. My father continued a similar interest and collected letters from the Civil War and old family letters. He had an interesting collection of letters from his aunt who was an artist. She had studied in Paris and was later commissioned to paint portraits of the Iowa governors. He also had a set of letters from family and friends written to my grandfather while he was in college. My father had a collection of 400 old letters, which I later divided among his six grandchildren.

It has been fascinating to discover that one of our family lines traces back to General Ulysses S. Grant. He was my sixth cousin, three times removed. I find it very interesting that the words on his tomb say, "Let us have peace." These words were of 130 years ago; however, with all of the world conflict we have today, he surely would have said the same thing in our current shrinking world.

This beautiful poem is one of my treasures from the family's letter collection. It was enclosed in an 1835 letter to my great, great grandmother, Mary Malina Grant. Her suitor, Eli, was in the service at the time. He wrote,

> *Dear Mary,*
>
> *One there is above all others*
> *Well deserves the name of friend*
> *His is love beyond a brother's*
> *Costly, free, and knows no end.*
>
> *They who once his kindness prove*
> *Find it everlasting love.*
>
> *Eli Pomeroy Wilson*

(Perhaps this poem won Mary's heart—Mary and Eli were married three years later. They had a daughter, Emma Marie Wilson, who in turn had a son, Ralph Emerson Reding. Ralph Emerson Reding was my grandfather.)

Another of my heirloom treasures is a newspaper clipping honoring the life of a family member by the name of Mary Graham, who preceded me on this earth by more than a century. She lived until the age of 96. These beautiful words were written in 1879 to honor her life and spirit. A portion of it reads:

> *She was light-hearted, generous, and unselfish in thought and deed, ever ready to lend a helping hand; full of earnestness. Interest in all that interested others or that could elevate the community in which she lived. She possessed a clear, strong intellect, a*

well-balanced judgment, and a remarkably retentive memory. In her disposition she was unassuming, in her manners genial and kind, and in her domestic relations affectionate. Her energy and her industry were most remarkable. She was, in brief, a good woman, serving her day and generation faithfully and acceptably and in death she is mourned as in life she was respected and loved. Like the strong oak, which had for centuries withstood the whirl-wind and the blast, finally bends and breaks, so at last bowed this venerable woman to the stroke of the Dark Angel and quietly passed to the world beyond. A kind son for many years saw that her every desire possible was gratified, and willing hands minis-tered her necessities. This aged Israelite has crossed the great arkana and gone up amid the ransomed to the beautiful hereafter.

What a tribute! Mary left quite a legacy to follow. It makes me ponder how others will review my life. We each leave "footprints in the sand." I may not have reached my dreams of becoming an aeronautical engineer, but I have always lived life to the fullest.

I have never forgotten an experience at Ames College my freshman year. In an English course, we were asked to write a theme about what we had done in our lives. My roommate didn't have anything to write about. I thought, "How sad!" At that young age I had already experienced so much . . . and it has continued ever since.

Throughout my journey, I have felt the thrill of diving from a 30-foot diving tower, camping beneath the stars, and flying a 40-horse Taylor Craft airplane onto the grassy airport runway at Ames, Iowa. At the age of 63, I attended a fitness camp for the body and soul, which included a mile-long challenge swim. A year later, I participated at an environmental learning center and went through a rope course 30 feet from the ground with a zip cord at the end of the course. Yes, it's been quite an adventure. I wouldn't have wanted to miss a thing. It's heartwarming to see my passions now being passed down to my children and grandchildren.

This remarkable woman experienced things that required a fearless and adventurous attitude. Her adventures led her diving deep into the cool waters and soaring high into the clear blue skies. She also dared to enter the world of computers—a world where many her age dare not tread.

Arlene's story reminds me that none of us is an island. We are each composites of little pieces of heart and soul from those in our own family history. Good or bad, these genes and personality traits are passed down through the generations. We all need to feel connected, and understanding more about our family history helps weave this interconnection. Peering into the lives of those who journeyed before us helps us better understand ourselves.

THE WINDING ROAD TO MONTEREY BAY

June McQuaid Usher

Nestled in the hills in Monterey, California, beneath the majestic pines, I discovered a pristine retirement community called the Park Lane. The fresh scent of spring flowers was in the air after an early morning rain, and from the outside walking path around the top floor I could see a breathtaking view of Monterey Bay.

It is also a special place in the evening, where dinners are an elegant event. The women are dressed in their finest dresses, and the gentlemen look dapper in their suits and ties. They ride the elevator down to the main-floor sitting room that is finely decorated with paintings and large potted palms. They are each served a glass of wine to sip during the cocktail hour. It is a time of mingling and visiting for the residents, all coming together with varied pasts. Some are in wheelchairs, but they look as refined as everyone else.

The residents later enter the circular dining room, with its floor-to-ceiling windows overlooking the gardens, and enjoy a dinner off the evening's menu. Ahh! It seems like a glimpse into another time.

Many world travelers have called the Monterey Bay area one of the most beautiful places on earth. June Usher calls it home.

The path that has led her to the doors of the Park Lane has been a winding and often adventurous one. She wasn't content to take the safe route. Her career in teaching led her to many parts of the world. Among other things, she survived a typhoon and getting shot at by snipers. I was fortunate to sit down with her on this beautiful spring day—amidst her busy schedule—to talk with her about her journey. This is June's story.

I was born in another beautiful part of the country in Salem, West Virginia, in 1918. My parents were Rex and Mary McQuaid. We were a large family—eight children in all.

I wanted to become a teacher. So, I decided to attend Salem College, where I received my teaching credentials. Coincidentally, I taught for a year in a one-room schoolhouse where my mother and grandmother had taught before me. I later received a bachelor's degree in Miami, Florida, and a master's degree in education at the University of Pittsburgh in Pennsylvania.

You could say I have had quite an eclectic mix of work and teaching experiences since that year in the one-room school. We were all struggling to deal with life during World War II. I left teaching for a while and worked in Dayton, Ohio, in a chemistry lab. This was about 1943. Then I was transferred to Hickam Field in Hawaii. I was also part of the special services in Japan for a time as a service club director. My path then led me to a one-year teaching position in an army school on the island of Saipan, which is near Guam in the West Pacific.

It was during this time that I met the man who later became my husband. His name was Thomas Usher, and he was in the service in Korea. We met and were instantly attracted to each other because we liked many of the same things. Everyone liked him. We were engaged for about six months. I came back to the United States for a short time, and then we agreed to meet in Hong Kong to get married. After we were married, we returned to the States and lived on Long Island in New York. I liked life in New York, but we found we didn't get along . . . so, after a year, I made the decision to end the marriage.

I was pregnant when we parted, which of course created some additional challenges. I was offered a job in Mexico at the USIS Culture Center (United States Information Service), which was in the process of being prepared for opening day. This would give me time to learn Spanish and prepare for my baby to be born. I went down there and lived for a while, but I decided I didn't want to live in Mexico. It was a good job with quite a bit of money, but I made the difficult decision to go to Tucson, Arizona, instead and stay there until my son was born.

Tracy was six months old when we moved to Monterey, California. This is where we made our home and where I taught until retirement at age 62. I taught first and second grades for a few years, then became a reading specialist and, later, a resource specialist for students with learning disabilities.

I've done a lot of things in my life—I mean, really a lot of things. My whole life is too much to talk about, but there are a couple of unforgettable life experiences from early in my journey that were quite exciting, thrilling, and frightening. These events are just as clear in my mind today as if they happened yesterday. I guess I was lucky to have survived them.

One such experience was when I was on my way to teach in an army school in Saipan. It was 1946, and I was traveling by ship with three other teachers. We boarded the ship in

Hawaii and proceeded to get caught in a typhoon part way into our trip. They had to turn the ship around and go back into the storm to make it to Guam, which was the closest island. The storm was pretty bad. They put us down in the bottom of the boat and told us to hold on tight. We didn't think about if we were going to live or die—we just held on tight! The dining room was up on the main deck. The water was so rough that some of the railings in the dining room broke like splinters. The storm lasted all day and caused a great deal of damage to the boat.

There were a lot of other people on the ship, but we were the only four who got off in Guam. When we got into Guam, no one knew the ship was coming into shore. All the power lines were down because of the storm, so there was no communication. On shore, there was only one man, an admiral, to see our ship come into port.

I had become friends with a man on the ship who was a radio operator. We were both standing by the ship's railing, just gazing out onto shore. He had been in the area before. He said, "Why don't we get off the ship? I could get a jeep and drive us around the island today." However, about that time, we got a message that we four teachers were going to be taken off the ship and flown the rest of the way to Saipan. The government was eager to get the school started there, so they needed to have us arrive as soon as possible. (The remaining passengers aboard the ship didn't arrive in Saipan for an additional six days.)

Another unforgettable experience was a few years later around 1952. I remember it was the day of Queen Elizabeth's coronation. I was teaching in Korea in another army school. There was an English company not too far from us that was located along the coast. Someone from this company invited my date and me out for a party. When we were returning that evening after the party, all of a sudden we were being shot at.

We were able to radio from the jeep to say that snipers were shooting at us. The radio operator talked to the officer on duty, Colonel Remel, and told him the two of us were out there. He said, "Miss McQuaid? What in the hell is she doing out there? If she doesn't have more sense than to be out there, she should be shot at!" Anyway, they did send an armored car out to pick us up, and we managed to get out of that jam. I don't remember my date's name, but I certainly remember that evening. It was some date!

So, that's a little glimpse into my life. I am fortunate that there are no dreams for my life that haven't been reached. Even since retirement, I have continued to enjoy the excitement of traveling. For example, there have been many return trips to Hawaii, and I recently went on a Mediterranean cruise.

Of course, none of us can predict the length of our life's journey or how it will play out. My own mother lived to 105 years old. She was quite a remarkable woman. She was born in 1885. She used to enjoy playing the piano. I discovered that I could play by ear. When I first sat down by a piano one day and started playing around, she said, "If you want to play the piano, I'll teach you." She could do anything.

At 104, my mother was living in an assisted-living home. One of the nurses who liked her a lot asked her, "Now what do you want to do on your 104th birthday? Is there anything you would really like to do?" My mother responded, "'Well,

I've always wanted to ride a motorcycle." They came up with a motorcycle, and she got to go for a ride. Of course, the press showed up for the event, also.

Maybe that's why I have always seen life as an adventure and have faced things head on—it's in my blood.

What a colorful journey! There must be a wide array of memories tucked inside June's heart from her travels throughout the world. I'm sure that she added richness to her years in teaching by drawing on these experiences.

It must have taken incredible courage to end her marriage and to forge out on her own when it became apparent that it was not a good fit, especially with a baby growing inside her. (June never did remarry but remained a single, very independent woman for the rest of her life.)

But . . . you may be wondering . . . what happened to the baby that she was carrying? Her son Tracy is now living in Palo Alto, California, and is a physicist. He apparently inherited her mother's love for adventure and travel. He has a passion for sailing and has been in many transPacific races, such as California to Hawaii. (June has been sailing with him on many of his boats—but not during one of his races.) Yes, the love of adventure continues into the next generation. Hopefully, he will stay away from the typhoons out there.

THE MASTER STORYTELLER

Verdi Grace Nelson

We were three women from three different generations gathered around Verdi's dining room table—I, in my forties, Ginny in her seventies, and Verdi, well into her nineties. Although there were years between us, we laughed heartily and our hearts were touched as Verdi shared stories and memories like a master storyteller.

Ginny had said, "You must meet my friend Verdi. She has so many incredible stories to tell about her life." Indeed she did. Now 98 years old, Verdi still lives independently in her own place.

She lives in St. Paul, Minnesota, in one of three identical buildings that were built in the 1930s. (I discovered these buildings were steeped in history. The story goes that the building next door was the home of Ma Barker and one of the places where Dillinger was shot. But . . . that's a story for another time.) Verdi's building has since been changed from apartments into condominiums, and it has been her home for many years.

Her dining room, with the morning sun streaming in through the light lace curtains, looked inviting. Verdi had her table set with china and silver, and she was waiting for us on this particular summer day. As we poured the coffee and passed around the cookie plate, she began to share the tales of adventure that were the essence of her being. She had lived—and amazingly survived—an adventurous childhood long before the days of seat belts, bike helmets, and all of today's protection from everyday hazards.

As a baby boomer, I fondly think back on carefree days of riding down the country gravel road at top speed with the wind blowing through my long blond hair, arms outreached to the sky as I learned to ride without holding onto the handlebars. I also think of the exhilaration of swinging higher and higher on the playground swing until my insides would tickle and I was sure I was going to fly completely over the top of the swingset.

However, I realized my childhood memories were tame in comparison to the stories Verdi was about to share. She talked about her journey through life, but the stories often came floating up from memories of her childhood. They included stories of learning to swing onto a moving freight train, dealing with the rattlesnakes sunbathing on the roof of her house, and many more fascinating episodes. I wish you could have heard her tell these stories with all the emotion of someone who has lived them. So pull up a chair at the table, pour a cup of coffee, and join us for this incredible journey.

A Visit with the Gypsy Queen

My story begins before I was born with a special trip to visit a gypsy queen. When my mother (Kate) was six years old, Grandma's neighbor took her to a gypsy queen to hear her fortune. (This neighbor lady cared for my mother each day while my grandmother worked.) The gypsy queen told this six-year-old girl that she was going to marry a man whose initials were FJG and that she would have three beautiful daughters. I don't know what else she told her. That's all I ever heard of this story.

My mother was too young at the time to remember this experience. After the neighbor lady shared with Grandma the details about her daughter's fortune, Grandma kept it to herself.

Years later my mother got married, and my father's initials were, in fact, FJG—Frank John Grace.

When I was on the way, my dad said, "It's going to be a boy, Kate. If it isn't a boy, we're going to take it back." I was born on February 29, 1904. When I arrived, I was a little girl. I was skinny . . . a horrible little thing, but Dad decided to keep me anyway. When I turned out to be a girl, Grandma couldn't keep her secret any longer, so she told Mama that she was going to have two more girls—and she did. I was the oldest; then Maxine and Pauline arrived.

We were each blessed with a head of thick beautiful hair. Maxine had red curly hair like Mama's—kind of a copper color; Pauline had brown hair with a soft wave; and I had straight hair—absolutely no curl—nothing, but I had so much hair. We all had lots of hair. So, this gypsy queen's prediction had come true—Mama did indeed marry a man with the initials FJG and they had three daughters.

The Naming Battle

When I was born, Mama suggested, "Since we're going to have three girls, we will have the three Graces. Why don't we name them Faith, Hope, and Charity?" My dad would have nothing to do with that. Mama thought it would be wonderful. He hated the idea! She said, "Then I'm going to name our first baby after an Italian composer." (Mama loved music.) He said, "I don't care what Italian you name her after, but she can't be named Faith." So Mama named me

Verdi (pronounced like Variday) after her favorite Italian composer. My middle name has a creative origin also. Mama had two girlfriends, Alice and Gertrude, who were disappointed when she didn't choose to name me after them. So she took the "Al" of Alice and "trude" from Gertrude and created my middle name of Altrude. My name became Verdi Altrude Grace.

Pauline was named after a storybook character. Dad had read a story where he liked the main character, Pauline. She was named Pauline Sumner after Mama's maiden name of Sumner. When the third daughter was born, we all wanted to name her after my dad, Francis. He wouldn't have anyone named after him, so we named her Maxine, after the actress Maxine Elliot. This third daughter became Maxine Frances. (The only way we could get dad's name included was as Maxine's middle name.)

In addition to the three girls, a boy was later added to the family. Again Mama tried to name my brother Francis after my dad, and they got into such an argument. Since Mama and Dad couldn't come to a resolution, a neighbor lady named my brother after her own brother. He became Bernard (Bernie) Leroy.

Marion Junction

I was born in Sanborn, Iowa, but lived there for only three years. Then our family moved to Marion Junction, South Dakota.

We had a big house in Marion Junction. A lot of families in the area were very large—10 to 15 kids. When the girls got to be about sixteen or seventeen years old, they would be put out to work for room and board. So Mama had two girls board with us. Ella was our "children's maid."

Poor Ella. She was supposed to look after me, but I would often try to get away from her. I suppose I thought it was fun. Then she would catch me and bring me back home. However, on this one particular day, she didn't catch me. I was about eight years old at the time. For some reason, I was fascinated by the town's water tower and headed right for it. I climbed up the water tower to where you could walk around, so I walked around it. The view was beautiful. I saw some cleats on the side of the tower, so I followed the cleats. They led right to a big gold ball on the top of the tower. So I crawled on over to the gold ball, wrapped my legs around it, and hung onto it with my arms. The wind was blowing, and the sun was shining—it was a gorgeous day. I don't know how long I was up there. I must have been pretty high. When I looked down, I saw these little ants . . . that were actually people. So I thought I had better start back down. They were pretty glad to see me come down. Here I learned that everyone in this little town had been looking for me. I had just lifted off the face of the earth. They hadn't thought to look skyward. They were so relieved to find me that I didn't even get a spanking.

Filing a Claim

During the time we were living in Marion Junction, the government was trying to populate the Dakotas, offering people a quarter section of land if they lived on it for three years. One section was 364 acres, so a quarter section was about 91 acres. When you went down to apply for it, they called it "Filing for a Claim." After you had lived there for three years, you "Closed the Deal."

After dad had signed up for a section, he contracted to have a house built. Etta Way, a good friend of Mama's, decided to file for the section next to us so we could all be together. We called her Aunt Etta because, when I was little, you couldn't call anyone by their first name, and the adults didn't want to be called "Mr." or "Mrs." I had a hundred grandmas, aunts, and uncles—even though they weren't related.

Another favorite person was "Grandma" Housesour, who lived across the street from us. She had a big house, and she also had a summer kitchen. (In the summer, all the cooking was done in the summer kitchen to keep the house cooler.) I remember she would make sauerkraut for her whole family and half the town. She had a big tub or something, and she made it in that. She would tromp it down with her bare feet. It was the best sauerkraut you ever ate in your life! [Hopefully, she washed her feet first.] Oh, she was immaculate. Everyone loved Grandma Housesour's sauer-kraut. [She certainly had an appropriate name for the queen of sauerkraut.]

Well, we were now living out on our new land. Mama was raising us alone much of the time because Dad stayed in town in Marion Junction and worked. He would come out every 28 days and see us. He spent much of the time while he was home chopping wood so that we could keep warm until he returned again.

Mama was much more timid than I and without my sense of adventure. There was a little store about eight miles away where we would get our groceries. It wasn't really in a town—the closest town was 90 miles away. We had a horse and buggy for transportation. Behind the buggy seat was a square where we could put groceries. On the way to the store, I used to sit in that seat and throw out Carnation milk containers so Mama could find her way back home. We raised the baby on Carnation milk, so there were enough containers to provide a trail for Mama's trips home.

Belle, Our Babies Are in Trouble

When we moved to this land, the ranchers initially threw up a sod house for us. We lived way up high on a hill, and there was a big ranch far down below us. Mama would go down every morning to help milk cows so that she would have milk for her girls. One day while she was down at the ranch, a huge storm came through. A cyclone came, picked up our roof, and just sailed it away! Aunt Etta was staying with us girls while Mama was gone. Well, Aunt Etta got all excited. She ran out, knocking the baby over. So I picked up the baby and carried her out of the house. Aunt Etta said, "We'll go where your mother is. We'll walk." So, in the midst of the storm, we walked.

Mama came outside and happened to see us way up on the hill struggling through the storm. She said to the rancher, "Oh, those are my babies! I have to go up there." He said, "The storm's too bad. You can't make it—you can't go." "Oh," she said, "those are my babies. I have to go." So, she talked to the horse, whose name was Belle. She put her arms around the horse's neck and she said, "Belle, our babies are in trouble. We have to go and get them . . . and you have to swim the creek with me in the buggy." With her arms around Belle, she pointed to us up the hill to show her and said again, "Belle, those are our babies." So Mama got in the buggy. (The rancher was madder than the devil at her for going out in the storm.) Belle swam the creek and came up to where we were, and mother picked us up. She brought us safely down to the big ranch. We had to stay at that ranch for six weeks until we got our roof back on. [I would say Mama worked past her fears that day and met the challenge head-on—with the help of trusty Belle.]

Snakes and More Snakes

Well, our roof was repaired, and we were finally able to return home. The only wood part of our house was the roof, and that was just held on with sod and stakes. How I remember the rattlesnakes that would like to rest up on top of our roof in the nice warm sun. There were big round bull snakes in our yard, too. We learned to be very good to the bull snakes, because they ate the rattlesnakes. One time my sister and I were going to go outside to play, and there was a snake lying right outside the door. So we hopped over it. Then we hopped back over the snake and told Mama. Mama hated the snakes too, so she tapped on the window to get Grandma's attention. Mama said, "There's a snake on the doorstep." Grandma picked up a little piece of wood and pounded on the snake. So that took care of that.

After that day, we couldn't play in the yard because of the snakes. Mama would put us in the buggy. We would play in the buggy, and trusty Belle would be nearby. Yes, I've always hated snakes with a passion—even garter snakes are too much for me. We never had any trouble with them, though.

My Father—the Railroad Man

My father and I had the same desire for adventure. Dad loved the railroad. He was a conductor for the Milwaukee Railroad for 57 years, but he preferred the freight trains.

One day he was going to take me with him so he could show me off to his brother, who was also a railroad man. I was all dressed up in my clean white dress . . . to be real cute for my uncle. Dad and I were riding up on the roof on top of a box-car and the train was rolling along in its rhythmic pattern. My dad could walk up there just as well as you and I could walk on the sidewalk. We were coming up to this bridge where they had put on long tines that hung down from the bridge for protec-tion. Well, they hung low enough so that they would knock us off. Dad said, "Oh-oh. Lie down." So we had to quickly lie down flat on top of the car, or we'd be swept off the railroad car. When I got up you should have seen my pretty white dress—it was white no longer. My uncle just laughed when we told him this story—he thought it was more fun. However, my mother never found out—we never told her.

When I was nine years old, my father taught me how to swing on and off of a moving freight train. Each day there would be a short time for switching tracks. When it got to be noon, the men working on the train would go out to eat. They always went to a restaurant that had a long counter with stools. They would set me on the stool and order my lunch. Of course, the men would gobble their lunches. They were working hard and were hungry. Being a little girl, I was eat-ing like a lady. That meant I was very slow. Well, when Dad was getting ready to leave to finish the switching he'd say, "You have 15 minutes. If you don't make it, don't worry. I'll pick you up on the way back." Believe me—I made it! I didn't want to be left behind. That's when he taught me to swing onto a rolling freight train. I have done it when they're moving, but they are very slow because they're very heavy. If I didn't make the first door, someone would pick me up on the last one. Of course, my mother never knew about this either.

Leland Tipton—the School Bully

I loved baseball when I was a kid. The boys would play base-ball, but the girls would have to play ball with a tennis ball on the other side of school. (There weren't enough balls or bats left over for the girls to use.) One day the boys were short one on their team. They said, "Verdi, come on—play first base." So that day I got to play baseball with the boys.

We had a boy in our school, Leland Tipton, whose dad was a state criminal lawyer. We girls would be hitting the ten-nis ball with our fists since we didn't have a bat. Leland would come over and take the ball from us, throw it, and run away with it. He'd also hit us with sticks—he was so mean. I told Grandma about it, and she told my dad. My dad said to me, "I hear Leland Tipton is bothering you girls. I want you to lick him." I said, "Dad, he's a boy!" He said, "I know it. You can lick him." I said, "But he's bigger than me." He said, "I know, but you can lick him. By the way, if you don't, I'll give you a lickin'." My dad had never laid a hand on me.

So I went to school the next day and sure enough, at noon out on the playground, Leland Tipton stole our ball again. I got it back, and he grabbed a big stick and started hitting me. I threw his cap up in the tree. I finally caught him and knocked him down and jumped on top of him. I hit him with my fists saying, "Got enough? Got enough?" All of a sudden this girl, May Ford, said in a real high, squeaky voice, "Hit him one for me." I was so mad that I hadn't noticed a big ring of kids had formed around us. They said, "Don't stop now! Don't stop now! Make him say he's got enough." So I did. Finally he said, "I've got enough."

I went into my class, and the teacher never said a word about it. I thought, "Oh boy." I kept waiting for something to happen. I never could get by with anything. When I got home that night, Mama never said anything either. The next night when Dad came home, he said, "Dade (that was his nickname for me), I hear you licked Leland Tipton." I just burst out crying. I sat on his lap, and I cried and cried. I said, "Dad, I hit him and I hit him until I made him say he had had enough." "Good for you," Dad said. Then Mama was worried because Mr. Tipton was a criminal lawyer for the state of South Dakota and he might try to get even. Dad said, "If he gets smart, I'll lick him too." Mr. Tipton never did say anything.

There's more to this story. My younger brother Bernie got polio when he was 11 months old and never learned to walk. Every Saturday night I had to push my brother in the buggy and walk down to the store and pick up the meat. Mama would have called in the meat order. I'd come home with my brother and the meat in the buggy. Well, all the boys were always hanging around outside Blair's, the neighborhood store. I'd have to walk past them to pick up the meat order. Not long after the episode on the playground, Leland said, "Good evening, Verdi. May I push Bernie home?" I said, "Sure." So for years, Leland Tipton pushed my brother's buggy home for me.

Ribbons for Christmas

Like I mentioned before, all three of us girls had a tremendous amount of hair. For Christmas, I would get three ribbons—each a yard and a half long and six inches wide—for my hair. That was my Christmas present each year. When I first had my hair cut, it had grown between my knees and my ankles. Grandma would cut our hair according to the moon. If Mama wanted it to grow faster, Grandma would cut it at one time of the year. If Mama wanted it thicker, Grandma would cut it at a different time of the year.

Grandma Sumner

Grandma Sumner and I were truly kindred spirits. We were much more alike than my mother and I. This leads me back to the story about the gypsy queen. There was a reason why Grandma was at work and her neighbor was caring for my mother. Grandma was delivering mail. She was the first lady rural mail carrier in South Dakota.

Grandpa (James) Sumner was in the Civil War. I was told the men came home from the war awfully discouraged and depressed. Grandma said they'd go off and be gone for a couple of weeks, but they'd always come back. So the women didn't worry about it—they just accepted it. Well, then Grandpa left when Mama was six weeks old, and he did not come back. Every time he had left before for these two-week periods, Grandma would take over his mail route. Well, when he didn't come back and didn't come back, it became her route. She drove that route for 17 years. Mama would be bundled up on the seat beside her until she was six years old.

Grandma Sumner had seven children. One of them died in infancy, so she raised six children all by herself. Twenty-nine years later, Grandpa returned. We don't know if he ever remarried or what he did during this time. He told Grandma, "I'd like to start over with you." She said, "After 29 years? Forget it!" She didn't need him, anyway.

Then he went to talk to Mama, who was about 30 years old by this time. Mama said, "Well, I never had a father, remember? This is my mama's home. If she doesn't want you, I don't either." So . . . he left. He went to Vermillion, South

Dakota, where three of his other daughters lived. They gave him a rough time, because they knew how hard their mother had worked to raise them. (My mother had been a baby, of course, so she didn't remember much of it.) So then he went to Kansas City, Missouri, where he lived until he died. When he died, Grandma was notified. Mama and my uncle went down to claim the body and had it buried.

We never learned what happened during those 29 years or where he spent his time or anything. It is too bad Mama didn't invite him to stay for a couple of days so we could have found out some of the answers to the mystery. We didn't know . . . and Grandma ruled the roost.

❧

We refilled our coffee cups, and Verdi continued on with her stories. It was now many years later, and she was a young woman. It was hard to imagine, but the stories we were about to hear were even more amazing.

❧

Assisting Dr. Cotton

My cousin's husband was a pharmacist. He and his wife wanted to go to a pharmaceutical convention one summer. They had asked if I would come to stay with their son, who was a little boy at that time. I said, "Yes, I would." So a month or so later I went into town to stay with him. While I was there, a woman came to the house and said, "Can you help Dr. Cotton?" He was a little country doctor. I said, "Sure, what's wrong?" She said, "I don't know. I guess the Methodist minister had an accident." She said, "Bring a tea kettle of boiling hot water and a spool of white silk thread to the minister's house." Here I was just a young woman . . . no brain. I brought the items and Dr. Cotton said, "Can you help me?" I said, "Sure, what do you need?" He said, "Well, we're going to sew this man's ear on." We took the spool of white silk thread, sterilized it and all that, and threaded it in one of those hook needles. The doctor stuck the needle in the ear, I pulled it out, and I pushed it back, and he'd pull it out. We continued this process until we had reattached the man's ear.

The minister had been in a car accident, and the car caught the ear. His body was also burned. Before we sewed his ear on, the doctor set me up with a can of medicated powder. He said, "Undress him and cover his body with this powder because he's burned with gasoline." Well, I didn't mind doing that, but I had gone to school with him as a kid. I hated to undress him . . . but I did as Dr. Cotton asked me.

A year later this young minister came back into town. He had come to see another doctor who was a nose, ear, and eye specialist. After his appointment he came to see me. I said, "Well, what did Dr. Bob say about your ear?" He said, "You sewed it on beautifully." When the doctor asked who did the work, the minister told him, "It was Dr. Cotton and Verdi Grace." The doctor then said, "That darn Verdi Grace can do anything!"

This reminds me of another accident. Dad, Mother, and I were riding in a car, and it was at night. Dad was the world's worst driver. He worked the railroad for so many years, and I don't think he was used to the motion of the car. As he was driving this car, a coupe passed us. We were going up a familiar hill where the road would turn when we got to the top of the hill. As this coupe passed us, Dad said, "There's an accident waiting to happen." He had no more than said it, and it happened. We heard it.

When we got to the top of the hill, we saw this coupe had smashed head-on into another car. It was a man, his wife, and baby. Dad had Mother wait in the car, and he said, "Verdi, come on." So I went with him, and I found the baby in the ditch. The baby and the husband didn't seem to be hurt. Dad got the lady up, and her clothes were torn off her back. Another car drove up right then, and the driver said, "I'm a doctor!" So he took over right away. Dad directed the traffic because, you know, railroad people are bossy. He knew just what to do.

The doctor looked at the lady, saw her chin was also injured, and said, "Oh boy, I need a bandage." (He didn't have his case with him.) I said, "Oh, I just put a clean hand-kerchief in Dad's pocket. I'll get it." So he pushed the lady's chin up and held it together with the handkerchief. (The fatty part was gone, but we found it.) The doctor said to me, "You come with me. We'll stop at this next little town a couple miles down the road and sew her chin on. Can you help me?" I said, "Sure." So Mama fussed and Dad said, "Be quiet, Kate. We're going to this next town." So I went with the doctor, this lady, her baby, and her husband to another doctor's office—Dr. Mitchell. The next day, Dr. Mitchell called Mama and said, "Mrs. Grace, was it your daughter who helped us after that accident?" She said, "Yes, it was Verdi who helped you." He said, "That's all I wanted to know. I want her to take nursing. She has the coolest head of anyone that I've worked with in a long time."

Some time later after graduating from Mitchell High School in Mitchell, South Dakota, I did sign up for nursing. This was 1922. However, my mother canceled it. She said I was too short—too little—to handle the work. I should have done it anyway. I guess I did have the knack. Years later my husband would say, "Anytime anyone in your family gets a belly ache, they send for you."

My mother also didn't think girls should go to college. For heaven's sake, how awful! I worked at the creamery and other jobs through high school to earn money for college. All these years, she took my money with the promise to keep it until I was eighteen. My mother had said, "I'll save your money for you."

So when I finished high school, I was going to go register for college, but my mother had no money. I said, "What did you do with that money?" I learned my mother had used the money I had earned to buy things for Pauline and Maxine. I said, "What about me?" Well, she dug up enough money for me to go to one year of college.

I went that year to Dakota Wesleyan College. Then instead of nursing, I went to six weeks of Normal School that following summer to get my teaching certificate.

Life on the Indian Reservation

I received my teaching certificate and applied for jobs with two different superintendents. The first job offer was on an Indian reservation, and I took it. This was a brand new way of life to me.

I got up to the reservation and stayed with a family, the Pilkers. Well, I found out they had a little child, and she had to sleep with me. (They just had the one bedroom, and the couple slept out in the dining room.) I had to go 2 1/2 miles to school. Mrs. Pilker would make my lunch every day. Do you know what kind of sandwiches she would make? She made cottage cheese sandwiches. They're terrible! I like cottage cheese—but not in a sandwich!

On Saturday nights, the lumberjacks down on the river would go to town and dance. They would come and pick up the teacher and take her into town. I remember they had a Ford with no top on it. When the car got stuck in the mud, these lumberjacks would just hop out, lift the car out of the mud, and continue on their way. So we'd go into town together.

The judge in town, Judge Martin, was a wonderful dancer. He found out I could waltz, so he'd say to the orchestra, "Every third number is a waltz." He would come to me and say, "I'll do every two waltzes with you and every third one with my wife." It was fun. We had wonderful Saturday nights. I loved it!

The lumberjacks would also come around during the week and shoot craps. I had never seen anything like it. Well, I played craps with them one time, and I won every game. I suppose they let me win, but I didn't know that. I wanted to give the money back at the end of the day, and the lumberjacks just had a fit. They said, "You won all that." I said, "I didn't want to win—I just wanted to play." "Well," they said, "you did and you won."

Then Mrs. Pilker got pregnant, and she didn't want me to stay there any more. So then I went down to the big ranch that was on the reservation and asked Mrs. Miller if she would take me in. Where else was I going to stay? She said that she would talk to the owner of the ranch. He said I could stay with Mrs. Miller if I helped her with her work. So I did. I had to churn the butter every Saturday morning and help do repair work on the cowboys' covers. Her daughter went to school, so she rode to school with me on my pony. (I had bought a pony when I was staying with the Pilkers. It was too far to walk, and I was afraid of the snakes. There were prairie dogs, too, and I was just as scared of them as I was of the snakes.)

In the evenings after we would get back to the ranch, I had to tie up my pony, and the little girl would sit there and wait while I did my chores. I had to drive a pair of ponies with a hayrack full of hay around to feed the cattle.

I remember I started working in September, but I didn't get my first paycheck until November. I did get all my money, but they were just slow in getting it out. I got $90 a month, which was a lot of money. I was about 22 years old at this time. I stayed the whole year. In fact, I was the only teacher that they were able to keep the whole year.

That year, there was a Southern white family with ten kids that moved into the area. One little girl had epilepsy, and she would periodically have a spell at school. I would get one of the Indian boys to drive us by pony to her mother's. Her mother would usually say, "Oh, I'll put her in the back room for a few days. She'll be all right." That's all they did. They said it was caused by something she ate. No one knew.

There were ten kids in that little house, but the mother was immaculate. You could have eaten off any corner of that house at any time. Then two of the children got diphtheria, so they couldn't come to school. As they began to get better, I would go up to their house to teach them. We held school outdoors, and I used the ground as the blackboard.

In those days, students had to take county tests at the end of the year. Their boy Harry was in the eighth grade. He had returned to school, but I knew that he wouldn't pass the tests since he had missed so much school from his illness. I went to his dad and asked if he would do Harry's chores so I could keep Harry after school to help him prepare for his tests. He said if I was willing to do that, he would be willing to do the chores. So Harry and I spent extra time after school. When the county exams came, Harry passed. I was so pleased.

I had 16 kids in seven grades and 45 classes to teach. It was a lot of work. I was teaching in the largest county in South Dakota. In October, we had to go for refresher courses. I went to an older teacher that I knew and told her I was having an awful time getting in 45 classes a week. She said, "Oh, what grades do you have?" I told her. Well, she sat down and wrote out the whole schedule of classes for each grade—from her head. I followed her schedule and didn't have any problems after that.

I was the teacher on the reservation, but I was also the warrant officer. When the children didn't come to school, I had to find them. This task could be challenging.

I remember two interesting characters on the reservation. We had a very old Indian out there. He was a wise and wonderful old gentleman. There was also a young Indian who got drunk once in awhile. He would ride bare-naked on his horse through what we called the lowland.

I went home at the end of the school year and got a call from a superintendent in Tyndal, South Dakota. There was a teacher there who had to be let go. He asked if I would fill her position. So, I went. My second teaching experience was in a Bohemian settlement. Again . . . what a change!

Do You Speak Bohemian?

This Bohemian community had an interesting tradition that would occur on the first Saturday after a new teacher arrived. They held a dance in the teacher's honor that would last from sunset to sunup. The teacher was supposed to dance every dance. Oh, it was rough. It's a good thing I knew how to dance. You had to do everything—all kinds of dances. If I didn't know some, they would say, "That's all right. We'll get you around. We'll teach you."

Not long after I started teaching there, I noticed the kids were having more fun on the school ground. I thought they were saying something naughty, because they were getting such a kick out of it. Of course I didn't know, because they were speaking Bohemian.

That weekend, I said to one of the women in the community, Mrs. Matuska, "Mary, you're going to have to teach me how to swear in Bohemian." "Oh, teacher!" she said. I said, "I don't want to swear, but I want to recognize the words. I think that's what the boys are saying out on the school ground. They don't think I know it." So that whole weekend, she taught me how to swear in Bohemian.

When we returned to school on Monday, there were two boys—two big boys—who thought they were pretty smart. They were swearing and laughing and having such fun. At the end of school, I dismissed all the students but those two boys. I let them sit there. "Miss Grace," one said, "we have chores to do. My dad is really mad if I don't get them done on time." I said, "You should have thought of that today on the playground when you said "such and such and such." They got all wide-eyed and said, "We didn't know you could talk Bohemian!" I said, "There's a lot of things you don't know about your teacher." So they sat there. Then they said, "If you let us go, we promise never to swear on the grounds again, and we'll supervise the playground." I said, "Are you gentlemen of your word?" "Oh yes," they said. So I said, "OK, I'll give you a chance, but if you don't live up to it, you know what will happen."

Well, it almost backfired on me when I saw one of their folks. Here they thought I could talk Bohemian. I said, "Don't tell your son, but I can't talk Bohemian. He was swearing on the playground, and I learned it was a swear word." His parents just loved it. They thought it was such fun.

I was there for the rest of the year and then went back home for the summer. I had a summer job in the creamery where I was in the butter room. They had 135 pounds of butter in this room, and what a tough job. One day this fellow got sick, and they asked each of us to do an extra hour that night. Well, Big Sadie was strong as a horse, but she couldn't stand another hour. So, I did it and then the boss asked me if I would take this man's job until he came back. I did that job for two weeks. I took all the butter out, and the older men rolled it out and brought me another one. Normally my job was to put the butter in the carton to pack it as it came down the line. When it got through me, it was all ready to ship. It was supposed to be two people's job, but I didn't know it. They didn't tell me that.

I didn't return to teaching after my year in the Bohemian settlement. After two years of teaching, my doctor wouldn't let me go back the next fall. He said that I was too conscientious. I worked on it 24 hours a day, and it was affecting my health.

⚘

After teaching, Verdi lived at home and earned money working at the creamery, the print shop, and things like that.
Then she left town and got married. The story about meeting Ernie was, of course, anything but routine. She was
doing fine by herself and wasn't looking for a man to take
care of her. Then along came Ernie. He was spirited and
spunky just like her, and he gradually won her heart.

Hi, Lard Ass!

Ernie and I met here in St. Paul. I just adored him. He was
a full-blooded Swede. I am Irish—actually Irish and part
Scotch/English. I told him it took a good Irishwoman to
keep this Swede in line.

I met Ernie through my friend Pearl. Pearl was a dear
friend of mine, and we did a lot of things together. (In fact,
we were lifelong friends. She just died this past January.) We
were young ladies at this time, and Pearl was interested in
Whoopee John Wilfarht. He was an entertainer. They had
known each other since they were kids.

On the night that I met Ernie, Pearl and I had taken the
streetcar to go on the boat by Harriet Island in St. Paul. We
got on the boat and then decided to go up on the deck. As we
were walking across the dance floor to get up there, Ernie saw
Pearl and yelled, "Hi, Lard Ass!" She said, "Hi, Swede!" He
was up on the stage whistling with Whoopee John. (We didn't
know Whoopee John was going to be entertaining on the boat
that night.) Ernie jumped off the stage and came and grabbed
me and picked me up. Oh, I was so mad! I didn't dare kick at

him, or he might see my underpants. He carried me up to the deck, and we ended up talking. He said to Pearl, "I didn't know you had such damn good-looking friends." She said, "You don't really know much about me, yet."

Well, we spent the evening together, and then he wanted to take us girls home. I said, "I'm not going to ride with you." Pearl said, "Oh, yes you are. Why should we take the streetcar when Ernie can drive us home in the truck?" I was living at 17 and Oak Grove. I had him drop me off down on Nicollet someplace so he wouldn't know where I lived, and I walked the rest of the way home.

The next night Pearl called and said, "Ernie wants to talk to you." I said, "I don't want to talk to him." She said, "He's crazy about you." I said, "Forget it. I don't want to talk to him." (I wasn't going to be hooked by anyone.) The following night, she said, "Verdi, he calls me every night two or three times."

One night about three weeks later, someone knocked at my door. There stood Ernie leaning against the door holding a cigarette butt. He said, "I know you don't want to see me, but I can't live without seeing you." So, I invited him in—what else could I do? We started seeing each other from then on.

I have always loved dogs, and I had a Scotty dog named Heather. For some reason, Ernie and the dog did not get along from the start. He said to me, "If you want to get along with me, you have to get rid of that dog." Well, I said, "Love me—love my dog." He tried really hard to make up with the dog, but Heather wouldn't have anything to do with him. He worked so hard at it. Finally, he said, "How are we going to get Heather to like me?" I had an idea. When Ernie came to the door each time, I'd give him a treat to put in the cuff of his pants. Heather would smell it, she'd go over, and she'd take it out. So that's how she learned to like him. Well, one time, he forgot and put the treat in his pocket. Heather smelled the treat right away. She got up on his lap and pulled his shirt. She tore the pocket right off his shirt trying to get at that treat. He never said a word, so then I knew he loved me.

Ernie courted me while skating at the roller derby. That was such a cool place to go on a hot day. We would often go to the roller derby in the afternoons when he was off work. Sometimes we would have dinner and then go to the roller derby at night. It was located in downtown Minneapolis where the convention center is now. (I had skated all my life and loved it. I skated to high school and I skated to college. After high school, I skated with the director of the roller derby so that we could bring in a crowd.)

Ernie and I dated for about a year, and we were married in a church here in St. Paul. Our wedding date was on July 29, 1936. We were both around 34 years old when we were married. It was just a small wedding with his family there. After we were married, we lived in a beautiful home in Roseville, Minnesota.

Ernie became an electrical contractor. There was so much electrical wiring in that house. He installed a panel on the bedroom wall. If I heard any noise, I'd touch the panel and everything would light up—the basement, the overhang out front—everything. The neighbors used to tease us and say, "Turn on your bedroom light so we can finish our lawn work after dark."

Ernie's Dream

Ernie saw the need for a fire department in the Lake Johanna area. The district was growing awfully fast. They had only a bucket brigade, and Ernie had a vision for an organized fire department. He called a bunch of men together and showed them his plan for the whole thing. The men laughed at him. He said, "Would you mind coming back in two weeks and give me a chance to talk to other areas and see what they do?" They did come back, and he eventually got it going. He started the Lake Johanna Fire Department. Now there are three or four fire stations, and every man gets retirement after 20 consecutive years. Isn't that wonderful... and to think this started with one man's idea.

Ernie and I would have to go to fire training in the summer to teach new groups of men how to become firemen. He would say, "I'm going to teach you people how to be firemen." He would throw me over his shoulder, walk up a ladder, and then carry me back down. Then he would say to this new group of men, "Now you do it." They would say, "With her?" He said, "Yes, just don't drop her." So each of these young firemen would throw me over his shoulder and up we would go. (It didn't bother me at all.) Then we'd go to the school grounds to practice jumping down the fire escape.

We worked awfully hard at it—we both did. Every time there was a fire, I'd make sandwiches and drive to where they were fighting the fire. I also took calls. We would get some of the dumbest calls. People think the fire department knows everything. One time Ernie took a call and he said, "Just a minute." He said, "You're going to have to take this call." The caller said, "Would you tell me how I can tell if my dog is in heat?" Well, I could tell her since I had raised dogs, but

Ernie was just flabbergasted. Yes, fighting fires and all that went with it was a big part of our life together.

The Story of Harry and Frank

After Ernie and I had been married for a time, I thought I was pregnant and went to the doctor. The doctor finally decided that instead of being pregnant, I had a big tumor. He called Ernie at work and told him to bring his wife in on Saturday. So we went. The doctor said to Ernie, "I think your wife has a fibroid tumor, and it needs to be removed. I don't know... well, I'm going out on a limb and saying that's what it is. Of course, if it's cancer, we're doing the wrong thing." This was on Saturday, and we couldn't get a hospital room until the next Thursday. All the hospital rooms were full. (This was in 1941—during the war.) Finally on Thursday we did get a room, and I was there for three weeks. It did turn out to be a fibroid tumor that was all intertwined. So that was the end of that business—I couldn't have a baby after that.

The doctor and my husband decided that we should adopt. I never decided anything—Ernie and I never even discussed it. When Ernie told me of this decision, I said that I didn't want a girl because he had a daughter from a previous marriage that he was really crazy about. I didn't want there to be any competition for his love. We went through an agency and said, "You better get started on a second one, because we're not going to raise one alone." "Oh," the woman at the agency said, "would you take a pair of boys?" We said we would.

We went to the Lutheran Receiving Home to meet the boys. They weren't to know that we were interested in adopting them. The adults in charge said, "Mr. and Mrs. Nelson would like to see our home." Harry came up to Ernie and said, "Come on, man." Frank walked beside me and said, "Harry is my older brother." Frank and Harry were 5 and 7 years old.

We talked it over and decided we would try this pair of boys. They came to stay with us to see how it went, and I noticed they would refer to each other by their whole name. One night after dinner when the boys and I were doing the dishes, Frank called Harry by his full name. I said, "You know, I had an awfully nice name when I came to live with Ernie. My name was Verdi Grace. I had to give that name up when I came here to live with Mr. Nelson. Mr. Nelson is very good to me, and I like it here." (This was my way of explaining to them if they wanted to be a part of the family, they should take the Nelson name, too.) Frank said, "I would like to live here, but Harry would like to come, too." I said, "You're going to have to ask Mr. Nelson." He marched outside and said, "Mr. Nelson, I'd like to live here, but Harry would have to come, too." Ernie said, "I don't know if the state thinks we're smart enough to raise children. We'll have to find out." Later Harry said, "I knew you were going to be my dad all along." We did adopt them, and of course, they took on the Nelson name.

It worked very well to take these two boys. They were the babies from a family of eight children where the parents were unable to care for them. They were big boys, but they weren't very well when they came to live with us. We had to go through a special doctor. He wouldn't let the boys be adopted unless he could meet the prospective parents. We had to take them back to him for another checkup a year later. Frank grew seven inches in that one year—Harry grew three. Their whole life had changed. We fed them well—we went places—we did things.

(Years later their other siblings located them through the adoption records. They had all been adopted into various families. Frank and Harry told us, "We had the best home of everyone." So I guess we did all right.)

Harry died in 1994 when he was about 50 years old. Frank was with the Navy for 23 years and lived out of state. I called Frank and told him that Harry had taken ill. I said, "I think you better come home to see Harry. If you don't and he doesn't make it, you'll probably be the saddest man around." Frank came and he sat at his brother's bedside hour after hour. He had always been very protective of his brother. (Frank still lives out of state, but he calls me every week.)

The Day Dickey Died

Mama was very musical, and she had the most beautiful voice. My sister Pauline took after her. Pauline could sing three octaves. You should have heard her. Years later as an adult, Pauline had a canary. When she would sing, the canary would join in. The way those two sounded together was gorgeous! The minute she started to sing, the canary would join her.

The rest of my family was still living back in Mitchell, South Dakota. The day the canary died, Pauline called me and said, "Well, Dickey died." I said, "Oh, Pauline, that's too bad." She said, "Now when will you be here?" I said, "When will I be there—for what?" She said, "Well, aren't you coming for his funeral?" I said, "For the bird?" She said, "Well, he's a part of the family." I said, "Where are you going to bury him?" She said, "Oh, I have a beautiful box I'm going to fix up, and I'm going to bury him in the backyard." I said, "I can't afford to fly from St. Paul to Mitchell, South Dakota, for Dickey's funeral." Oh, was she mad. She didn't have anything to do with me for quite awhile.

I might fly back to Mitchell for a dog, but not for a bird. I continued my love for dogs and raised Scotties and Sealynams over the years. I had a black and white pair. Heather, my Scottie, would always sit in the kitchen watching me while I baked. She was just wonderful.

One time after Ernie and I were married, we went to my sister's house in Mitchell for Thanksgiving. We got about 20 miles toward home and Ernie said, "Did you put the dog in the car?" I said, "No, didn't you?" So we drove all the way back to my sister's house. There sat Heather eagerly waiting for us. My sister said, "I was hoping you wouldn't come back to get her." I said, "No, Ernie turned around in the middle of the road and went right back. He had to go and get our dog!" [It appears Ernie and Heather had definitely bonded from their original encounter.]

Ernie and I

Ernie didn't care to travel, so the only place he would take me was home to Mitchell, South Dakota. Later when my mother was ill, we went to Mitchell ten weekends in a row.

I was very involved with the Eastern Stars. I did take one trip to Europe with the Eastern Stars in the 1960s. I remember we were traveling on the Autobahn, and our bus was pulled over to the side of the road. Here was this big herd of cattle. They stopped the bus and all the traffic for the cattle. We had to sit there until all the cattle had been taken across. Our group also went to Paris. That's where I learned what a bidet was. I didn't try it. I did try to get my girlfriend to try it, but she wouldn't either.

Ernie and I loved to joke with each other. I used to kid Ernie about the fact that he was older than I. Actually, it was only by three months. When he turned 52, I said, "Gosh, it must be terrible to be that old. How do you feel?" Then three months later, I turned 52. We used to have a lot of fun with silly things like that. He had a great sense of humor. (Little did I know that this would turn out to be his final birthday.)

Ernie and I were married for 18 years. He had never been sick in his life. I still clearly remember the day he died. I got home from running some errands. Harry had written us a letter. His son had enclosed a drawing of a house with a six-car garage. Isn't that a kid for you? We sat there and laughed about it. Then he said, "What did you get Maxine for her birthday?" (Maxine was a neighbor lady.) I told him, and he said, "How did she like it?" I said, "Oh, I'll take it over tomorrow after church." He said, "Oh, no. You're going to take it over now. A birthday present should be given on a person's birthday or not at all." So I took the gift to Maxine's. I didn't stay but just a little bit. When I came back, he was gone. He had dropped dead of a heart attack! I tried to give him a pill, and I even put whiskey down his throat. I called for help right away, but he was gone. It was awful! We didn't even get to say goodbye.

Even though it's been 46 years since he died, I think of him often. Ernie was handsome and full of hell. Our anniversary was yesterday so, of course, I thought of him even more. I always do. I have an awful time on his birthday—the third of December.

On his first birthday after we were together, when he came home from work, I had a beautiful gift and a cake on the table. We sat down for dinner, and he said, "What's this?" I said, "That's your present and your cake." He started to cry. He said, "We never got birthday presents when

we were kids. My mother couldn't afford to buy us gifts."
(She was left with five children to raise alone. They didn't get
gifts, but they did always have a birthday cake.)

I think of that little boy sitting there without gifts and
then I cry. I can't help it. So every year I had a birthday gift
for him, and birthdays were always special. [Now I under-
stood why, on the day that Ernie died, he thought it was so
important for the neighbor to receive her gift on her birthday—and not the day after.]

My Philosophy of Life

My philosophy of life is what my grandmother taught me
before she died. I was sixteen at the time. She called me to her
side and she said, "Verdi, you have no philosophy in life as of
now. I want to tell you what to do. You should treat others as
you want to be treated." I said, "Well, that's the Golden Rule.
I know you have always taught me so." "Well," she said,
"there's something that goes with that. As ye sow, so shall ye
reap. If you follow those two things, you'll never go wrong."

So that is how I've tried to live. I've helped everybody as
much as I can. I even read the *Bible* through three times to
old people. My mother insisted. I'm so glad that I did it,
even though I couldn't understand all the words at the time.

I've had lots of fun in my life. There have been some bad
times, too. It was hard getting over my grandmother's death.
As a child, I would spend two months every summer with my
grandmother. My mom would say, "Grandma needs you."

I have wonderful memories of those summers with my
grandmother. They would have a Chataqua there in the
summer. A group of people would come into town, and they

would put up these big tents. There would be preaching in the tents. It was like a revival, but there was much more to it. It was entertaining, too. In a little town, it was often the only form of entertainment that they had. I heard some wonderfully talented people in these tents.

They also had races and things for the kids in the mornings. I would beat all of the girls in the girls' races, and then maybe I would run in the boys' races. My cousin Alba was just a little older than I. When we would get home, Grandma would ask him, "Alba, did you run in the races today?" He said, "No, I held the ribbon for Verdi to break."

My grandmother was a wonderful person—just wonderful! She was good to everyone. What she knew—she taught you. She treated everyone just alike. She didn't favor anyone.

Yes, Grandma was a wonderful lady—and very smart. She came from Indiana to South Dakota. She could do anything. One time a man came to see us; he was looking for Grandma. (Grandma had died the previous October—the 21st of October, and we buried her on the 24th—on her 77th birthday.) We told the man how she had recently passed away. He said, "Well, let me tell you about your grandma and what she's done for me. Years ago, I went to Hurley, South Dakota, to be a mortician. I got my first person to embalm, and I just couldn't do it. I called the doctor and told him I couldn't do it, but he just told me to call Grandma Sumner. I told the doctor that I didn't know Grandma Sumner, but the doctor just said to tell Grandma Sumner that he had told me to call. So, I did. She said, 'OK. I'll be right there.' So she came right over and said, 'Now, what do you want?' I told her that I couldn't embalm this person. She said, 'Oh, pshaw . . . of course you can.' (That was her favorite expression—"Oh, pshaw.") 'Where do you begin?' So I told her what they do first. Your grandmother stayed with me, and we embalmed my first person."

Grandma had never done anything like that before, but it didn't bother her. I take after Grandmother in a lot of ways. I'm a cuss.

Planning for the Future

I bought six cemetery lots in 1941 and paid $75 apiece. Ernie and Harry are both buried there. I will be buried there, also. Back when I found the spots, I said, "I want to be buried with my feet to the east and my head to the west." The man at the cemetery said, "That's an odd request." I said, "My grandmother told me that we need to be buried with our head to the east and our feet to the west. This is because when the Lord comes he will come from the east. We have to rise up to meet him. I don't want my back to him—I want my face to him." He said, "Well, that's unusual. We've never had a request like that."

So that's what we're all going to do. When the Lord comes and sees us, we'll all be ready. Our family tradition is that we're always buried fully dressed, including shoes.

It's Been a Wild Ride

A couple of years ago, I went to the Mall of America with my granddaughter. I had never been to the Mall. My granddaughter has a little boy, and he wanted me to go on a ride with him. He asked, "Can you go on the roller coaster ride?" I said, "Sure." My granddaughter said, "I'll ride behind you and hold onto Travis. It's really a wild ride." So we took the ride, and it was wild!

A short time after that, my doctor said, "Well, Verdi, have you done anything different lately?" I said, "No. Oh, I was on the roller coaster at the Mall of America." He said, "You what? You were on the roller coaster? Don't you ever do that again! That's no place for you! You're too old for that stuff." I said, "I had a wonderful time." He said with a small grin, "The things you do—you drive me nuts!"

Somehow, I have survived a lot of things. I seemed to have had every childhood disease—and for some reason I would get them severely. My sister had chicken pox; she had one pox on her tummy. Me, you couldn't touch with a pin— I had so many. My sister had whooping cough; she whooped once. I was in bed for ten weeks! I got so bad that I couldn't turn my head or I would whoop. I also had measles and scarlet fever. I had everything. I think I built up resistance, because everyone in my family is gone but me. My sister Maxine was 34 when she died of cancer; Pauline was 80 when she died. My great grandmother and great grandfather lived to be 96 and 98. I've also outlived both of them.

Throughout my life, I have followed my grandmother's advice that she gave me right before she died. I have had a wonderful time, and people have been awfully good to me. Remember, all you ever get out of this life is memories. That's all you ever get. You can't take your money with you. Have you ever seen a Brink's truck in a funeral procession? No, you never do. You can't take your money with you. You might as well give it to others so they can enjoy it.

❧

The hours had slipped by quickly, and we had arrived at the end of this fascinating journey. Verdi gave us a tour of her home and showed us some of her favorite possessions collected over a lifetime. There were no old photographs of her, but she did have a framed photograph of her father in his conductor's uniform. Her walls displayed more recent plaques of appreciation from the St. Paul Winter Carnival and Governor Jesse Ventura. A shelf held Minnesota Twins bobblehead dolls and other mementos from a special day at the dome. (It was an unforgettable day, when she even got a hug and kiss from her favorite baseball player of all time, Harmon Killebrew.)

Her bed was filled with teddy bears. One, in particular, held a special place in her heart, and there was yet one more story to be told. It touched my heart, as had so many of the others.

❧

Teddy

When I was just a little girl, my mother and I, with my younger sister in the baby carriage, would go strolling down the road on our morning walks. Every day on these walks, we would pass by a store where I would see a special teddy bear in the window. I loved that teddy bear. One day the store-owner came out and said, "I'm going to give you the bear." My mother said, "Oh, no." He stooped down and said to me, "Every day I see you stop by my shop. Your little face is pressed against the window, just peering at that bear. I want you to have it."

Teddy is now 95 years old and has the prime spot on my bed. He still wears the brown coat made for him by a neighbor lady when I was a child. He has been with me through this entire journey, and he will be buried with me.

Just like Verdi, Teddy was showing some of the physical signs of aging. Through these many years, he had been lovingly cared for by the one who picked him out in the storefront window back in 1907. I can imagine her holding him tightly as she fell asleep each night after yet another adventurous day.

The Final Party

Verdi's niece is planning a 100th birthday party on February 29, 2004, and has already reserved the location. She said, "I hope this place is big enough to take care of all your friends." Verdi said, "I'm looking forward to it. It should be a wonderful time!"

Verdi's upcoming 100th birthday celebration is sure to be a day to remember. (It will be made even more special because of the fact that this will actually be only her 25th birthday. Verdi was a leap-year baby, in case you didn't catch it from her birth date at the beginning of the story.)

The stories will no doubt be told in abundance. There will be laughter, hugs, and oh, so many memories as they celebrate the life of this remarkable woman. Grandma Sumner would be proud. It truly will be a wonderful time.

4

THE MYSTERY
OF A PHOTOGRAPH

I mourn no more my vanishing years;
Beneath a tender rain,
An April rain of smiles and tears,
My heart is young again.
And so the shadows fall apart,
And so the west–winds play;
And all the windows of my heart
I open to the day.

EXCERPTS FROM A QUAKER POEM
BY JOHN GREENLEAF WHITTIER

THE MYSTERY OF A PHOTOGRAPH

*E*very photograph captures a specific moment along the journey of life. It is fascinating to look at old black and white or sepia photographs and ponder what may have been happening behind the photograph. The participants of the photograph are like actors in a movie—suspended in time. As viewers, we can only guess as to what story may be behind the faces gazing back at us.

If we are fortunate enough to be able to go to the source, we can learn little tidbits about the events that prompted the photograph or what was taking place behind the scenes. These tidbits can reveal humor or other emotions that remain tied to that photograph even years later.

The two women in this photograph both have a quiet, calm beauty. They seem to share a love for one another and to portray gentle spirits. Are they mother and daughter or mother and granddaughter? Like so many others, this photograph has become cracked and brittle through the passage of time. The edges of the paper are broken and beginning to curl, yet the women's faces seem resilient and determined not to fade away. I wish I could sit down with them and peer into their world . . . but, sadly, I don't even know their names.

The following photographs are some that have touched my heart for their grace and beauty. They aren't the quick snapshots that we take today. Photographs in the past were often taken on a special occasion. Since most people didn't have their own personal cameras, they depended on a photography studio or traveling photographer. Some images will always remain a mystery, and others have a story to tell.

MOTHER AND CHILD

This photograph tugged at my heart and made me long to know the story behind it. It happens to be a photograph of Annette Scherer Robbins (from "The Fortunate Four") as a baby, being held by her beautiful mother. It appears to be a proud moment.

Annette had this to share about the photograph:

"My mother was a clothing designer. I'm sure she probably made the garments in this photograph. I was her first child. Sadly, she died after giving birth to her third child—all within three years. It was just too hard on her body."

How sad that this beautiful and talented woman had such a short life. I can clearly see where Annette got her full head of dark hair. Annette was three years old when her mother died. She was raised primarily by her grandparents and maiden aunts.

THAT SPECIAL DAY

*C*onfirmation—being accepted into the church—has always been a spiritual and special day. It marks the beginning of a girl's journey into young womanhood. In the past, it was a day of white lace and bows and celebration with family. This wonderful photograph preserves this day in the life of one young girl.

I discovered this photograph in one of my grandmother's old albums, and I just had to learn its story. She was my grandmother's childhood friend, Anna Anderson. What young innocence. Anna's hair is beautifully swept back and held with a large bow. She is adorned with a lace-covered dress. The intricate backdrop and woven chair provide the perfect setting for this special moment. I imagine the locket hanging around her neck to be a gift from her parents or perhaps an heirloom passed down through the family. This was Anna's day to feel pretty and special.

I can't help but wonder how the rest of the journey transpired for this beautiful young girl.

NO REGRETS

Phyllis Ranallo

This photograph of Phyllis and Elmer Ranallo was taken in 1942. I knew the final chapter in the story of Phyllis and Elmer, for I had seen the photograph for the first time at Elmer's funeral service in 2001 following his death from lung cancer.

After seeing this exquisite photograph from when they were a young couple, I had to learn from Phyllis just how their love story began. Here is the story that lies behind the photograph.

❧

Elmer first asked me out during my senior year in high school. I was raised on a farm near Turtle Lake, Wisconsin. Then, in my senior year, I moved into Cumberland, where I was rooming with three other girls so we could attend Cumberland High School. I was only 17 years old at the time, and Elmer was four years older than I. My friends and I went to a lot of dances, and I had seen him at some of them. I knew he had been engaged to Janice, who was a friend of my girlfriend Dola.

I was quite surprised that this "engaged" man was asking me out. Well, Elmer didn't actually ask me out. He waited in the truck and sent his cousin J. P. up to the door to ask me out. I told J. P., "If Elmer wants to ask me out, he's going to have to ask me himself." So J. P. brought me out to the vehicle where Elmer was waiting, and Elmer asked me himself if I wanted to go out on a date. I said, "But you're engaged!" He said, "Not anymore. I'd like to take you bowling." I said, "I don't know how to bowl." He said that he would teach me and that he didn't bowl very well either. That first date he bowled a score of 200!

We continued dating after that first bowling date. When Elmer proposed, I laughed at him. We were sitting in his car in the park by Beaver Lake. He was always joking around, so I thought he was kidding. I didn't believe him. He did finally convince me of his sincerity, and I later received an engagement ring. (I thought my dad would be upset at my getting engaged at such a young age. Fortunately, when I told him, he just said, "Oh, good." He really liked Elmer. He did add, however, "You better watch out. He's a popular guy. Lots of girls will be after him.") Our first date was on February 27, 1942. We were married one year later to the day on February 27, 1943. I was a young bride of eighteen years old.

Elmer was drafted into the service a short time before we were married, and he was sent to Japan. I remember he was seasick almost all the way over. The men were strapped into their bunks as the ship traveled through a terrible typhoon. When he did feel well enough to write, he wrote me love letters on toilet paper. I don't know if that's all the paper he had or what—I never did ask him.

We made our home in St. Paul, Minnesota, and for many, many years our morning routine would be to have breakfast at Serlin's Cafe. We would be there by 6 a.m. Oh, we made a lot of friends there among the other "regulars." Then by 7 a.m. we would be out walking—up to six miles a day. We walked together a lot over the years. When we were young, we even walked to our first jobs after we moved to St. Paul—Elmer to Booth Cold Storage and I to Trudeau Candy. Later it was walks around the lake or in the mall during the winter. We also spent numerous hours together creating and caring for our beautiful perennial garden behind the little house that we shared.

Elmer and I were married for 58 years, and we had a wonderful life together. When my daughter Candace was young, she thought we were rich because we took a trip every summer. We went to New York, to Europe three times—we had some memorable trips. She didn't realize that all year I had been putting money away out of my small paycheck to pay for that year's trip.

I miss our morning breakfasts and walks since Elmer passed away. I can still sense his spirit out in the garden and everywhere around me. Yet, I have no regrets. Not a day went by that we didn't say, "I love you." We never had much money, but we enjoyed life and we had lots of friends. Isn't that what life is all about?

THE WEDDING ALBUM

Wedding photographs are often filled with mystery and wonder. They catch a moment in time that is overflowing with love, excitement, and anticipation over what the future may hold. It is especially interesting to look at the images of couples who lived generations before us, for they hold incredible history. Did their dreams come true, or did tragedy lie ahead?

Nameless Faces—Sealed Wedding Dreams

This simple and elegant wedding photograph triggered my desire to begin recording and writing these stories more than ten years ago. I discovered it years ago in a box of forgotten black and white photographs at an estate sale. I was drawn to it and must have studied it and put it back in the box three times. I thought, "Am I crazy? Why would I want to buy this wedding photograph taken in the past of a couple whom I don't even know?"

Yet, their faces held such innocence and hope that I just had to buy it. I couldn't imagine this photograph—taken on their wedding day—being tossed into a box of useless items for the garbage. So, I paid the hefty $2.00 price (half price since it was the final day of the sale) and took it home.

To me this young couple represented all of the uniden-tified faces in old black and white wedding photographs. Many such photographs are gathering dust in a box in the attic and are eventually thrown out because no longer is any-one living who shared their history and memories.

This sweet young couple appeared to be no more than about 18 years of age. They couldn't continue to be name-less, so for years I have known them as Emma and Charles. I have imagined several scenarios as to how their lives might have unfolded.

But what is the truth? All I know is, based on Emma's wedding dress, they were probably married in the early 1900s. (When I showed my grandmother the photograph, she said that her sister Arvida had worn a similar style during this time period.) The photograph is set in a mat that tells us it was taken at the S. H. Neperud Studio in Blair, Wisconsin.

This is where reality ends and the dreams begin. I hope that someone out there will be able to identify this wedding photograph as a part of his or her family so that the mystery can be solved. I also hope that "Emma and Charles" had a joyful journey together.

❧

My grandmother had an old, worn leather album that con-tained cherished wedding photographs of friends and rela-tives. This album was stored in a large trunk with other albums and keepsakes. I have many fond memories of my grand-mother, my sisters, and me sitting close together on the couch with the photograph album on our laps. We would be huddled over the album, peering through its pages, as she would share the stories connected with the images in the photographs. Of course, none of the photographs were labeled since she knew all of the people in these photographs so well. They were all dear to her heart, and there would be tears and laughter as she shared the stories connected with each of the images.

I was drawn to two beautiful wedding photographs in her album. Wanting to include them in my book, I thought I had better confirm their identity. I opened the pages of that old worn album once again and this time wrote down my grandmother's responses. By the way, this was on the day of her 106th birthday. She was ready to celebrate her life with family and friends over ice cream and cake. I would say that this would be living on the edge of time, wouldn't you? (She passed away a month later, so I am glad that I didn't pass up this last-minute opportunity.)

Here are the stories that go with those two special wedding photographs.

Dave and Mabel Johnson

My grandmother Eva had talked about her best friend Mabel for many years. They grew up in the same rural community. She had met Mabel when they were both in first grade in the little country schoolhouse, and they immediately formed a special friendship and connection.

This romantic photograph is of Mabel and her husband Dave taken April 1917 on their wedding day. He looks like a handsome young man, and she is beautifully surrounded by silk, sheer netting, and flowers. What did the future hold for them?

As a child, Mabel had frequently struggled with health problems. Sadly, her life, her marriage, and her friendship with Eva were cut short when Mabel was yet a young woman. Mabel's daughter walked home from school one day as she always did. Upon arriving home, she found her mother dead. Mabel had died of a heart attack, leaving behind her husband and eight-year-old daughter.

Even after many decades, and now as an old woman, my grandmother's eyes would well up with tears whenever she shared this story about Mabel. She would start out by saying, "This is Mabel, and she was my best friend."

Not even the death of one of them could erase the emotional bond between these two women whose special friendship had begun when they were young children.

Swan and Lydia Carlson

What a handsome couple! The photograph was developed in rich sepia tones. Flowers adorn her hair, and the veil cascades to the floor. The abundant bouquet of flowers in her hand is trailing with ribbons as she is shown seated next to her new husband. I learned the couple was Swan and Lydia.

Lydia was my grandmother's sister. (You can read about Lydia in "Hilda and Eva—The Little Girls" and "Lost Love.")

Lydia Emelia Gerdin met Svante (Swan) Malcom Carlson while she was living in Duluth and doing housework for families.

Lydia and Swan were married just before Christmas on December 23, 1917, on her parents' farm. The house was beautifully decorated with evergreen boughs. Lydia continued to make Christmas a special time each year—she loved to decorate her home and make homemade candies.

Lydia and Swan had five children during their marriage. She was a strict mother but also loving and kind. She was game for almost anything. She went ice-skating with her children on the little creek behind their home. She also loved walking through the woods looking for wild flowers.

Apparently, Swan tried to teach his wife how to drive one day. They made the mistake of taking their five children along. There was so much laughter that she never tried it again.

Swan died in 1944—27 years into their marriage, only a few months after he was diagnosed with cancer. Lydia lived exactly 27 years more and passed away in 1971 at the age of 84.

The images Lydia's children remember about her are her pleasantness, her wonderful smile, and the toss of her head as she laughed. Her daughter Helen said, "Her laugh was always with her when we visited Grandpa and Grandma's farm. She and Aunty Hilda would sit on the old trunk in the upstairs hallway and visit and laugh until early morning. We all have wonderful memories of that smiling, happy person—our mother, Lydia."

What a wonderful tribute—to be remembered for your laughter and joy of life.

There is yet one more wedding photograph to be included. It is quite a contrast to the previous ones.

This happens to be a favorite photograph from my own wedding day in 1975. It reflects the feeling of free-  dom that was such a part of my growing-up years in the 1960s and '70s—just sitting in a tree amidst nature. The final chapters in my own journey are yet to be written.

We truly are each a prod- uct of our own era, and what reflects that era more than a wedding photograph.

PEARLS, LACE, AND THE GIFT OF MUSIC

Lucile Reding Johnson

While I was interviewing Arlene (Johnson) Graham, she laid out cherished family photographs all over her table. We talked about some of the stories connected to them. I was so drawn to the beautiful black and white photographs of one particular stunning woman who appeared in several of the photographs spread before me.

Who was this beautiful young woman? She had a serene gaze with a subtle smile. The flowing lacy dress and string of pearls around her neck in this first photograph reflected a sense of beauty and refinement. Her gentle spirit showed through in each of the photographs, and I was drawn to learn who she was. What were her dreams? Where did her journey take her after these photographs were made?

I learned the young woman was Arlene's mother, Lucile. Here is a brief journey into Lucile's life as told through the eyes of her daughter Arlene.

My mother, Lucile, was born on September 9, 1900, in Des Moines, Iowa. She was the second daughter of Ralph and Josephine Reding. She was always active in tennis, golf, dance, and music. When she finished high school, my mother wanted more than anything to be a dancer. However, this was around 1918, and the profession was frowned upon. "Nice girls" didn't do that. So she chose another love—music—and

Lucile and Stella

she enrolled in what is now the Julliard School of Music in New York. It was called the Damrausch Institute of Music at that time. Her older sister Stella was a student there already, so it was natural that my mother should follow her.

In fact, both of my mother's parents were also musical. Her mother played the piano, and her father played the coronet. Her father was a postal clerk. Her mother taught piano at Drake University in Des Moines, so this explains how they were financially able to send their daughters to such a fine music school. Stella and my mother shared an apartment where they each practiced the piano for five hours per day. (I can't imagine what the other apartment dwellers thought. I hope they liked music, or it must have driven them crazy.)

After finishing music school at the Damrausch Institute, Mother taught piano to students who were going to college to be kindergarten teachers. At that time, kindergarten teachers were required to learn how to play the piano in order to be able to play and sing with their little students. She had a third-floor studio in Cedar Rapids, Iowa. She received a wonderful gift from her grandfather. "Grandfather Johnson" was the head of the family, and he wanted to give her a Steinway grand piano. In order to get the piano up to her third-floor studio, however, they had to pull it up from the outside of the building and bring it in through the window. Apparently, things didn't go as smoothly later when they were trying to get the piano out via the stairway. It got away from them and, unfortunately, a man broke his back in the process.

Mother married my father, Robert Emmons "Bob" Johnson. (Ironically, my father was tone deaf.) He was born in Waterloo, Iowa, but only lived there until about the age of seven. I don't know many details of his life after that or how they met, other than that the best man in their wedding had introduced them to each other.

My parents were living in Omaha, and they had a strong desire to bring culture to the children of the community. So through the Parent Teachers Association, they brought the Junior Theater Production to town from New York over several years for plays and musicals. I was in grade school at this time, and I felt very privileged to be allowed backstage at the high school auditorium where most of the productions took place. The cast parties were normally held at our large home after the last performance. This was pretty exciting for a young girl. (I also remember helping count the mounds of coins brought to school by the children for streetcar money and admission to the productions. Admission was about 5 cents per student.)

Of course, as I was growing up, my mother wanted me to share her love of music. She had to pay me to take piano lessons, and she tried EVERYTHING to get me to practice. I remember that as I would practice and often hit a wrong note, she would call down from upstairs, "That should be a B flat." *B flat! I didn't know where there should have been a B flat!* I had no interest in practicing. I just wanted to run outdoors and play.

It had been recorded on mother's report cards while she was in music school that there was a "stiffness in the fingers." I now understand that this was the beginning stage of arthritis, which I also inherited. She was able to teach music, but due to the arthritis it would have been difficult for her to perform very often. Unfortunately, in later years it became too difficult for mother to play the piano at all.

My mother died on September 9, 1967, which was 67 years to the day from when she was born. After my mother died, my father found a good home for her beloved grand piano.

Lucile seems to have had the same artistic and poetic life that her portraits exhibit. She may not have been able to pursue her first dream as a dancer; however, she was able to spend a lifetime in her second love, music. It is sad that the pains of arthritis prevented her from stretching her musical talents to the extent she might have otherwise achieved.

I also got a chance to catch a glimpse of the woman from whom Arlene may have inherited her strong sense of adventure. I learned that in youth Lucile and a friend, both wanting to experience the intensity of a storm, had gone out on a boat on Lake Michigan. Of all the passengers, they were the only ones who appeared on deck the next morning. The other passengers were too ill from the storm, but these two adventure seekers had slept through the night. They had missed the storm entirely.

Lucile and her daughter Arlene

Lucile brought beauty, grace, and the gift of music to many who had the fortune to cross paths with her. She also helped touch the lives of many children through the theater productions that she brought from New York into her small community. The world is much richer for the gifts that she brought to it.

5
LOVE LETTERS—SWEETER THAN CHOCOLATE

I was born when she kissed me.
I died when she left me.
I lived a few weeks while she loved me.

HUMPHREY BOGART

WORDS FROM THE 1950 FILM:

IN A LONELY PLACE

HELLO, SWEETHEART

*L*ove letters are a feast to the senses—the texture and scent of the paper and the sight of the familiar handwriting. They are meant to be read slowly, drinking in each word, and then tucked away to be read again at a later time. With the addition of email, may the passions recorded through love letters not become a treasure of the past.

The author of this love letter wishes to remain known only as Charlie. This is appropriate since it could have been written by any number of the men shipped overseas during World War II. Even though his wife received this letter more than 50 years ago, it reflects the same yearning for home of men and women today who are separated by the war on terrorism. (The more things change, the more they stay the same.)

The Philippines   *Sunday, August 26, 1945*

Hello, Sweetheart

How are you today? Just fine I hope. I am OK but gee I'm homesick and blue. Boy, what I wouldn't give to be with my darling wife and kids. But maybe if I'm lucky I'll get to go home before too long from now. The sooner the better!

Gee I hope when we leave here we go back to the states but I bet we go somewhere else. Of course that's just what I think. I don't know for sure. You know I wouldn't mind being home where it's cold. It would be nice to come home to a nice warm house and a nice sweet wife. Boy oh boy. Say darling, do you still love me a little? I love you and miss you darling . . . honest. Well, I'll close for this time. Don't forget I love only my wife and kids. I am sending you all my love and kisses. Forever I'm yours and only yours.

Charlie

MY BUD,
YOU WOULD HAVE JUST LOVED HIM

Lorna May "Chloe" Hulbert
Story told by Elaine Johnson

Special friendships and connections are not always dictated by age. This story portrays the mutual admiration between two women with nearly a 45-year age span between them. One was beginning her journey as a young mother, and the other was filled with wisdom and humor that could only be acquired through years of living. A little touch of fate one white snowy day caused their paths to cross. They discovered an understanding and appreciation for each other even though they had grown up in such different times. A beautiful friendship was formed and numerous stories shared.

I had heard many stories from Elaine about her colorful and unique neighbor woman, Chloe (pronounced Chlo-e), and looked forward to talking with Chloe about her life. Unfortunately, she was one of the women whose journey on earth ended before I had the opportunity to visit with her. However, while Elaine and Chloe had morning visits over coffee or sat enjoying the blooming spring flowers, Chloe had often shared stories about her life and her love for her husband Bud. This is a recollection of some of the stories she shared. It includes a beautiful love letter from Chloe to Bud. These stories, combined with her letter, give us a glimpse into the journey of Chloe Hulbert. This story is a tribute to her and the life she joyously lived.

How fondly I think of and remember this dear one today. I met Lorna Mae (Chloe) Hulbert during a blizzard in November of 1992. I remember it was Election Day. I was catching a ride to downtown St. Paul, Minnesota, with my neighbor, Cindy, to go to my job at Minnesota Museum of American Art. I was 35 years old at the time.

An all-night snowfall had blanketed the city in pure white. Cindy and I drove north on Point Douglas Road through a good 8 inches of the thick, fresh white snow. As we neared Highway 61, I suddenly, and perhaps guided by fate, decided that I was not going to go in to work after all. I told Cindy to pull over and let me out. I was going to walk home, which was now about a mile behind us. As I walked back, I remember feeling free and happy about being out on such a day, enjoying the not-too-cold white world around me.

As I neared Chloe's house, I could see that she was out shoveling, and I knew that I would go up to her and introduce myself. She had been a familiar figure in my neighborhood over the years. I would often see her shoveling, weeding her bank of creeping phlox, iris, and lilies, or crossing the road from her mailbox. How strange—wrong—that in the ten years that I had already lived in this St. Paul neighborhood I had never stopped. I guess that's the downside of being trans- ported by a car rather than by one's feet. Isolation and anonymity are so easy when one moves through the neigh- borhood in a car.

Well, my connection with Chloe was immediate. I don't remember exactly what we talked about, but we liked one another right away. The fact that it was an election day came up at some point, and she mentioned that her son usually picked her up to take her to vote but that she hated to ask him to do so on this day of such deep snow. I happily offered to take her later in the day. I wanted the opportunity to spend more time with this older woman who, I could tell, was a special person. There was a brightness to her eyes and an intelligence and wit that was apparent right away.

That first trip to the polls together became a tradition that continued on for the rest of her life. We never missed one election. We'd usually go in the morning, and it became a habit for us to go out for breakfast afterwards. Sometimes it would be just the two of us, but as our circle of connections with others in the neighborhood grew, we would often be a group of four or five. We'd talk politics, fearful that our candidate wouldn't be able to pull it out, hear stories from our friend John, the river boat mechanic, laugh, remember past elections, and just enjoy the simple friendship of neighbors. Oh, we were lucky.

Chloe had been a Democrat her entire life. Talking about the state and national political scene was one of the prime topics in our conversations. Every day she would read the paper and then do the crossword puzzle with her morning coffee. She was often disgusted with the current state of affairs. She would tell me how, in the retired years of their marriage, she would comment or complain and her husband Earl (Bud) would say to her, "Chloe, you're getting crotchety." Then she'd laugh and say, "Oh, I wish you could have known my Bud. You would have just loved him."

Chloe's niece, Lilly, described her aunt as "the original hippy." Chloe was a free-thinker all the way. She usually voted for the Democratic candidate, but she was not bound to this. She voted for Ralph Nader for President two times, and she wrote in Mark Dayton for Governor once.

My friend Chloe was born and raised in St. Paul. She told me she was the daughter of a German mother and a French father and grew up with her three sisters and two brothers in a house on Portland Avenue east of Lexington Parkway. When Chloe was eight years old her father, who traveled cross-country in some sort of sales work, died. This was the year of the great flu epidemic, which I believe was what brought on his death. My recollection is that her mother had to take the train out to Oregon to retrieve his body.

Now a widow with six children, Chloe's mother raised the family with the help of her own mother and a sister who lived up on Thomas near Lexington Parkway. Investments provided the financial means. During the Depression, these investments were lost and the family entered a period of great struggle to make ends meet. Her mother took on some sewing and millinery work to try to earn a little, but food was still scarce.

In spite of their financial struggles, Chloe described their home as one that was always full of life. Friends of hers or her siblings would come and go with the doors always unlocked. Sometimes they would all be gone and come home to find a friend or two just sitting about contentedly. They were a family who read a lot and discussed a lot. They were thinkers, writers, and painters who made what they needed, pulled pranks on one another, argued about literature, art, and politics, and were competitive with one another intellectually.

As a student at Central High School, Chloe was separated out into a group that received greater challenge in their coursework. She didn't like being separated out and felt some awkwardness socially during her high school years.

It was during these teen years that her mother's attorney and friend, "Uncle Louie," got Chloe a part-time job with an office that handled the paternity and child support issues of unwed mothers. Chloe told me many times how her boss was a tight-laced woman who did not approve of her. Chloe's dress, the manner of her hairstyle, her stockings—these and perhaps other things became issues of disapproval. I would guess that it was really Chloe's spirit that was the problem. Her intelligence, wit, and passion must have been too much for this woman who wanted things gray and contained.

Chloe also worked at the Pioneer Press during these early adult years. She would refer to this job sometimes in our conversations when she was disgusted with women for claiming harassment in the work world. She said, "Of course there was harassment. You just dealt with it. I used to have to walk down a hall at the Pioneer Press and would always be hassled by a particular man, but I just ignored him. You learned to not let it affect you."

As a young adult, Chloe and other siblings continued to live at home with their mother. They all contributed to the financial needs of the household. In the end, though, her mother lost the house. During the years that I knew her, Chloe wrote an account of how the house was lost to them. It was Christmastime and the house was all decorated, including the "snow dolly" in the tree. One evening as they sat visiting with friends and family, a man from the bank came in to show the house to a buyer. They could not imagine that this would ever happen. This was their home!

As a resident of St. Paul, Chloe fondly remembered Sunday afternoon strolls on Summit Avenue. Men, women, and children would all be dressed up. She described her

Uncle Louie as being somewhat of a dandy, with a vested suit, bowler hat, and umbrella. As he and her mother would walk along, he would swing his umbrella and tip his hat to the ladies that they met along the avenue. Chloe told me she knew the names of all the families that lived in these mansions.

Walking as a means of getting around was the common way in Chloe's life as a young person. She and her sisters would regularly walk to the river, to Lake Harriet, to Lake Nokomis, or out to Battle Creek for a day of picnicking and then back home. A walk totaling 15 or 20 miles was not considered unusual. A yearly family treat was when her mother would get them all together for the streetcar ride out to the amusement park in White Bear Lake.

Sometimes, Chloe would tell me stories about her aunt and her "little" German grandmother. These two women lived together in a house with a vacant side yard nearby that became a garden space for flowers and vegetables. She remembered her grandmother pulling a wooden wagon full of goods from the garden over to their house. Chloe as a little girl would sometimes accompany her grandmother on these walks, and she would be "mortified" when her grandmother, wearing a little black hat and dressed in clothes that were not "modern," would pause on someone's stoop for a rest.

It was in her grandmother's yard that Chloe learned her love of gardening. She would tell me of sending her son Al off to school, stooping to pull a few weeds, and being stunned to see that the bus was there dropping her young son off from his morning at kindergarten. A few hours in the garden had slipped away like minutes.

She loved digging in the soil. Time spent pulling, planting, and pruning was the delight of her heart. During the last two or three years of her life, back problems and her aging body prevented her from doing the gardening, mowing, and snow shoveling. She missed this outdoor work life so much. She couldn't even bear to sit on the steps outside her front door anymore because it made her so unhappy knowing she couldn't do the chores she loved. She used to tell me, "You know, I've never been depressed during my entire life, but now I am. It drives me crazy that I can't do this work."

A few years before I met Chloe, her husband Earl (Bud) had died of cancer. I'd seen him out in the yard at times but regret that I never stopped to meet him. Chloe loved Bud. She would say, "I wish so much that you had met Bud. I can't stand that you lived here all those years before you met me and you never knew him. Well, you would have just loved him. You wouldn't think I was anything special if you had known Bud."

Chloe would go on to say, "Bud could do anything. He was such a good writer. He was both a thinker and good with his hands. That's why John reminds me of him so much." (John was the neighbor who is a writer, storyteller, riverboat pilot, and mechanic). She would add, "Oh, how I miss Bud."

Chloe often told me the story of how she met her husband Bud. It would go like this, "My mother-in-law used to say she picked me for Bud, and you know she really did. It was through her and Bud's sister that I met him. I was taking a writing class that they were also taking, and she used to tell me that she wanted me to meet her son. Well, at the time he was in Mexico working as a laborer on some project. When he returned, she set it up that after one of these night classes, we would all meet at a bar."

I don't remember what details she might have recounted to me of this first meeting, but I know that it did not take long for the two of them to decide that they were strongly attracted to one another. I believe that Chloe and Bud married sometime after she turned 25 years old.

She used to tell me of how she had girlfriends that she thought were so silly because they were so focused on getting married. She recounted with a mocking, moony tone how an acquaintance had said, "Maybe I'll marry Tom" after a first date. As for Chloe, she was very happy, thank you, being an independent female and would only change that status if there was a man fine enough to make her think that such a partnership would be a better life.

Chloe would sometimes refer to how she and Bud were meant to be together. They had so much in common. Both had come from families with four daughters and two sons. Both families lost their fathers while the children were young and the mothers were the sole support in the ensuing years. The intellectual life was an emphasis in both households. Both Chloe and Bud were natural writers. She liked to say he was so much better at writing than she was. In their work lives they did not earn their living from writing, but Bud had had some short stories published in *Harper's* magazine.

She and I would spend time together fairly regularly, especially during that first year. I quit my job shortly after meeting her to have more time for my family. So, I also had more time available for running errands together with Chloe, visiting over coffee and the paper, or admiring the blooming lilies or irises.

Not too long after meeting her, my husband and I decided it would be fun to start a book group that, of course, included our new friend Chloe. Starting small, the group eventually numbered 10 to 12 friends who were mostly from the neighborhood. This group became a highlight of life in Highwood for us all. (Highwood is an historic neighborhood in the bluffs overlooking Pig's Eye Lake southeast of downtown St. Paul.) Chloe was the wise matriarch of our group and often reminded us to consider our reading from a critical perspective. "But what was the theme? It's got to have a theme," she would say. This emphasis on theme came to her from writing classes that she took with a Minnesota writer and activist. This Minnesota author became friends with both Chloe and Bud and actually spent one summer living in a small trailer in their backyard.

My friendship with Chloe was pretty amazing. We had a mutual admiration. Though there was a nearly 45-year age span between us, it did not prevent us from having a closeness that is a treasure whenever one finds such a friendship. I believe I was meant to come into Chloe's life at a time when she was struggling somewhat with loneliness. She used to say, "You are the closest thing to an angel that I've ever met—and I have met a lot of people." She missed the companionship of her husband and did not at that time have any neighbors who provided a social connection for her.

"You understand me," she would say. How lucky I was to have her as a friend—someone who was born near the turn of the century, had lived through all the changes of time since then, had loved deeply and lost many of those most dear to her (a husband and adult son to cancer, and her only daughter-in-law to diabetes), continued to live a life of intellectual pursuit, loved a good joke, and cared so deeply for me.

My dear friend Chloe passed away on March 20, 2001. (She had been so convinced that she wasn't going to live to see the year 2000, but she did.)

How fortunate I am for having in my collection of cherished possessions a beautiful letter that Chloe wrote many years ago to her husband Bud. Their love for each other is apparent as she shared descriptive memories of their first summer together as husband and wife. This letter touches my heart each time I read it.

✿

Dear Bud,

I remember the long stream of cars that flowed around Lake Calhoun and the colored lights that played on the fountains and the way the lamps looked against the trees at the side of the lake. I remember sitting with you on the benches and kissing and stopping on the path to kiss . . . and kissing again in the dark under the trees.

I remember the sweet smell of flowering bushes, the smell of the lake, and the smell of the rain. I remember how we walked in the rain until we were sopping wet and your Aunt Lizzie peering at us out of a closed car. We didn't care, did we?

I remember how you sold all the magazines at the magazine stand on Lake and Hennepin and reading the funnies and looking at the New Yorker cartoons.

I remember the soft way our footsteps and the jukebox sounded in the beer joint with the padded walls . . . and sitting holding hands across the table.

I remember the way my blue slacksuit looked in the long mirror outside of Walgreen's. I don't remember seeing you in that mirror, being very vain and always looking for myself because it was a wonderful full-length mirror. I could walk at it from a distance and think delightedly and secretly that no one had the least idea that we had a baby under that blue slacksuit.

I remember just how it feels to go into the Chinese place with tables very close together and white table covers and air condition-ing after being on the hot street and how it feels to reach the Hasty Tasty and go in out of the rain. I remember the harness shop and the store with nothing in it but old magazines and books, another one that was called Wade's Rotisserie, and the Jewish Delicatessen where we bought Kosher corned beef. I also remember the Uptown Theater with the pink striped top and the fancy pink toilets.

I remember how quiet our new apartment looked when we would first step into it and the curtains all in a row billowing out at the same angle in the breeze. I remember the twilight always there when I came home and how I would hear the soft pong of tennis balls across the street. If the paper was gone, I knew you were home. I would come in quietly so I wouldn't wake you. You would be lying flat on your stomach on the bed. I remember how you held me. It got dark sometimes, and we forgot about dinner. We let the door-bell ring and ring.

It used to be fun taking a bath with the window open over the bathtub, feeling the wind or rain coming in, and then coming out in my bathrobe just as you came in from work. I know just how that apartment smelled. I certainly cleaned it clean, scrubbing the woodwork every Saturday and trying to live up to the good exam-ple the industrious five had set. But you cleaned it cleaner—wash-ing the floors, which was a thing I never knew until later and was probably very bad for the varnish. I wondered how you could always mop the floors so much shinier than I could.

We had fine Sunday breakfasts and would then lie on the beaches of Lake Calhoun, go swimming, and watch the sailboats. It was good that summer, wasn't it, with the electric fan clanging, your white flannel pants and the cleanest shirts you ever saw, and candles on the table every night.

Our writing class was just a few short blocks away then. I used to come all the way over from St. Paul for it and wouldn't think of missing class, but when it was just a few short blocks away, we never went. Who cared about the writing class anyway?

Do you remember how you took me canoeing right in your backyard, so to speak? The lake was all black and mysterious with the lap, lapping of the water against the boat. The nausea of pregnancy was rocking my vitals, so it wasn't half as wonderful as it should have been. Only, I didn't want you to know. The pipe that you had cultivated just to please me suddenly set my stomach swaying, also. I didn't want to tell you that either.

I remember your wearing your green gabardine pants and white shoes and how you sat on the chair backwards holding your pipe in your hand. I still remember how wonderful you looked the first time I saw you without a shirt with your suspenders over your naked skin. You were wonderful and sweet, and I loved you very much.

In our other apartment, I remember how you had stood in the doorway at the end of the closet during the night to protect me and show me the way back to the bathroom. I also remember the hot water in that apartment and the skylight, which made it seem as if it were always raining outside. (Remember how we had looked for an apartment while ankle deep in soft wet snow with snow melting and running off our hats?) I remember the girl coming in to clean when we were lying in bed and the smell of gasoline from the buses outside our window.

I remember you brought home those white plates and the goose liver stuff whose name I can never remember. You protested when I washed your socks. I remember we once paid 65 cents for breakfast because it included a salad of lettuce, tomatoes, and French dressing. That was at the Happy Hour. I remember the tall blond girl who was a hostess there and who worked with you at the Ramona Café.

I remember the times I had my head in your lap and you would lightly stroke your fingers over my eyelids. We read short stories, and you told me some of the poetry you knew. A piano tinkled from another apartment.

That was a wonderful apartment, too, and I remember just exactly how it smelled. Do you remember one night when our friends Vic and Kay called on us? I thought, "These people have been married for several years!" That seemed incredible!

Once after we moved, we went to see the Garwicks, Kenneth and Izora. I thought it was wonderful because their house was so big and bare with nothing in it but the two of them and their piano… but they didn't even seem to know it was bare. We played the piano and talked. Only, Kenneth shut you up when you started to say something that sounded very learned. It impressed me enormously. They told us when the honeymoon was over we would become bored and start to play cribbage.

I remember wonderful things about you. I can think of you and know exactly how it feels to touch you and how warm or cool your skin smells. I know how it feels to carry your baby inside of me (his buttocks next to my heart) and how my heart almost stopped when

I felt him move the first time. I remember the look of wonder on your face when I let you feel him. I remember wonderful things about you. I am happy because I love you.

Chloe

Both Chloe and Bud won my heart. I was touched by the intimacy they shared. Chloe's letter is such a visual glimpse back into a simpler time for them as newlyweds. I like to picture the two of them curled up on an old couch while Bud softly stroked her hair and recited poetry to her. A warm summer breeze would be blowing through the curtains and piano music from a neighborhood apartment would be drifting into theirs. They just totally enjoyed being together and were oblivious to the rest of the world around them.

Throughout her life, Chloe's passions were many—writing, discussing politics, gardening and, of course, her love for Bud. Their love that started out in this little apartment only grew stronger because they challenged each other intellectually, loved passionately, and appreciated the individual spirit of one another.

My thanks to Elaine for sharing this beautiful story about her friend Chloe and their most unusual friendship. Perhaps many would have seen Chloe and simply seen an old woman shoveling snow. What unexpected gifts Elaine was given by taking a moment to meet Chloe and connect with her spirit. Both of their lives were enriched by the friendship that began one snowy day in 1992.

THE LITTLE RED RAMBLER

Eva Gerdin Olson

Story shared by Joy Kuby

My mother was going through an old family trunk recently and discovered the wedding announcement belonging to her parents, Eva and Herman. It was on plain paper that had become brown with age, but the wording was simple and elegant. It announced to their family and friends the beginning of their lives together in 1921.

This is their announcement and wedding picture. It portrays a handsome young man and his beautiful bride.

Mr. & Mrs. John Gerdin

announce the marriage of their daughter

Eva Eleanor

to

Mr. Herman Olson

Saturday, July the sixteenth

nineteen hundred and twenty-one

Maple Ridge, Minnesota

In the same trunk was also discovered the following note that Eva had written and slipped into an anniversary card to Herman many years later in 1992.

Herman,
This is our 71st wedding day.
How nice it would have been if
you could have taken me for a ride
in the old red Rambler.
Eva

Again, they were such short, simple words, yet Eva's tender note expressed the reflection of a lifetime together. Somehow, 71 years had quickly slipped by since their wedding announcement. They were no longer that handsome, vibrant young couple in the wedding photograph, but her heart was filled with love and rich memories. Herman and Eva now found themselves in their nineties and no longer able to drive. I'm sure that she longed for a carefree ride in Herman's treasured shiny red Rambler—a simple ride like they had experienced so many times over the years.

Herman and Eva were from the wonderful era when couples would go out for a Sunday afternoon drive through the countryside. The cool summer breezes could be felt through the open car window, mixed with the scent of dust trailing behind the car from the gravel road. It was a chance to appreciate the natural changes of the seasons, observe how tall the corn had grown in the fields, and perhaps stop in to visit the neighbors. The visit would usually be combined with coffee and a fresh-baked cake that was ready "just in case" someone dropped by.

The words in Eva's note also seemed to reflect a longing for the closeness they had once shared. Herman had suffered a couple of slight strokes, which had affected his memory and mental clarity. He was most likely unaware that it was their anniversary.

I am Eva's granddaughter and this note, meant for only my grandfather to see, brought a smile to my face. I remember all the times I would be happy to see them come driving up our long country driveway in that same little red Rambler. It also created sadness in my heart for the changes and loss of freedom that are inevitable for each of us toward the end of our own life's journey.

This 71st anniversary turned out to be their last one together. Herman passed away later that year in 1992. I'm sure Eva never imagined that she would live an additional ten years.

LOVING YOU, EMIL

Donna and Emil—you read their tender love story in "The Bride and Groom Show." Theirs was a romance that developed at the Glen Lake Sanatorium through love letters secretly passed through the help of cupids—particularly that of a Latvian woman. Donna looked forward to receiving the sealed love letters handwritten by Emil, usually on light blue stationery. Donna's love for this sweet, gentle man grew as she was drawn to his spirit—mainly through his letters.

Today Donna has more than 25 letters that she received from Emil, written primarily between January and May of 1952. They have been safely tucked away in a box for the past 50 years. The blue ink has begun to fade over time, but it is still legible. Each letter is treasured and tells a part of their story. The spelling of some of the words, such as the word "fahr" for "far," and some of the interesting sentence structure only add character and reflect Emil's challenges to learn the English language. I thank both Donna and Emil for being willing to share excerpts from them.

The letters tell the story of how their love quickly grew. They also tell the story of Emil's past and of life in a tuberculosis sanatorium, much like being in prison with its limited "privileges." They tell of an era that thankfully most of us know nothing about. The letters refer to names such as Mrs B., Pappy, and Ma Swallender. All were part of the staff at Glen Lake that became like family to Donna and Emil. The letters tell of how much Emil missed Donna on days that she was not working and during the period of time that she was away following her mother's death. They tell of the sorrow over the death of her mother and the support she received from Emil. As Emil wrote, "Shared sorrow is half sorrow." Best of all, they are sweet love letters that resulted in a happy ending.

This first letter is the earliest letter in Donna's collection. It reveals she and Emil were just beginning to "fall for each other." It also tells of Emil's past struggles in life.

January 2, 1952

Dear Donna,

I'm so happy about your letter and your honest way to tell me everything about your problems. I sure will be glad to answer you because your problems might be mine and vice versa. I hope you'll understand my poor English and forgive that.

Yes, Donna, Mrs. Brachmann is right. I'm loving you like no one before. Don't ask me since when and why. My heart feels like that and I can't help it. I'm thinking of you all the time, and you come even in my dreams. I'm just wondering how Mrs. Brackmann knows that. I haven't told her or anybody else a single word, but I feel that you like me. So, now you know . . . I like you, too.

There isn't much to tell you about my past, but I'll try my best. As I told you once before, I was born on a farm. I started to work for my dad at seven, taking care of all the farm creatures.

Later I had work in lumber camps and railroad stations driving horses and loading lumber until finally I turned to be a mechanic. In 1944 the Russians came back to Latvia, so I joined the Latvian Army to fight against them. I served as a machine gunner and mortar man in Latvia, Poland, and Germany until at last 1945, April, we were in Berlin. All of us that were left decided to go west over to the Americans and surrender. I spent eleven months in different P.O.W. camps in Germany and Belgium. When they did let me go free, I started to work for the U.S. Army in their auto garages. After three years in that business, they gave me an A1 degree. Of course, when I came here, I started all over from the bottom again.

My plans for the future are pretty dark yet, because I won't be able to work my old job. So I would like to be a tool and die maker because I love to work with my hands.

Dear Donna, maybe this letter will help you decide where to go. I'm alone in this country, without friends, and my relatives from Australia can't help me much. As you see, I can't promise much for my little girl except my best thoughts, my love, and my two arms. I'm so depressed sometimes about my helplessness that I'm losing hope. But now your letter is giving me new strength because I know for sure that you like me. That would be so wonderful to go together with you, to love you, and keep you warm. It doesn't matter how hard that would be.

Well, I better finish this so I can meet you at the show.

Emil

January 3, 1952   Oak Terrace

My dear little girl!

I think I was kind of confused yesterday too, that it all came so sudden—your letter, the movie, and your hands. Donna, I didn't *realize that a girl's hands could be so wonderful. I didn't sleep much last night because of my thoughts . . .*

Donna, I'll be missing you these days. I'm missing you every day you don't work. Thanks for the address you gave to me. I know my little girl will be thinking of me while reading this.

Please write to me, that is if you feel like it and have the time. I was going to send you a little picture of me, but I'm afraid you wouldn't like it. It's poor looking.

Good night!

Love, Emil

January 5, 1952   *3rd East*

Dear Donna!

I'm sitting here alone and writing. Everybody else is asleep and snoring. Thanks for your letter. I'm not worried anymore, and I'm glad we are coming closer and closer together. Also I'm thankful for your telling your parents about me. Forgive me that I haven't written my mom and dad about you yet, but it's only a couple three days ago since we sat in the movie. I sure know my mom will like you very much. She's always been understanding about the way I'm going, and she's never been disappointed in me or in the rest of her kids. I wrote to her some time ago that the girl I'll marry will be American-born. She said that's up to me.

Donna, could you spare a little picture of you to send to Australia? I know how delighted my people would be for that. I have one of you but I hate to send that away. I would then have none left to look at when you aren't around.

I don't feel that you would be cold towards me, Donna, while you are on duty. That's natural. You should be like that, and you're right about that Nursing Office, too. I'm happy enough just from seeing you every day, and from now on we'll be sitting in movies together. I'm thinking a lot about going for walks, too, when I have some exercise. I can imagine how wonderful that will be together with you.

My little Donna, I haven't enough words to tell you how happy I am just because I can call you mine. I don't think you'll miss the other fellow's diamond either. After all, there are things that are worth more than all the world's diamonds and gold put together.

Be good, you are a darling!

Emil

January 7, 1952

Dear Donna!

I should have written you sooner. I know you're waiting for this, and I shouldn't let you wait. Thank you for the invitation for a ride on your birthday. I sure will be there. I kind of planned that before but didn't have a chance to ask you.

After my discharge, I would like to go to a vocational school to learn something to make a living with. I can't go any place like I am because I can't do even paperwork in an office. Auto repairing and welding would be too heavy to start again. I don't have a heart to think about your making a living alone for both of us. The other version I have is to find some job right here in Oak Terrace, and we could stay here for a while.

So, I said it's just planning, and we can't make any decisions yet unless we have sure grounds for them. First of all to get more privileges. One thing I know for sure. I wouldn't want to see the girl I love crying and disappointed if things wouldn't go like they're supposed to.

Donna, I love you. I'm longing to put my arms around you and hold you tight—forever. But God only knows when that time will come. I'm glad, Donna, you are a Methodist—I'm a Lutheran. That's right. I was worried you might be a Catholic. I don't like that kind of worshipping God very well, because of those ceremonies and sacrifices. I'm not a special churchgoer, but it doesn't stop me from going God's way and living right.

I'll be missing you more from now on because I'm not allowed to stay in the hall after the privilege. They sure broke my hours yesterday. I blew off some steam too, but there is some left inside me and I have a suspicion that I did lose my sweet ol' pal, Miss L. Maybe I'm a bad boy after all, but I didn't mean to.

I'll see you again, Darling. I have a little gift for your birthday. (It's not a ring.)

Love, Emil

January 9, 1952

Dear Donna!

You sounded kind of sad about that Mrs. B. talk. Donna, don't listen to them. She is just an old lady and her mind must be different than ours, and maybe she didn't mean that so bad after all. Anyway, she didn't want to hurt you.

Once before Christmas we had a talk about you. She said that she likes you the best of all the girls on our floor. I was in love with you long before that. I can tell people's characteristics pretty well by the expression of eyes and face, so I liked you right away. I haven't ever thought of you as being dishonest. I wonder what people might say about me. So, it isn't worth it to worry your sensitive soul about that there might be some more talk. I have faith in you and I'm trusting every word you say, and I know you'll believe me.

Yes, we haven't talked about marriage yet, but I'm sure which way we are going. I know you would like to marry me and I like you, too. Donna, you're the only one for me to marry with, and I'll do that as soon as possible, though I don't think it would be wise for us to get married before my discharge. But I would be willing to do that even if that would be the very first day outside here. What do you say?

I have a pretty strong feeling that one chapter of my life is closed. It was the darkest one with long and endless nights, but you have brought a light into it with new hope and love in my soul, and you have your hand to help me out. Donna, I can't describe my feeling towards you. Just a plain "love" isn't enough.

I'm sitting here in my corner and thinking of you. I saw you last night in my dreams. I wrote my mom yesterday all about you, but I didn't mail the letter yet because I hope to get the picture from you.

Well, see you in the movie tonight. Be my good girl until then.

Love, Emil

January 14, 1952

Dear Donna!

I can't explain my feelings right now, but I know there goes something wild (inside me). One thing I know, I'm very, very much in love with you. I need you all the time, but still there's the cruel life between us that keeps us, at least for a while, apart. Darling, I thought about that plan for going to your house for the weekend, but it's impossible right now. I'll tell you why. I'm afraid I'm still positive. That was about three months ago when they took a culture while I had a bronchoscope in my lung. Seems to me they can't find out what's wrong. X-ray is clean and also my bronchial tubes. Now, about a month ago, they started to give me a "strep." Maybe it will help. So I think it's better for every one of us if I stay here until we are sure.

Darling, don't mind this talk, but God only knows how much I love you and how dear you are to me. I don't want any harm to happen to you or your relatives.

Darling, take good care of yourself and don't work too much. It seems to me that you do sometimes and you look tired.

Love you, Emil

January 15, 1952

Darling!

Thanks for the letter. You have such a wonderful way to write them that I wish I could do the same. But I have a feeling that my letters sound kind of cold. Do they? If they do, darling, I hope you'll understand my difficulties expressing my thoughts in a foreign language that I've been talking only two years. But you should know by now that my heart is full of warmth, even if I haven't a chance to let you feel that. Darling, I feel almost like physical pain, because we are so near to one another, but at the same time, so fahr away. We can't even hold hands. I sure will be glad when I'll be gone to the cottage, so we'll be able to arrange our dates more often.

Donna, you are so sweet and wonderful, and you care so much about me that I'm so happy I could cry. (The roughest ones sometimes do.)

Love, Emil

Sunday Afternoon

My Darling!

I'm trying to read my history book for tomorrow and writing to you at the same time. Anyway, I can't get my thoughts on history. How are you doing, Darling?

Donna, I made about one-third of that purse. If it turns out all right, it will be for you, my girl. And I'm sure I'll finish it before your birthday. Darling, please tell me the color you want, because I don't have any idea what color clothes you wear outside of here. You have the last word to say because I don't know much about things girls like.

Darling, I have been pretty lonely without you around. We don't have much time to talk of course, but I'm feeling different when I know you're here all the time. Last night I had a dream about you. It's not a long time ago since we met, but I have a *feeling that we are standing so near to one another that no one can part us. No one can stop us from making our life together. It's just a matter of time.*

We had a little wine the other night. Phil opened his jug, but we didn't get drunk. Darling, do you like wine? I hope you do.

Well, it's time again to say "good bye" sweetheart. I hope to get some news from you soon. I'm loving you very, very much because "Ich Hab' Nur Dich Allein." [The English translation to this German quote would be "I'm yours alone."]

My love, Emil

January 17, 1952

Darling!

I'm going wild about you, especially since last night. Darling, I have a thousand things to tell you, but when I'm near you I just can't find the right way. I'm full of love, and I feel it growing every hour greater towards you. I love every little thing about you—the way you talk, the way you act and look. You look very sweet and pretty. Please believe me. I'm not telling you compliments because you don't need them. And there's still a long week ahead of us when we will meet again.

Donna, I asked my doctor this morning about the ride. He says it is all right if the weather is good. But I think I'm going anyway. Even if the weather is bad and nobody will be out, we still can spend a couple hours down in the Blue Room together. Tell me, how's that?

Did you write me, Darling? I hope you did. I'm going to write you with that address you gave me. I'm expecting a letter from you very much, and I know you do the same. That sure is God's way that led me over here near you from so fahr away, and I hope all good spirits will keep us together.

I'll be 26 on May 15. Pretty old man, isn't it? My pa got married at that age and had his first baby when he was 29. Do you think I shall do the same?

The boys were teasing me a little this morning, but they think the best of us anyway. Darling, the dinner is here so I have to stop. Be good, as all ways!

My love, Emil

January 18, 1952

Hi Darling!

How's my little girl this morning? I'm freezing to death in my corner—the wind is from this side. How about warmin' me up a little?

Darling, you're in my thoughts all the time, and I'm smiling when I think about those happy hours we have spent together. Arneson (Ralph Arneson, the married patient) can't figure out why I'm smiling once in a while as I read my history book. He thinks there's something funny about that, but he doesn't know where my mind is wandering. I think it's kind of romantic to sneak around a corner with you and to steal kisses from you.

Everyone thinks that I have the sweetest and best-looking girl in this place. I know it's true. Also, I had a compliment about you from Mrs. Arneson. My sweet little girl, maybe you don't realize that yourself—how lovely you are. If I wouldn't know that you're trustworthy, I would be jealous all the time.

See you, Darling.

Love, Emil

January 19, 1952

Hi!

How's my baby? It's cold outside this morning. Darling, I haven't finished my breakfast yet, but I wanna get this letter ready before the mailman comes. I'm thinking of you, my darling girl. How are you dressed and how are you looking while you read this? I know the answer! You look pretty as always. That's too bad—I look like a bum this morning. I haven't shaved yet, so I got some "compliments" from Miss Grattan and Ma Swallender already. That's the thing girls won't understand—the poor man's soul. It sure feels wonderful to wear three-days-old whiskers. I know you won't be on my side either, so I'll grab my razor as soon as I finish writing this.

My Old Man Doctor has written down in the "Book" that I can go for a ride anytime I want. It's pretty good, isn't it? He is sometimes like my good old Pappa to me. One guy told me that Dr. Mattil gives a privilege every ten days after that six-month period in bed. We sure will be going for a long walk at the time of my birthday if he will do the same with me. I bet everything is romantic here by that time.

Darling, I'll finish this. I'll write you again at your local address. Be real good now and take care of yourself!

My love, Emil

January 21, 1952

My Darling!

Thank you so much for all you have done. Those trousers sure look pretty, and I like them very much. They are just the right size, too. I'm trying to find somebody in this place who could hem them up. So, I think, Donna, the best way would be when you'll be going to Minneapolis next time, to take the trousers back to the store and have them finish them. They do that without extra charge, too. Darling, I just can see all those troubles you are going through because of me. You are such a brave little girl, and I appreciate that very much.

Donna, it's a good idea to buy yourself a skirt like that. We'll be a couple of swell looking kids when we'll be going out together. I almost can't wait. I'm glad that the 28th is coming up. Hope things will start moving better then.

Darling, I'll ask Dr. Matill for those couple extra hours. I don't see a reason why they would hurt me. There's many much worse patients that go for vacations. Anyway, he wouldn't hang me just for asking and even if he wouldn't agree, we can stretch out those hours a little longer. Everybody else does.

Darling, Donna, I was expecting to see you today but didn't. You know how that is to be in love, and you are just the right kind of girl to be crazy about. I'm feeling sometimes like starting some troubles and to get kicked out of this floor so we could meet much more. But I don't think you would like me to do that. I wouldn't like that either. It was just some thoughts. Maybe it's best to wait.

(January 22)

I didn't finish the letter yesterday so here goes some more. Darling, I'm thinking of you even in my dreams.

How do you like the name, "Mrs. Grinvalds"? That's what your name will be. I'm feeling like you would be my little wife already. Do you think the ceremony would bring more differences in our emotional feelings? It might and it might not because we are so much in love.

Even our present names are some sort of relatives. "Woods" and Grinvalds." My name comes from German "Grinwald" meaning green woods or green forests. Darling, it sounds like "sweet nothings" but there's some truth, too.

Well, I suppose I won't see my baby today, either. Couldn't you come to see me even for a minute or so today? If not, we'll be seeing each other tomorrow at the movie. I'll take a seat about the same place where we sat last time in case you'll be late. By golly, I saw you!!! It took the breath out of me. Goodbye!

Love, Emil

January 24, 1952

Darling!

I didn't sleep either. I woke up about four times and every time my blood was just boiling. I kissed you, Darling, and I'm full of happiness but I'm kind of confused, too. I still think it's a crime to kiss you on the lips, and you're the last one in the whole world that I would like to get hurt. Darling, isn't there any records at the nurse's desk of all the patients?

Please find that out—am I positive or not? I've been trying to find out for the last couple of months myself, but you know how my doctor is. I hate to get real tough on him. I haven't been for a check-up for more than four months. It's my only chance to get a look in the records down in his office. Every time he comes he says that he doesn't know or doesn't want to know.

Donna, please don't think of me as being silly or scared. It's only for your sake. I care so much about you and TB isn't for taking chances with. My God, how I wish I would be negative.

Be good, Darling. You are wonderful! Good night.

I love you, Emil

p.s. I'm going to send one of your pictures to my ma because she wants to see you so much.

January 25, 1952

Darling!

I'm wondering how my girl is that I'm loving. I'm thinking of you, Donna—your wonderful arms and lips, and your brown eyes. I did receive a letter from my mom. She tells me to say "hello to the little brown-eyed girl." Darling, she tells me to be a good husband to you and to keep you warm because life is so rough sometimes. She is very glad that I have a girl like you to go together. She says also that for husband and wife "shared sorrow is a half sorrow, but shared fun is double fun." I think she's right. Also she sent this money order. Please, Darling, if you're going to the P.O. today would you take the money out for me? Thanks, Honey. There'll be eleven dollars. It's signed already, too.

I had a talk with Al Dahlgreen tonight. He says that he likes you and me going together and he stands for us. Ma Swallender teased me this morning and asked who I'm making the handbag for. When I didn't say the name, she started questioning me about the "sweet little chick" I was sitting in the movie with. She's one of the nurses I like the best. We were fighting some times when I was still in the surgical room because I didn't want to exercise my sick arm and hated so much to sit up and have a back rub. It was kind of fun, though.

Well, it's time for bed now. It's 9:30 p.m. For you, too. I think in the future I should make you to go in bed earlier, about 9:30 or 10, instead of doing that 11:45 or 12. How's that? I just would love to pinch you if you wouldn't listen to me.

Good night. Emil = heart. I'm giving you all my love and thoughts. See you smiling and with love in your eyes for me now.

Love, Emil

January 27, 1952

Darling!

Darling, I asked for a second privilege yesterday. My doctor groaned something about next week (which is now this week). So when I get this privilege, I may go to make a phone call with the nurse's permission. I know Mrs. McDonell would allow me to do that. Tell me, Darling, how can I get you by the phone? I could do that about 2–3 nights a week, after 7 p.m. Maybe we could meet some place and be alone for some 10 to 15 minutes. Wouldn't that be wonderful? Darling, I'm missing you so much that it almost hurts me. To put my hands around you and to hold you tight even for a short while would be like heaven.

Yes, Darling, my mom is a good and wise woman. She has not much education and schooling but education from the great life helps a lot. She has always been honest and unselfish to other people and has taught her kids to be the same way.

I know, Donna, she would like you like one of her own children because you're the same way we all are. My family is just a middle class one, too, but we were highly respected among our neighbors in Latvia.

She told me that she is going to write you, and she will because I told her that we are going to be married. (Aren't we?) I just couldn't tell her when.

My Darling, Donna, I would like to get engaged and I'm wondering about that every day, though I can't ask you. You can guess why. No, it's not my TB, and it's not because I couldn't make up my mind. I have done that a long time ago.

Listen to me, Donna, and tell me if it's all right with you to wait about two to three months. Please, Honey.

Well, I think I'm just talking too much.

Love you, Emil

January 29, 1952

Darling!

Yes, Donna, I would like to meet your mom and the rest of the family. We could arrange it in the auditorium or when I have a ride again after two weeks. How's that? And also I could meet you one extra time during the week. I can't ask for it this week because there will be two passes already. Darling, I'm so upset sometimes because we can't make a certain date. We can't be sure about anything because those rules can be interpreted in many ways. Or maybe we are rushing things too fast. But we are wild about one another and it's natural to be so. I sure know if we both would have been outside we would have been married in the first couple of weeks after we met. It doesn't sound sensible, but when one is so much in love — why wait.

Darling, I wrote to the rest of my family and a couple of my friends in Australia about us. They sure will be surprised because they don't believe in real love. They say that girls in Australia go for a moneybags and for an easy life and they are hard to please. They think that Americans are the same. If they just would see the difference.

I'm telling them that there isn't any more perfect country and prettier girls than ours and it's the truth.

Yes, Honey, I want a wife for next Christmas and no one else but you, my Donna. I hope all the best spirits will help us to become a husband and wife. 'Til then we must be patient too, because things won't turn out well if rushed.

I'm giving all my love, Darling, and I'm just feeling your arms around my neck too.

Love you, Emil

Donna and Emil had to be careful about their time together. They didn't want it to threaten the security of Donna's job. This letter is in response to some apparent gossip on the floor.

January 30, 1952

Darling,

> *We won't give a chance for anyone to complain about us while you're on duty. On the other hand, it is nobody's business what you are doing on your time off. Nobody has a right to say something about your private life. It belongs to you even if they would hear some gossip. If they are going to kick one of us off this floor because of that, they'll do that anyway no matter who tells them. And if they won't, they won't. Well, it's just my point of view.*

> *This letter is going to be a short one. I'll be seeing you tonight and I have still plenty of algebra to do. My teacher is coming at 11:15.*

> *Yes, Donna, Carey is right about you and you have the prettiest ankles, too. A girl can't be more perfect than you. You can be proud about the way you look. I love you so much, and I'm proud of you, too.*

> *Since I met you, I don't see other girls anymore and my eyes are for you only. I don't care much about the whole world because I want to care for you only, my girl and wife to be.*

> *Darling, it's time to finish. Don't mind the rush, but I hear the mailman.*

'Til tonight. Loving you, Emil

February 1, 1952

Hi Darling!

How's my girl? I'm pretty happy, too. I got the pass for 12 hours from 8 a.m. to 8 p.m., and I'll be all yours for the entire time (if I last that long). Now I'm praying like hell there won't be a blizzard tomorrow. They can cancel the pass.

No, Donna, I don't have any special plans except to be with you for your birthday. It's your privilege to make the plans and have all the fun you want. We could go to church, have dinner together, maybe even a movie. Well, 12 hours isn't very much time to be together, and we shall make the best out of it.

Darling, please don't make me too popular. Somebody may get disappointed because I'm not that type at all. Especially I have hard time with strangers. I wish myself that I had a louder mouth and a lot of wild stories to tell. That's what my sisters tell me—that a girl can't get any fun out of me.

Well, I guess my x-ray must be OK. They wouldn't let me go otherwise, and God bless my Pappy's ol' hide, too, for being so good. Darling, you do that and tell him sometime. Let's see what he has to say.

Now be my good baby 'till we meet.

As always loving you, Emil

February 12, 1952

My Darling!

How's my little girl today? The place feels kind of empty without you around, my Donna. Even if I don't see you, but when I know you are here, it's different.

Oh, baby, I'm puffing and tired out. Just changed the linens on my bed and took a bath. Mrs. Stratten promised to give me another reading of the rules. I don't mind that so much. The privileges alone are worth it. One privilege after another and pretty soon I'll be able to meet you every night.

Donna, I wish we were married. It's too much strain on us, and we don't dare even to talk in front of other people. Everyone seems to think that we are fit to be good mates. And now good-bye 'til tomorrow.

Love, Emil

February 16, 1952

My Darling,

Darling, I am so happy that Matill says you may work 8 hours a day. I bet you are, too. It's better to be careful for a while. You know, Darling, I am thinking that you could gain some 5-6 pounds before you start the 8-hour days. That wouldn't change your looks. You would be just as lovely and there's some protection then. Tell me, what do you think?

Darling, I'm so crazy about you already even though we aren't married yet, and I'm trusting in you and have a feeling that nothing will ever get us apart. You're the one I want to live for and for any price. I don't want to lose you.

Be my baby! How about a little kiss for goodnight?

Love you, Emil

p.s. My Darling, try to get over your loneliness. I'm lonely, too, but days full of happiness will come for both of us.

February 19, 1952

Hi!

Darling, yesterday when I came from my class I wanted to kiss the little charge nurse at the desk. Crazy thing, isn't it? I think you would be a wonderful charge nurse all the time.

Baby, "the door to my heart is wide open." That's a song some cowboy is singing. It's true, but for one girl only and she has already entered. I'm speaking of you, Donna, from my heart. And I'm going to keep you there forever. You will be like a little cheerful canary in a golden cage.

Darling, you don't mind my getting romantic, do you?

Well, it's 6 p.m. You must be here soon and I'll see you. I still say you're the prettiest one in the whole place, and I'm the lucky guy you're loving. A man just can't be more lucky than I am.

All my love is for you, Emil

Emil mailed the following two letters during the dark days after the sudden death of Donna's mother. Donna had gone home for the funeral, and Emil was missing her desperately. (Unfortunately, Donna's mother died before Emil could meet her.)

February 24, 1952

Darling,

Please forgive me if you don't feel quite like reading my letter now, but I'm thinking of you all the time and I would like to be with you to say something and to share part of your sorrows.

Since Friday morning, when Margaret came, I haven't heard anything from you, my darling, so I'm wondering how you are and what you are doing. I don't expect letters from you—just a couple of lines.

Donna, there has been so many dark days in your life and these maybe are the darkest ones, but I know you'll get over it. You're the quiet, serious type of a girl that is able to stand up, no matter what comes. I'm telling you, there are still plenty of sunny days left, though. It's always like that and I believe in that myself.

It's time for sleep now, Darling. Everyone in porch is broke down with colds, including me.

(continued on February 25, 1952)

Hi! Today is the date for the 4th privilege. At least we may be happy about that. Donna, every time I'm thinking of your mom I feel a lump in my throat, just like it would have happened to my mom. You'll be lonely without her, because no one can replace a mother. Maybe my mom could, but she's so far away.

Darling, please write me just a couple of words.

Love you, Emil

February 26, 1952

Dear Donna,

Did something happen to you or are you angry with me? I don't think it's either one. I'm feeling kind of sad lately because there's no news from you. Darling, I'm not the only one that cares. We all are thinking of you. Some nurses want to send flowers, but we don't know where the funeral is. I don't know what they decided to do after all.

Donna, maybe it's not fair to interrupt you like this in your sorrow. Some people want to be left alone in cases like this, but I still believe that "divided sorrows are half sorrows."

Darling, do you understand me? I don't have sweet words, but it doesn't mean that I don't have a warm heart and warm feelings towards you or any of your family. I often thought of your mom and wished to be a good kid for her, like one of you—but it's too late now and I didn't even have a chance to see her.

There isn't anything new around here except almost everyone has colds and noses in bright red color. I had a letter from my Australian mom. She has some good news and some bad news, too. She tells me to give you all her love. She likes you very much and says that you look "lovely and sweet." (Darling, you do.) She did spend her free week with my ill sister in Adelaide—it's a 1,300-mile trip from Sydney. Doctors haven't decided yet to give my sis a surgery or not.

The bad news is that something terrible is happening to my grandpa (mother's dad) in Germany. He got sick about a month ago and now they had both his legs amputated. I can't think of anything worse that can happen to a 78-year-old man. She couldn't say what the cause was. How cruel a life can be.

Darling, it wasn't a very good letter. It seems that all the worst happens at the same time. But so it is. We sometimes think we are out of luck, but when we take a good look at the fellow next to us he always seems to be a little worse.

Please write me, Darling, if you have a spare minute. Hope to see you soon.

Loving you, Emil

February 28, 1952

Darling,

I finally got your letters. Thank you! I surely was worried about you. It seems that I can't live any more without you around, and the mail is so slow.

I'm a little tired today from working and running around too much. I made one $9 billfold and started another one—a fancy one, too. I'm feeling my old strength coming back in my weary bones, and I'm glad that I've something to do.

I went to the movie last night dressed up in my blue jeans and plaid shirt. I was lonely without you, but I "saw" the movie. It was "Smuggler's Island" with Jeff Chandler.

Donna, I have a class Monday afternoon, but I'll be going for the ride anyway if your uncle will be coming. And from now on we may arrange dates more often down in the auditorium or Blue

Room. I'm not asking anybody's permission anymore and nobody minds if I'm going to the store, O.T., or the movies.

Darling, better days are coming for us. I have been thinking about us getting married, but I still can't get a place and can't set any real plans. I'm thinking about going to school, but I don't know how I could arrange that—to get married and go to school—or to go to school first.

Honey, would you tell me your thoughts, please. You haven't told me anything yet. Of course, it's wrong to build a dream house before the time comes. I'm never doing that, though we must plan something. I have been used to things for me alone, but now we'll be two and it's different. It's like a strange world we're going to enter. The worst thing is that I haven't been living a normal life for the last eleven years.

So long, my loved one. 'Til Monday.

Loving you, Emil

Time has passed and it is evident that Emil is getting stronger every day. Along with that, of course, come more freedoms and "privileges."

April 4, 1952

Darling,

Dr. Matill was here for a visit this morning, too. He's nice and kind to me just like a father. I asked him for some days off. He wanted to know what I'm going to do and where I would stay. He doesn't want me to tear around and "paint the town" for a whole day if I don't have a place to stay.

Bill Odden invited us to his place for some days this summer. We often talk about life and serving in the army and P.O.W. camps. Baby, I'm kind of lonely without you—still four more days to go.

Well, I have to get the letter down to the P.O. in time. This was not a good one, but I should say like my "buddy" Bill always says that I just don't feel so "hot."

Love, Emil

April 14, 1952

Hi Darling!

Goodie, goodie! Good news today! My purse has been sold, so we'll have a "big" roll of money to spend. At least we'll have a big juicy steak for dinner, and I can't even think of what else we'll have.

Also, I had a letter from the "lil ole man" (Waldemar Strantins). He seems to be kinda excited about us. He likes you and says that you're for me and wishes us both the best of luck.

Darling, I mailed your package. I'm very glad to do something for you. I don't have much chance to help you—so never mind the sentiment. Just give me the works.

Love you, Emil

May 1, 1952

Darling,

Donna, I also like the way you are and wouldn't like you to be different. We're enjoying being with one another and never in my life has time gone so fast. I love every little thing about you, and I like very much the way you choose your dress.

Maybe I'll see you in my dreams. Good night.

Love you, my Darling!

Love, Emil

It was a short time later that Donna and Emil became engaged. These beautiful letters had helped them through the various stages of Emil's recovery from tuberculosis, the death of Donna's mother, and daily frustrations and celebrations. Many feelings and dreams were written in the letters that they perhaps felt too shy to speak of during their limited time together. The letters had been their daily connection to one another and had forever united their spirits.

The year, 1952, was a most memorable one for Donna and Emil. Their romance began through these letters in January, they became engaged in May, and they were married in New York on the "Bride and Groom" show in December. The rest is history.

6

LOVE AND LAUGHTER

Laughter is wine for the soul.
Laugh soft, loud, or deep.
Comedy and tragedy step through life together, arm in arm.
Once we can laugh, we can live.

SEAN O'CASEY

IRISH PLAYWRIGHT

THE ICEMAN

Inez M. Kullberg
1889 to 1984

Some family stories are just too priceless to be forgotten and are repeated throughout the generations. Avis Carmody Kuby shared this story about her mother, Inez.

Mother was an artist and a free spirit. When I was growing up, we would spend wonderful summers at our cabin on Lake Minnetonka in Minnesota. She enjoyed the freedom of doing housework in the nude. I remember many times my mother would be down on her hands and knees in the nude scrubbing that old wood cabin floor.

I also remember one time the neighbors at our cabin were making a trip to Florida. I said, "Bring me back an alligator." Wouldn't you know—they did just that. Mother usually "went with the flow of things," and she let me keep the baby alligator in a small pond that we dug near the lake. (It got loose one summer in Lake Minnetonka and scared some folks half to death.) In the winter it found a home in our

Inez's free spirit shows through while she relaxes on the beach. (She signed the photograph with "Inez, 1916".)

bathtub. We had Alex, the alligator, for years until it got too big, and we donated it to the Como Park Zoo in St. Paul. But I'm getting sidetracked with my story.

Several years later, my mother's free spirit got her in a bit of trouble on a particular day back at our house in the city. The house was set up so that the milkman, iceman, and meterman could access the porch and cellar without entering the house. The back porch to the kitchen had a door to the outside as well as a door to the cellar and a small door/hatchway on the wall between the kitchen door and the basement door. This hatchway led directly inside into the back of the kitchen icebox.

Mother had been doing some morning housecleaning in the "buff" when she suddenly realized the iceman would be coming shortly. She hurried down the long hallway that led to the kitchen and grabbed some money out of the cookie jar to put in the porch side hatchway to the icebox. Reaching for the hatch, she heard the outside door open to the porch.

There wasn't time to get back down the hall, so she jumped behind the cellar door with the "money in hand" as she covered her private parts. Much to her surprise, the door opened. It was the meter reader—on his way to the cellar. "Oh!" she said in surprise, "I was expecting the iceman!"

I think she got even more embarrassed when she realized how that sounded. Our family has had many laughs over the years with that story. It is a gem!

Inez was a delightful woman, with a sparkle in her eye and a love for life. She continued to live her life as a free spirit and artist. She taught watercolor classes almost until her death at the age of 95. (Inez also married an artist. Her husband Ernie was a commercial artist. Some of his well-known artistic contributions include the Indian maiden on Land O' Lakes butter cartons, the first "Land of Sky Blue Waters" waterfall theme for Hamm's Blue Waters beer, and one of the Betty Crocker portraits on the side of General Mills cake boxes.) Their combined artistic talents were passed down to their children and grandchildren in an abundant supply.

Inez's grandson Mitch had this to say about his grandmother: "She was always my mentor from ever since I can remember. She even went with me when I applied for and was accepted at the Minneapolis College of Art and Design. I still miss her. She was always my best friend. She was the best!"

I only knew Inez as a woman in her 90s, so it was a surprise to hear this humorous story from her daughter Avis. Thanks for the laughter.

WHERE'S THE BEEF?

Hilda Swanson

1893 - 1996

Throughout the generations, sharing a household with the in-laws has never been an easy task—especially when they are older and often set in their ways. This is a humorous story of how my great-aunt Hilda coped with her situation.

My husband Charlie and I were busy raising a family. His folks (simply referred to as Grandpa and Grandma) were getting up in years, and it was becoming obvious they were no longer able to live on their own. I suppose Grandma was about 86 and Grandpa about 83 at this time. We knew they needed to move in with someone . . . but no one wanted them. They could both be quite difficult to get along with—they had a dose of that Swedish stubbornness, I think. In their later years, Grandpa was bossy and always arguing about something and, oh, how Grandma liked to complain. They had a daughter living in St. Paul, Minnesota, but her husband wouldn't have them. They also had two sons living in St. Paul, but neither one of them would take them. Therefore, it was up to Charlie and me. The family agreed we would get the family farm for taking care of them as long as they lived. We also had to pay the other siblings a certain amount in exchange for the farm.

So . . . Grandpa and Grandma sold their house in town, and they came to live with us. I had never worked so hard! We fixed up the living room as a bedroom for them. It had doors, so their room could be closed off in the evenings. They would sit in their room, and Grandma would be complaining. She didn't want to come back to the farm, so she was always complaining about something.

Of course, I can be kind of mean, too. One time their oldest son brought a great big roast for us to cook. I used to bring supper in to Grandma because it was hard for her to get out to the kitchen. So I put a piece of this roast, vegetables, potatoes, and roll on a plate and brought it to her on a tray. She always left something. No matter what you gave her . . . she left a little bit. She'd *never* clean her plate. Well, that evening I overheard her complaining to Grandpa about the small portion of meat that had been on her tray. She said all she got was a tiny piece of meat—just a corner, with some potatoes and gravy. That's all she got!

I was steaming mad, so the next day I took a platter and filled it . . . I mean really filled it . . . with potatoes, gravy, vegetables, and the biggest piece of roast beef you've ever seen. I set the platter down on the table in their room. Grandpa was going to help her. Then he looked at the tray and said, "Vad i hela varden!" (This was Swedish for, "What in the world!")

Grandma never said a word about it, and Grandpa helped her eat what was left. It was probably childish of me . . . but it certainly felt good!

Grandma lived with Hilda and Charlie until she died eighteen months later, and Grandpa was with them for a total of six years. Hilda had to make many adjustments and learn to deal with an issue that we will all face—caring for aging parents. Humor certainly helped her deal with some of these stressful times with her in-laws.

Hilda herself enjoyed a long life and lived to the age of 104. The cycle of life repeated and she, in turn, lived with her daughter for many years. I feel fortunate to have captured this little vignette from everyday life before she passed away. Thanks for sharing it, Hilda.

STROLLING WITH A STRANGER

Ruth Swanson

*T*his little story happened many years ago, but Ruth remembers it well. She is a petite woman married to a taller husband, which you will see has its ups and downs.

Some years after our marriage, my husband Ken and I were attending a wedding at the Baptist Church in Stanchfield, Minnesota. After the wedding ceremony and reception were over, we were walking out to our car. I tucked my arm into my husband's arm. We walked a bit, and when I looked up I saw that the face of the tall gentleman beside me was not my husband, but a stranger to me! Ken stood back a ways—just smiling. Oh, how embarrassed I was! Ken said that I had given this bachelor a thrill.

A CHANGE OF PLANS

Irene Christiansen

When Irene met Bob more than 50 years ago, she was attracted to his good looks and nice personality but especially to his great sense of humor. At the time, neither of them could predict just how much they would need to draw on this sense of humor in their first few weeks of marriage.

Bob and I met at South High School in Minneapolis, Minnesota, in the 1940s. The school was getting ready to celebrate its 50th anniversary. Plays and stage shows were being put on as part of the celebration. We were both performing in what was called the Floridora Sextet, in which we sang and danced. We got acquainted during these performances, and Bob asked me to his senior prom. (He was a senior, and I was a junior.) So I went with him, and we had a very good time. We had dinner at the St. Paul Hotel in downtown St. Paul, which was very exciting for a 17-year-old girl. We attended the prom with another couple. After the dinner, I remember, we drove around and around the downtown streets in this other guy's car . . . with no particular destination in mind.

Bob graduated that spring. Then I didn't see him again until the next September when his class was having a reunion at a place called Eaton's Ranch. He invited me to this reunion where there were hayrides, a wiener roast, and horseback riding. We started dating steady after that. We seemed to bond right away—we completed each other. I guess you could say we were a matched set.

The following January, Bob joined the Navy Air Corps. He began his training to be a pilot. A third of the way into his training, a bunch of the guys that were in pilot training were washed out. Bob's folks received a discharge letter from the Navy saying that their need for pilots had been reduced. (In the beginning, pilots were being killed off left and right.) The majority of men in Bob's class got washed out of training. Bob and many of the others went into the regular Navy instead. The worst part about this was that they had to go back and go through basic training all over again. Then the Navy wanted Bob and his friend to be gunners—on the underside of the plane—where they would be sitting like ducks waiting to be shot. The men said no to this assignment.

Bob and I had been dating about a year when we became engaged later that fall. I was 18 years old, with the same dreams as most young girls—dreams of a special wedding day surrounded by my family and friends. I would never have imagined that I would be getting married in a room full of strangers. Let me tell you how this came about. We had made plans to get married when Bob was home on leave, and then his leave was canceled. You can imagine our disappointment. We decided that I would go out East, and we would be married where Bob was stationed, at Neumann's School in Lakehurst, New Jersey.

There wasn't much time to prepare, but I did purchase some items for my wedding trousseau. I bought a beautiful gold suit with a cardigan neck and three large brown and gold buttons. I also bought a kelly-green, brushed-wool coat at Young Quinlan's, a brown felt hat, and brown leather sling pumps. For lingerie, I purchased blue silky pajamas and a blue quilted jacket with peach lining to wear over them. New Daniel Green satin slippers completed it all.

On December 16, 1944, we got married in the chapel where Bob was stationed. Of course, Bob looked wonderful in his uniform. He had a good friend, George Scott (no, not the actor, George C. Scott), who served as his best man. Since I was far away from home and knew no one, I didn't know what to do about a maid of honor. The guys just flagged down a WAVE (a woman serving in the Navy), and she stood up for me.

We were limited on time, and in our rush the Justice of the Peace had forgotten to sign the marriage license. The priest laughed and said, "This is the most illegal marriage I've ever performed. We've got to get this marriage license signed." (It did get signed later after we were married, so our marriage became official.)

Our best man, George, lived in one of those big brownstones in Jersey City. Talk about a generous spirit—George and his family put on quite a reception for us. George's parents were Scottish. (They spoke with a strong Scottish accent.) To make room for our reception, they had taken all of the furniture out of their living room and had even set up a phonograph in the corner for dancing. Several tables had been shoved together out in the kitchen. George's mother was busy in the kitchen along with a few Jewish women who were fussing around. You could hear an interesting mixture of Scottish and Jewish dialects as they prepared the wedding dinner. These women were cooking and laughing—just having a ball. They prepared a big chicken dinner for us—quite a wedding feast. George's relatives and some of his neighbors were there and ate with us also. After dinner, the sweet sound of music filled the room as the old phonograph played its tunes, and we danced and danced. Even though our reception was made up of a room full of strangers, it was wonderful. The room was filled with warmth, laughter, and good wishes for the two of us.

Then George's parents surprised us with a room at a nearby hotel for our wedding night. The only problem was that since we hadn't known we would be staying overnight, we hadn't brought any bags. When we got to the hotel without any luggage, the hotel manager questioned if we were really married. We had to call George's mother—the one who had made the reservations—to verify for the hotel manager that we were indeed married. It's funny now, but it was embarrassing at the time.

Bob and I were able to spend two weeks together as husband and wife before I had to return home. We were honeymooners, and this was our first Christmas together. Being far away from home, our place seemed empty with no signs of Christmas. Bob went out and cut a Christmas tree (illegally, I'm sure) and made a wood stand for it. We put it on the table, and the smell of fresh evergreens filled our small living space. I tried to find ornaments for our little tree. Because of the war, there were no ornaments to be found. It was time for some creative thinking. I found some artificial poinsettias with silver petals. I took these petals apart so they looked like individual silver leaves, and I hung them on the tree. Then I got some green and red yarn and made little yarn people and hung them on the tree, also. When Bob got off the base and came into our room, he was happily surprised at the sight of the decorated tree. This was our first Christmas memory together.

Our brief honeymoon had to come to an end, and I returned to Minnesota. I had probably been back home for only a few days when I received a call from Bob. The men were getting their orders. They would be going down through the Panama Canal and then coming into the port of San Francisco before being shipped overseas. He said that we had to try to see each other again before he was shipped out, so he asked me to meet him in San Francisco.

I got on a train and this time headed west. The trains were so crowded during the war. They didn't want to have much to do with civilians—service men and women had top priority. The railroad car didn't get cleaned once during the entire trip out to San Francisco. I remember there was a young woman who had a baby with her, and she needed to have a bottle warmed. The conductor could have easily taken the bottle back to the kitchen, but he wouldn't. It was just a zoo.

No food was being served to the civilians on the train. When the train stopped in Reno, Nevada, for about 20 minutes, the conductor said, "There's a restaurant about two blocks down." Everybody got off the train, and we ran to that restaurant. I stood in line looking to see what they had to eat. It would have to be something I could take with me back to the train. The only lunchmeat they had for sandwiches was headcheese. It was the worse looking stuff I had ever seen in my life. So I left without a thing to eat and ran back to the train.

When the train was pulling into San Francisco, people threw banana peels and garbage at the conductor. They were so mad at him because he wouldn't do anything for that poor woman with the baby. All of us had received hardly any service the whole time.

It had been a three-day train ride from Minnesota out to San Francisco. By the time I got there, I was both exhausted and famished. Bob and one of his friends met me at the train depot and took me over to the hotel. Since I was starving, Bob went out to get me something to eat right away. As hungry as I was, exhaustion took over. I collapsed on the bed and quickly fell fast asleep. When Bob returned with the food, he couldn't awaken me. I was comatose, I guess. He finally just gave up. The next thing I knew, he was calling me at 5 o'clock in the morning. The men were being shipped out—he was going to war to some unknown place in the South Pacific. I had traveled three days to get to see him before he left, and I had slept right through our time together. I couldn't believe it!

I lost the hotel room the next day because they found out that my husband had been shipped out. (The hotel didn't cater to civilians either.) So then I went to the traveler's aid and managed to get a room for one more night in a different hotel.

My aunt lived in Redmond, Washington, so I decided to buy a train ticket to go visit her before I started my journey home. This train trip was a zoo, also, let me tell you. My train car was like an old smoking car—filled with wooden benches and with a potbelly stove over in the corner. This was an overnight trip, but traveling coach, as I was, I had to sleep sitting up in my seat. I remember there was a couple on this train car who were just as drunk as skunks. The woman was very well-dressed. It would have been interesting to know their story. They could have been somebody famous for all I knew.

After visiting with my aunt, I left for my train ride back home. A year and a half passed before Bob and I were able to see each other again and celebrate his safe return home. We were then finally able to really begin our life together.

Now, 58 years later, we have welcomed 11 children, 21 grandchildren, and 8 great grandchildren into our family. The laughter and sense of humor that carried us through those first few weeks of marriage have certainly sustained us in the many years that have followed.

THOUGHTS ON AGING

When I'm an old lady
I'll sit on a stool,
I'll paint pretty pictures,
And wear my muu-muu.

The sun shining down,
I'll plunk on a straw hat
That folds up in the front
And droops down in the back.

I'll look rather stylish,
Old fashioned and quaint,
I hope that my neighbors
Don't grimace or faint.

Each stroke of my brush
Will create a real treasure,
For in my old age
I'll enjoy all my leisure.

While others are fussing
At afternoon teas,
I'll be by myself
Doing just as I please.

Irene Christiansen
6/15/02

Riding the Streetcar

Ginny Elmer

There is one family story that always puts a smile on my face, especially around the holidays.

My parents, Beulah and Dana Lawrence, were gathering some friends together for a New Year's Eve party one year. This was many years ago—before World War II. They lived in Minnesota in the St. Anthony Park area. Perhaps my parents didn't own a car—I'm not sure. At any rate, they were taking the Como-Harriet streetcar down to Eisenminger's market, a well-known meat market, to buy some Limburger and Leiderkranz cheese for the party. These were both delicious, but very smelly, cheeses.

Well, the streetcar was bustling full of holiday passengers, all traveling to their own destinations in preparation for the New Year's Eve celebration. In fact, it was so full that my parents weren't able to get two seats together. Mother found a seat many rows behind Father. As passengers got off, my mother would move up to a vacant seat and gradually get closer to where my father was sitting.

A seat next to my father finally became vacant, and she sat down next to him. She said, "Everyone that I sat next to had such bad body odor!" He thought for a brief moment, smiled, and said, "Take a smell of that package you are carrying." Here she was the smelly one with her package of smelly cheese. What a hoot! Just think what the other passengers were thinking about her.

Father would often set the package of cheese on the radiator to make it nice and soft. Would that stink! He loved it.

7

DREAMS IN A BOTTLE...
AND OTHER BURIED TREASURES

We shall not cease from exploration
and the end of all our exploring
will be to arrive where we started
and know the place for the first time.

T. S. ELIOT

THE LEGENDS OF XANADU

*"There is a place where late summer breezes
whisper in the old maples and the setting sun casts a
magical golden light. This place is Xanadu Island."*
—Alice M. Vollmar

❧

At times it is a location rather than a specific person that
has had a very romantic and intriguing past. I felt com-
pelled to include the following fascinating story about
such a place.

The romantic and magical place of Xanadu Island is
located, surprisingly, on Elbow Lake, which is in west-central
Minnesota near the quaint town of Battle Lake. Xanadu
Island's stately trees and deep, clear water have held a secret
for decades—the mystery of the lost diamond.

This story actually begins back in 1922 when millionaire
J.C. Jones of St. Louis discovered this secluded and wooded
five-acre island while on one of his annual fishing trips. He
named this romantic spot Xanadu after the poem "Kubla
Kahn" written by Samuel Coleridge. Coleridge wrote, "In
Xanadu did Kubla Kahn a stately pleasure-dome decree."
J.C. fell in love with the beauty of the island and purchased
the property to use as a summer retreat for himself and his
wife. His wife happened to be Clara Morgan of the well-
known J.P. Morgan family.

Ed Everts of Battle Lake worked for J.C. Jones in the
1920s and early 1930s as fishing guide and general

groundskeeper. His father owned the lumberyard in town. Ed remembered the day that J.C. arrived at the lumberyard and said that he was going to build a little shack out on Battle Lake. They didn't hear anything more until a few months later when plans for his "little shack" arrived in the mail. Ed's father started asking around since no one knew who J.C. Jones was. A millionaire by the name of P.D.C. Ball, who had owned the St. Louis Cardinals at one time, knew of him. He said, "Jones is good for the money. Build what he wants. Anything he doesn't pay for, I will." So the building began . . . and went on and on. Apparently J.C. had to have everything just so—no expense was spared.

His little shack proved to be a mansion-sized stone and cedar home that contained three large stone fireplaces and beautiful vertical-grain paneling. He included six French doors that led from the wraparound porch to the large living room. The house had a warm and rustic elegance. He also included servants' quarters on the grounds—the maid's cottage, the groundskeeper's cottage, and the housekeeper's cottage. There were buzzers installed in the house connected to the servants' cabins. The servants were on call 24 hours a day and were paid at the end of the summer.

This story takes place during prohibition, so J.C. also included a secret trapdoor in the master bedroom closet. It led down to a room in the basement where boxes of bootleg whiskey were hidden. From time to time, J.C. would give Ed, his groundskeeper, contraband with instructions to "do something with it," saying, "Hide it. Don't tell me where it is." So, Ed got to know that basement quite well.

However, Ed Everts thought of Mr. and Mrs. Jones with only respect and affection. He said, "The Joneses were the most generous people I ever met. Sure they were rich, but they weren't stingy. Mr. Jones had the policy of always asking the going rate for things—then he would offer 25 percent more." He added, "I remember one episode. It was the 3rd of July, and Mr. Jones and I were making a trip into town together. Mr. Jones saw some young boys walking into town, and he asked the driver to stop. Mr. Jones asked, 'Are you boys going into town tomorrow to celebrate the Fourth of July? Then you will need some money.' He gave each of the boys $25."

The 1920s and '30s were a wonderful time for J.C. and Clara. She was the love of his life, and they often enjoyed entertaining their special friends on the island.

Legend has it that on a warm summer afternoon they and their guests walked down to the lake for a refreshing swim. One of the guests that day was a wealthy young woman from the city who was wearing a walnut-sized diamond ring on her finger. Sometime either during the swim or on the walk up the path from the lake after the swim, her sparkling diamond was lost. Where could it be? Everyone, including the maid, the gardener, and the housekeeper, joined in the search. They peered into the clear, cool water and scoured the land, but it had simply vanished.

Ed Everts, the groundskeeper, also had recollections of that lost diamond. He said, "The Joneses always had company—usually other millionaires—and that was in the day when a millionaire was a millionaire. One guest, a wealthy woman from back East, had gone swimming wearing this huge diamond ring. She said that she remembered seeing it when she got out of the water, but by the time she walked up the path toward the house the stone was gone. I must have spent three days on my knees looking for that diamond. Never did find it."

Just as in the fictional story of the Titanic where the elderly Rose Calvert returned the coveted sapphire necklace to the sea, it appeared that this mystery guest's diamond had returned to the elements of the earth.

As far as we know, her walnut-sized diamond has never been found. Is it lying at the bottom of the lake or buried in the sandy shores? Perhaps it is lying near the path under the protection of a half-century of leaves that have fallen in preparation for the many winter days. The mystery of the lost diamond will probably remain a mystery forever. If you listen carefully, perhaps you will hear the answer to this secret. It may be whispering in the rustling leaves of the golden maples of Xanadu.

Even though J.C. and his wife Clara had abundant wealth, their lives did not prove to be without sadness. Clara Jones had been married before, and she apparently had a son who had been accidentally killed. Every year on the anniversary of his death, she would stay confined in her room all day. She wouldn't even come out for meals, as she grieved for her son. On this day once a year, Xanadu Island was the place of solace for healing her heart from the loss of her son.

The story also goes that Clara Morgan Jones became very ill at some point and died. J.C. was so distraught at losing his wife that he locked up his beautiful summer home and servants' buildings and left the island, leaving everything behind.

He never returned to his beloved Xanadu—a place of laughter and sunlight, which had become hushed by his sorrow.

However, this story does have a happy ending. Xanadu Island has had a few owners since the days of J.C. Jones. Romance, light, and laughter have again returned to the island. It was purchased by a couple in 1960 who converted the servants' cottages into summer rentals. The rentals were never advertised, but for a few select families the island held over 40 years of rich summer memories.

It is currently a bed-and-breakfast where guests can catch a glimpse of a time long gone when this area was a playground for millionaires, near what was then the edge of the wilderness. Xanadu's stately stone mansion continues to sit proudly on its bluffs, half hidden by majestic maple trees. At night, the moon shines through the leaves and casts a warm glow over the lake and onto the massive stone walls of the cottage. Some of the original furnishings, including a trunk bearing J.C. Jones's initials, still remain as another reflection of a bygone era.

This wooded island estate has become a getaway for many for a time of reflection or romance. It is the perfect setting for wedding celebrations. Who could think of a better way for a couple to begin their life together than by spending a romantic night in the original master bedroom with its fieldstone fireplace and four-poster bed? (One can peak into the closet and still see the trap door that led to J.C. Jones's secret room in the basement.) Morning then greets visitors with an inviting view of the sun coming up over the lake and the aroma of soufflé omelets prepared and served by the gracious hosts.

It's impossible to walk along the path to the lake or peer into the clear blue waters without dreaming—just perhaps, I'll catch a glimpse of the lost diamond glistening in the sun. The diamond may be long gone, but the story of Mr. and Mrs. J.C. Jones and the dreams of Xanadu live on.

My thanks to Bryan and Janet Lonski for granting permission to use stories they have shared and the information that they have recorded on their Web site about the romantic history of Xanadu Island. Also, special thanks to Bryan and Janet for the wonderful memories of my own escape to Xanadu. My heart longs to return.

DREAMS IN A BOTTLE

The Lake Street Bridge Letters of 1924

If you saw the movie *Somewhere in Time* starring Christopher Reeve and Jane Seymour, you were no doubt fascinated as I was by the intriguing thought of stepping back in time . . . even if only for one day.

The letters you are about to read will enable you to do just that. This is a wonderful, true story about four young women and coworkers—Verona Camille Bangs, Marcella Flory, Helen McKinzie, and Violet Rehnberg—who had large dreams that did not include continuing their lives working in post-high school clerical jobs at the Washburn Crosby Company in Minneapolis. They gathered together on a rainy August afternoon in 1924 for a farewell luncheon for Marcella, who was the first to break away to pursue her dream of a music career. Verona was hosting the luncheon at her house.

Each woman had hopes and dreams for what the future would hold for her. They decided to record these thoughts in letters to themselves and place the rolled-up "manuscripts" or "scrolls" in a canning jar and bury it by the Lake Street Bridge in Minneapolis. (They were creating their own time capsule.) They all vowed to return in five years, dig up the jar, and compare their current lives with these dreams and aspirations.

They finished their letters, walked down in the light rain to the Lake Street Bridge, and buried the jar near the bridge. However, it remained there for 67 years until it was discovered and unearthed in 1991 by construction workers demolishing the bridge. Can you imagine the workers' surprise? The lid had rusted off the jar, and one letter was quite damaged from water, mold, and the elements of time. However, portions of all four letters were still legible and in remarkably good condition. The Minnesota Historical Society is now preserving this collection of letters.

These letters give us a wonderful opportunity to step back in time and peer into the lives of young women in the 1920s. The letters describe their environment and what they were wearing, as well as the dreams that were in their hearts. As I read the faded letters that the elements of earth and time had damaged, I fell in love with each of these women and hoped that all of their dreams had come true. They had lived much before my time, yet I could connect with their anticipation and apprehensions of the future and the exciting dreams of youth. I was also deeply touched by their love and friendship for one another. The following is a large portion of each of their letters.

VIOLET REHNBERG — AUGUST 3, 1924

My greatest ambition is something seemingly unattainable—
if I were to become a concert artist—a soloist who would hold
hundreds spellbound!

Presently—it's raining! Raining!

*Seated today at the table, I am "weary and ill at ease." For I
wonder what the future holds for me. But that is a little ahead of
my outline, so you will have to wait for that.*

*After having finished a most delightful lunch at Camille Bangs'
at 3328 45th Avenue South, Minneapolis, Marcella, Camille,
Helen, and I have seated ourselves at the table and are forthwith
writing—well, as for appearance, they may be called manuscripts or
scrolls, for they don't appear ancient now but intensely interesting.*

*Marcella is the guest of honor at present, as she is about to
leave for St. Cloud for a two-year course of music, after which she
intends to teach. She is absolutely the sweetest, loveliest, and most
likeable girlfriend I have ever had. I have spent many happy
moments with her, all of which can never be erased from my mind.
She is very big-hearted.*

*She plays the piano and she has a very good voice. She drives a
Haynes. And I almost forgot to add that she has long hair, which is
unusual for the day and age.*

*Camille is the artist of our group, along lines of painting and
drawing. She, too, works at the Washburn Crosby Company, as do
all of us. She has a very striking personality—oh, so different—so
sweet and considerate. Yes, and she has a kitten, just adorable.
Well, it fits right in the family.*

Camille dances, and one would not have to question it, for she's as graceful as can be.

The only one left is Helen McKenzie, a more recent acquaintance. Helen is so likeable that words fail to express. She is engaged to Allen Belden, and I assume she will be married when this manuscript is recovered.

Well, last but not least is me. At present, my mind is all made up to take violin and vocal lessons—starting this coming September 1924. Time will only tell what success I have. If I only had a little more backing in courage, confidence, and money, I feel I could be a success but—well, we shall see!

At present, I am living at 102 Eighth Street, Minneapolis, and I will be for another year according to present plans.

I was born in Minneapolis and went to public school as well as high school here. I started to take violin lessons when I was young, and I have played for various types of entertainment. I love my music! If I could only be in the right mood so as to practice when I should.

The future seems so uncertain for me. Oh, for a real wonderful future! There is the popular slang phrase, "Not much of a future but oh . . . what a past." I would like to be able to say, "Not much of a past, but oh, what a future!"

Who knows, perhaps five years from now I'll look back and say, "I told you so. Your future was rosy, but time could only reveal each rose bud as it opened."

My greatest ambition is something seemingly unattainable—if I were to become a concert artist—a soloist who would hold hundreds spellbound!

Oh, for the applause of an audience who truly enjoys me and mine. Not for what I might stand for but for what I really am! My thought just now . . . Marcie playing the piano, Camille dancing, me playing the violin, and Helen with her family in the audience.

Is all this absurd? Perhaps, but just wait. Wait until we speak of this "future" as "now!" Oh . . . Thrills!

Oh, that I may someday make a life with William E. Dahl, son of the late Judge Dahl. We were once dearest friends, but through some foolishness of mine we broke it off. I've forgiven myself; now might he. I have met several who have taken my breath away, but they have never gotten my heart for any length of time.

Oh, Helen, Camille, & Marcella, I love you now and will always. Marcella, I must think of you as sort of going out of my life, for you will meet other friends.

Well, my ladies, "arrivederci" until we meet again in August 23, 1929.

Violet Anne Rehnberg

August 23, 1924

⚘

VERONA CAMILLE BANGS

I could write all about my friends, how good they are to me and how interesting each and every one is, but it would take ages.

What could be more interesting or wonderful than to see four perfectly normal, modern girls on a rainy Saturday afternoon writing letters to themselves. It might seem silly to some folks, but nevertheless, it is fun to be silly sometimes, isn't it?

I suppose you are just squirming with curiosity by now to know what it is all about. Well, I'll tell you how it started . . .

You see, for over a year now, we four have been palling around (Helen McKinzie, Violet Anne Rehnberg, and Marcella Flory—my pal and dearest friend). We have been working in the same office— all equally disgusted with the humdrum of it all—until Marcie made the first break and decided to go to school to study music. This all started while we were having lunch the other day. Marcie was at the office when someone said, "I wonder what we will all be doing five years from now." Helen suggested that each one write a letter telling something of her present life, include what she would like to do in the future, and then bury them all in a box. At the end of five years, we would return and dig it up and see how near our desires have been fulfilled. Quite a novel, thrilling idea, don't you think?

At present, I am living in a pretty little bungalow near the Mississippi River, which is between the two cities of Minneapolis and St. Paul. Things have not been as pleasant and agreeable at home as they might be. Mother is all that a wonderful wife and mother could be—always agreeable, unselfish, sympathetic, and true, and she tries so hard to make a go of everything. But I—what have I done to help? Nothing, except help in a small financial way with the house and try to give Mumsie a few of the pretty things that I would love to see her have.

It would be quite impossible to ever repay her for all the sacrifice she has gone through to make me happy and put me through high school. I have been happy, especially this summer. If only things had run more smoothly for her. But every cloud has a silver lining, and things do seem to be working out better now.

I could write all about my friends, how good they are to me and how interesting each and every one is, but it would take ages. So I must say "arrivederci" until five years from now when I hope we will all be able to meet again.

Verona Camille Bangs

HELEN MCKINZIE

This is how I hope the Helen McKinzie or Helen McKinzie Belden of 1929 to be—the happy, always happy, wife of Allen.

August the twenty third, 1924

To me—Helen McKinzie in 1929 (five years)

My, how foolish this sounds now. So sort of solemn and all—but then—here goes. This is how I hope the Helen McKinzie or Helen McKinzie Belden of 1929 to be—the happy, always happy, wife of Allen. (Such a love—comradeship—almost a worship of each other—as we now have.) God has been good to us. Sometimes it seems almost too good to be real—to last forever—this Big Fire of ours. But God helping—may it grow and become richer as time goes on, and may I always be worthy—ever appreciative—of Allen.

I hope to be married in 1925. I shall have work in the city. By 1929 we shall have a house of our own and a little love nest, as we like to think of it.

I want to help make our home a haven of rest—a place of happiness to all who come within its doors. May Allen always call me his "Queen." May I learn the art—as my mother has—of over-looking little differences.

    May he always remember to tell me if he loves me and may I tell him, too. I know we shall. And then may we have a little one by 1929.

    This fall may Allen find work in the city. If he does, I know it would be so much easier for him to be happy. Just to know that in my heart we are moving toward being One.

    May his mother have no hard feelings if he leaves her. I do want to do what is right. I admire her. May we always be friends.

    May the Lord bless these wishes.

Helen McKinzie

⚘

MARCELLA FLORY

The fortune-teller, Mrs. L., told me I would be married in two years. I wonder what will really happen. She also told me I would make a big success of music, traveling a lot after I was married.

To myself, Marcella J. Flory

    This day, the 23rd of August 1924, I went to a luncheon—a farewell dinner to me. I am going to S.C.N.A. a week from Tuesday, September 2, for three years or maybe two—all depends.

    The fortune-teller, Mrs. L., told me that I would be married within two years. I wonder what will really happen. She also said that I would make a big success at music, traveling a lot after I was married. I am now going with George S. She told me that I was going to marry him. In five years, I suppose I'll be married as this is August and I'll be married in June. I'll most likely be on my honey-moon, as we have planned to go abroad. Oh! Thrill!

Mother and I are planning to go to Yellowstone Park next summer, June 1925, and work during my vacation. We have a Haines car now—hope to have a new one next summer.

Here is a tour of we girls—we are all sitting around the table at Camille's house. Helen, Violet, Camille, and I are all writing fast and furious. Camille's mother is over to Mrs. Metcalf's. Mitzie, the cat, is having fun playing with Helen's belt on her pink voile dress. Violet has on a pongee dress, yellow stockings, a black and white tie, an amber bracelet, and her hair is done high. She just said that she had washed her hair. She is a darling girl and a wonderful violin-ist. Hope she goes on with her music.

Camille, the dear, is wearing a red jacket, white blouse, skirt, shoes and stockings, and is wearing her hair very odd—sort of vampish like.

Helen, the only one of the four of us who is engaged, is very small and dainty, just as sweet as she can be, has a pink voile dress, an engagement ring, and wears her hair high. By the way, I must mention that all four of us have long hair—very unusual as the style is now to have it bobbed.

Grandmother is living in Hastings now on the old homestead. We go down there almost every weekend now.

Aunt Lizzie lives at 155 Exeter Place. They have three chil-dren—Donald, Anne, and Grove, Jr. They are the dearest children, although Donald is a case. Hope he grows better with age.

Aunt Dot lives in Elgin, Illinois. Aunt Daisy lives in Iowa. Judd lives at 3429 First Avenue South. He has Barbara June—just 5 months old. She is going to be my flower girl when I am married. I am much in love now—hope it lasts.

I am sealing this up with all good faith that we four will meet on August 23, 1929, at the Lake Street Bridge and read each other's manuscripts.

M. J. F.

4243 1st Avenue South

Minneapolis, Minnesota

Can't you just picture these four "modern girls" gathered around a solid oak table in the cozy dining room—wearing their long dresses or skirts, with their hair swept up off their necks, listening to the falling rain, and watching Mitzie, the cat, play with the belt on Helen's dress? I imagine that they were probably deep in thought and also giddy with excitement over contemplating what their lives would be like in the faraway year of 1929.

After reading these four letters, so many questions remain unanswered. Why did the jar remain buried for 67 years—why didn't these four young women return to recover their letters as they had vowed to do? Had they seen their dreams come true? Also, had they remained close friends as they were at the time of these letters? One of the women held the key to these answers.

Camille Bangs had the surprise of her life when she picked up the paper one August morning in 1991. She was now 86 years old and living in Minneapolis near Lake of the Isles. She couldn't believe what she was seeing! There on the front page was the story about the letters that she and her friends had buried near the Lake Street Bridge. She just couldn't believe it—it had been so long.

It was hard to imagine that now—67 years later—construction workers had miraculously unearthed their jar of dreams from where they had buried it at the base of the old Lake Street Bridge. The bridge had been demolished a few days earlier.

Why didn't they return to dig up their time capsule as they had promised? In an interview with a reporter from the Star Tribune newspaper, Camille said that they did indeed return to dig up their letters, but they were never able to find them. Apparently, the jar wasn't where they thought they had buried it.

❧

Here is a brief portrait of what transpired in the lives of these four women after preserving their hopes and dreams in a jar by the Lake Street Bridge:

Verona Camille Bangs, who was the artist and dancer of the group, was married for a time earlier in her life. After her clerical job at the Washburn Crosby Company, she went on to work in sales and promotion for General Mills. She later worked for Munsingwear for 18 years.

Marcella Flory, the guest of honor at the luncheon, was planning to leave for music school. Unfortunately, the

Depression came along, and she was forced to forego her dream of developing a music career. She had to make more money than what a career in music would provide at the time. Instead she got an office job with the United States government. After living in Minneapolis for a time, she moved out east with her husband and son. Sadly, Marcella had passed away before the letters were discovered.

Violet Rehnberg, whose dream was to become a concert artist and hold hundreds spellbound, fulfilled her dream but perhaps not to the extent that she had wished. Music was always her dream, and it remained an important part throughout her life. She played her violin for family gatherings, for church, and even for a governor's ball. Violet also worked as an executive secretary for General Mills for 47 years.

How did her lovelife unfold? Violet was engaged twice and broke it off twice—to the same man. (Perhaps she still carried a torch for the young man she wrote about in her letter.) Apparently, her career and obligations to her mother as an only child played a large part in breaking off the engagements. She later gave her engagement ring to her cousin. At the time the letters were discovered, Violet was 86 years old and living in a Minneapolis nursing home.

Helen McKinzie had written that she hoped to be the "happy, always happy, wife of Allen D. Belden." She did indeed marry Allen, and her dreams seemed to come true. They were happily married for more than 60 years. The couple shared a home—their love nest—in Red Wing, Minnesota. Helen died in December 1990 at the age of 87— just eight months before the letters were discovered. She remained a true romantic and idealist throughout her life according to her daughter, Margaret Mason.

Did the friendships of these young women remain strong? Yes, Camille Bangs and Marcella Flory remained best friends throughout their lives. Helen McKinzie's daughter had also heard the name Camille Bangs from the time she was a little girl.

It is unknown if Violet stayed in contact with the others throughout her life. She had written in her letter, "Oh, Helen, Camille, & Marcella, I love you now and will always. Marcella, I must think of you as sort of going out of my life, for you will meet other friends."

I like to think that all four young women remained connected throughout their lives. I hope they enjoyed the love and friendship that they felt on that rainy day in August of 1924 as they sat around the table in Camille's house recording their personal hopes and dreams. How wonderful it was that they dared to dream big—"to hold hundreds spellbound." They had individual dreams of a career in the arts, travel, love, and a happy marriage—many of the same dreams as young women of today—decades later.

How fortunate for us that these letters were miraculously discovered and unburied near the Lake Street Bridge so that we could catch a glimpse into the hearts and lives of these four "modern" young women of 1924. Now in the twenty-first century, perhaps there are four "modern" young women of today who will also bury a time capsule of their hopes and dreams in anticipation of what the future may hold. The miracle may unfold once again in the distant year of 2070.

[My thanks to the Minnesota Historical Society for granting permission to use the material in the Lake Street Bridge Letters collection.]

ON A FINAL NOTE

All of these spirited women have shown us that life is a journey to be savored each step of the way. This final note provides an update into the lives of some of these women.

THE JOURNEY OF A LIFETIME

The Fortunate Four—In The Summer of 1935
Initial interviews: Irene (May 2000) and Annette (July 2000)

Annette Scherer Robbins continues to enjoy an active retirement with her husband Orem. They spend winters in Naples, Florida, and enjoy summers in Minnesota and at their cabin in Wisconsin.

As noted, Betty Klein Bridgman died suddenly in July 1999. Irene Holth Hoebel passed away in February 2002. I attended a memorial service and reception held in remembrance of the life she lived. Family and friends from across the country gathered to share touching memories and humorous anecdotes. One person commented, "There was always a reason for a party when you knew Irene."

Garneth Holth Buchanan died peacefully in February 2003. Her children said, "After two and a half years apart, our mom has rejoined our daddy. Both of them died peacefully at Birchwood Health Care Center; both of them died on a Sunday; and both of them died at exactly 5 p.m. Maybe that was just a coincidence, but we doubt it. Theirs was a perfect bond, before and now."

A BRUSH WITH DESTINY

Let's Have a Picnic
Initial Interview: January 1999

Jeanette Scherling has since moved from Minnesota to a retirement community in Washington, D.C., to be closer to her daughters. There was a special celebration in May 2002 for Jeanette's 90th birthday.

I learned of yet another interesting twist to the Naftalin/Scherling story. Her daughter Beth met, fell in love, and married a third cousin and took back the Naftalin name.

Bouquets of Daisies and Wild Asparagus Fern
Initial Interview with Dorathy Lysne: July 1999

Dorathy passed away in May 2001 at the age of 93. Her daughter said, "Mother was alive with the joy of living until near the end. Throughout her life, she continued to write wonderful little jingles and slip them in with gifts. This is one of our special memories about her."

Destiny Through Time
Initial Interview with Ruth Swanson: May 2001

Ruth's journey on earth ended in November 2002 from cancer. She will always be remembered for her vibrant smile and sparkling eyes.

The "Bride and Groom" Show
Initial Interview with Donna Grinvalds: July 2002

Donna and Emil celebrated their 50th wedding anniversary in December 2002 with a party in their home. In February 2003, Donna celebrated her 75th birthday and, unfortunately, Emil also suffered a second heart attack. He is currently going through physical therapy following surgery.

A Celebration of the Journey

Caught Between Two Worlds
Initial Interview with Winifred Miller: March 1999

At 97, Winifred continues to do well in her own apartment. She keeps busy by knitting baby blankets.

The Journey from Hollywood
Initial Interview with Dr. Chris Matteson: September 2002

Chris has since experienced both joy and sorrow. In November 2002, she flew back to Hollywood to attend the funeral for her dear niece. In January 2003, Chris enjoyed two weeks in Hawaii as the guest of one of her painting students. While there, she also made arrangements for a future showing of her work at a prestigious art gallery. Her creativity continues to flow.

Viola Gets a School
Initial Interview with Viola Daetz: March 1999

Viola turned 87 in January 2003. She is living in an assisted-living care center. Unfortunately, her quality of life has been affected by the loss of her short-term memory.

Sing from Your Heart
Initial Interview with Charlotte Sonnichsen: March 1999

Since my interview with Charlotte, it became necessary for her to move into an assisted-living facility.

The Journey on the Train
Initial Interview with Lee Anderson: March 1999

Lee and her husband Oscar continue to live independently in their apartment. Lee now gets around by wheelchair or cane.

Clear Blue Skies and Cool Deep Waters
Initial Interview with Arlene Graham: March 1999

Arlene lives in her own apartment. She is still spunky but says she has physically slowed down from "go go" and is slipping into "no go." Arlene plays bridge twice a week and recently ordered a book called *How to Keep Your Brain Young.* In spite of recent sorrows within her family, she maintains her positive spirit and sense of humor.

The Winding Road to Monterey Bay
Initial Interview with June Usher: March 2002

June continues to live in the beautiful surroundings of the Park Lane retirement residence.

The Master Storyteller
Initial Interview with Verdi Nelson: July 2002

Verdi's dreams for her 100th birthday celebration were indeed realized on February 29, 2004. Over 200 family and friends joined with her to celebrate her spirited journey. Verdi looked smashing in her lavender dress, and she truly enjoyed the day. The stories were flowing, and I was thrilled to be a part of the celebration. The story of this special leap-year baby was even captured by the local newspaper and TV media.

THE MYSTERY OF A PHOTOGRAPH

No Regrets
Initial Interview with Phyllis Ranallo: December 2002

Phyllis stays active by going for early morning walks with her dog Sadie. She enjoys the time spent with family and lifelong friends.

LOVE LETTERS—SWEETER THAN CHOCOLATE

Hello, Sweetheart! Anonymous

Charlie, the author of this letter, passed away in January 2003 at the age of 88. He spent the last two years of his life in a nursing home afflicted with Alzheimer's.

My Bud, You Would Have Just Loved Him
Initial Interview with Elaine Johnson: March 2002

As noted, Chloe passed away in March 2001. It turns out that she died in her home. Knowing her love for politics, it was most fitting that two politicians (a family member and a neighbor) lovingly watched over her body in wait for the coroner to arrive.

Love and Laughter

The Iceman

*Initial Interview with Avis Kuby about Her Mother Inez Kullberg:
September 1997*

Avis passed away in November 1999 from lung cancer.
Her children had a beautiful memorial service at the
Como Park Conservatory in a room filled with
poinsettias. Avis had a great love for flowers, so this was
a fitting celebration of her journey. There were also the
live sounds of Dixieland music. She was a spirited, fun-
loving woman just like her mother Inez, and I would
guess they both approved.

A Change of Plans

Initial Interview with Irene Christiansen: November 2002

Sadly, Bob was recently diagnosed with cancer, and he
passed away in February 2004. Irene is blessed to have
the support of her large family.

Dreams in a Bottle and Other Buried Treasure

The Legends of Xanadu

I discovered the beauty and serenity of Xanadu Island
during my stay in the summer of 2000. The mystery of
the lost diamond continues.

ABOUT THE AUTHOR

Joy Kuby is a personal story preservationist and the owner of Joyful Images. Her quest is to gather stories from women who have journeyed before her—women who have experienced much of the twentieth century. She resides in Minnetonka, Minnesota, with her husband Keith and her dog Lindy.

❦

Joy is currently working on her next book. If you have a spirited story of lifelong friendship, love, or adventure that you would like to share, please send any correspondence to the address below.

Joy Kuby
Joyful Images
P.O. Box 49
Wayzata, MN 55391

More information can be found at her website.

www.joyfulimages.com

COMMENTS FROM READERS

There is a tug and pull for me to sit down and do a straight-read of your book. But there's also a feeling of no—slow down—savor each story and the essence of each woman. I've looked through the pages and already feel I don't want the book to end.

—*Camille Crandall, National League of American Pen Women*
—*Minnesota Branch, Board Member*

What a wonderful read! It was hard to put the book down, as I wanted to capture more heartwarming stories from the enlightening Fortunate Four. These women lived their passion as they journeyed together. I suddenly felt I was a part of their journey. As I read of their growth, my own heart and soul evolved.

—*Kian Dwyer, Author of "Living Your Chosen Eulogy"*

Fantastic! Hail survivors and adventurers! Heartwarming, joyful, adventurous, and honest. Congratulations on a wonderful book. What a work from the heart! You have written a true treasure.

—*Janice Alexander, Bloomfield, CT*

I finished reading your book, *The Fortunate Four*, and I thank you for the many hours of pleasurable reading that it provided. You were able to capture the many joyous as well as sad times of your characters as they traveled life's journey. I wish I had known some of the women. I will certainly recommend *The Fortunate Four* to my friends.

—*Joy L. Peters, Hopkins, MN*

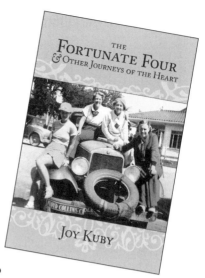

How to Order

Did you enjoy reading about the
spirited women in *The Fortunate
Four & Other Journeys of the Heart*
and would like additional copies to
give as gifts to the spirited women in your own life?
Copies of the book are available in several ways.

1. Ask for *The Fortunate Four* at your local bookstore.
   *(If not currently available, resellers can order it through
   Ingram, Partners, or Baker & Taylor.)*

   - ISBN: 1-59298-007-4

   - $18.95

2. Order via the web at *www.BookHouseFulfillment.com.*

3. Telephone orders are available by calling
   1-800-901-3480. *Follow the prompts to
   Book House Fulfillment.*

To contact the author directly to request signed copies or
for book club discounts, personal engagements, interviews,
or special events, send an email to *jkuby@earthlink.net.*

For a current schedule of events and for more
information about *The Fortunate Four*, go to the author's Web
site at *www.joyfulimages.com.*

Keep the stories alive.